IN LIMBO

IN LIMBO

The Story of Stanley's Rear Column

TONY GOULD

READERS UNION
Group of Book Clubs
Newton Abbot 1979

To SIMON GRAY
in gratitude for so many things, and
in the conviction that the play will
long outlive those London critics
who treated it with so little
sympathy or understanding

CONTENTS

ILLUSTRATIONS

From left to right, Major E. M. Barttelot, J. S. Jameson, Herbert
Ward, J. Rose Troup, William Bonny, H. M. Stanley and
Tippu-Tib
The Emin Pasha Relief Committee
The steamers *Stanley* and *AIA* on the Aruwini river
Jameson's plan of Yambuya entrenched camp
Beehive huts in Yambuya camp
Stanley giving final instructions to Barttelot
Interview of Barttelot and Jameson with Tippu-Tib
Arabs raiding a native village opposite Yambuya
Tippu-Tib's fleet of canoes on the Congo river
Jameson's Christmas card to Barttelot, 1887
A Congo Warrior by Herbert Ward
From left to right, E. J. Glave, Alfred Parminter, Herbert Ward
and Roger Casement

HISTORICAL INTRODUCTION

THE STORY of the Emin Pasha Relief Expedition has always aroused great interest. There have been several books written about it and only a few years ago two came out more or less simultaneously. Its attraction lies in the phenomenal vicissitudes of Stanley's journey through 'Darkest Africa', in the contrast between the philanthropic goal of the expedition and its rigorously militaristic conduct, and in the latent comedy of the long-delayed meeting of Stanley and Emin, two such contrasting personalities as to be mutually incomprehensible.

In all accounts of the expedition, therefore, the story of the rear column, of the five Englishmen Stanley dumped in the very centre of Africa along with the bulk of the expedition stores and left to fend for themselves while he went on in search of Emin, forms merely an episode (invariably seen retrospectively), a single chapter which, for all its intrinsic interest, interrupts the flow of the main narrative. By taking this episode and making it the main narrative, one gets quite a different perspective: the story of the rear column comes to be seen less as a part of the Emin Pasha saga and more as a significant moment in the history of the Congo Free State and that State's relations with the Arab slave traders and the Africans who became its subjects.

Leopold II, King of the Belgians, had always wanted a colony. He dreamed of creating another Indian Empire—and it was to the Far East that he first looked to realise this dream. But there were two sizable problems: colonies were not to be had just for the asking; and although Leopold might crave one, it was not a craving shared by his countrymen. If the King were to acquire a colony it would be in spite of, and not because of, Belgium.

When he had failed to gain a foothold in China, the Pacific Islands and North Borneo, Leopold made a bid for the Philippines; but they were not for sale. Only then, after ten years of looking, did he turn his attention to Africa. That was in 1875, before the 'Scramble' had begun. He called for an international geographical conference to be held in Brussels and this took place in 1876. His ostensible aim was to make Brussels the headquarters of an international body devoted to the advancement of science and the suppression of the slave trade in Africa. As he said, in his opening speech at the Brussels Conference: 'To open to civilisation the only area of our globe to which it has not yet penetrated . . . constitutes, if I may dare to put it in this way, a Crusade worthy of this century of progress.'

At first the *Association Internationale Africaine* seemed to have little substance, to be merely an idealist's plaything. But then, a year later, the news reached Europe that Stanley had succeeded in descending the Congo river, and Leopold found a focus for his colonial ambition. He sent two envoys to intercept Stanley at Marseilles on his return to Europe and to encourage him to return to Africa and work for the new Association. But Stanley resisted Leopold's initial advances; he was intent on getting Britain to annex the Congo. With this purpose in mind he had written in 1877, for the *Daily Telegraph*:

> The question of this mighty waterway will become a political one in time. As yet, however, no European power seems to have put forth the right of control. Portugal claims it because she discovered its mouth; but the Great Powers— England, America and France—refuse to recognise her right . . . If it were not that I fear to damp any interest you may have in this magnificent stream by the length of my letters, I could show you very good reasons why it would be a politic deed to settle this momentous question immediately. I could prove to you that the power possessing the Congo, despite the cataracts, would absorb to itself the trade of the whole of the enormous basin behind. This river is and will be the grand highway of commerce to Central Africa.

Stanley pleaded in vain. Britain was not to be seduced into another colonial adventure at that moment; and Stanley himself was the victim of snobbish distrust. He was still the 'American' upstart, the newspaperman who had stolen a march on the Royal Geographical Society and been on his way to find Livingstone before that worthy body had even thought of sending an expedition for that purpose.

Such parochial matters were of no importance to the King of the Belgians. What exercised his faculties was a diplomatic question, how to secure for himself 'a slice of this magnificent African cake' without offending the English. 'I think if I entrusted Stanley publicly with the job of taking over part of Africa in my own name,' he wrote to his ambassador in London, 'the English would stop me. So I think that at first I shall give Stanley an exploring job which will not offend anybody, and will provide us with some posts down in that region and with a high command for them which we can develop when Europe and Africa have got used to our "pretensions" on the Congo.'

And that was precisely what happened. Stanley accepted Leopold's commission to return to the Congo and set up stations along the river in the name of the *Association Internationale Africaine*, or rather, the *Comité d'Etudes du Haut-Congo*, as it was now called. A year or two later it became the *Association Internationale du Congo*. These bewildering changes of name were all part of Leopold's policy of mystification. One person who clearly understood the King's real aim (and could not be bought off by him) was Stanley's great rival in the Congo, the French explorer (Italian by birth), Count Savorgnan de Brazza, who wrote:

Mr Stanley acted in the name of the King of the Belgians for Belgium, which at that time wanted to found in Africa a sort of international factory, of which it would be in supreme control. Doubtless the King of the Belgians was quite disinterested. He gave his millions with the sole aim of civilising the savage tribes. I thought, however, that there was a political idea at the base of the humanitarian sentiments of the King of the Belgians. I was far from blaming him for this, but that did not prevent me from having a political idea of my own, and mine was very simple. Here it is: if it was advantageous to take possession of the Congo, I preferred that it should be the French flag, rather than the Belgian 'International' flag, that floated over this magnificent African country.

In the end, of course, both flags flew over that magnificent African country. The Berlin West African Conference of 1884–85 ironed out the details. This conference took place at the instigation of Bismarck and the French, partly in response to Leopold's activities in the Congo, partly as a result of Bismarck's own sudden awakening to the diplomatic advantages to be gained from having colonies, but mainly because of the dispute between Britain and France stemming from the French occupation of Tunis in 1881 and Britain's unilateral invasion of Egypt in 1882—as well as their long-standing rivalry in West Africa.

Faced with the nationalist revolt led by an Egyptian officer, Arabi Pasha, in 1881, Britain and France had intended to act in concert to protect their financial interests in Egypt and, in particular, the Suez Canal. But the fall of a government in France meant a reversal of policy. So Britain went in alone. And once in power, of course, found it impossible—despite repeated promises—to withdraw. Worse than that, it was impossible not to expand. In order to protect Egypt itself, Britain was drawn ever further into the Sudanese hinterland. Again, the intention was to withdraw; but it was not so easy to do, especially when the man on the spot had very different ideas from those of Her Majesty's Government. General Gordon was sent to Khartoum with orders to abandon it and withdraw, but he preferred to remain and die a martyr's death at the hands of the Mahdi's forces.

The French naturally resented Britain's unilateral action in Egypt; they had built the canal, after all, and now it had passed out of their control. So they acted together with Bismarck (who wanted to divert them, after the humiliation of the Franco-Prussian war a decade earlier, from all thoughts of recapturing Alsace and Lorraine) against the British. The British, reluctantly, had to accept that their dominance in Africa no longer went unquestioned. In return for her support of British policy in Egypt, Germany demanded virtually a free hand in the disposal of the remainder of 'unclaimed' Africa.

If Bismarck only acquired colonies for diplomatic reasons— that is, to incite Anglo-French rivalry outside Europe—Leopold went about it the other way round. He used his considerable diplomatic skills to acquire a personal empire. He played off the British and Germans against the French, representing himself as the lesser threat to the balance of (European) power in Africa, and at the same time won over the French themselves with a promise that, should he be forced by the enormous expense of the undertaking to sell out, they should have the right to buy the Association's assets—in other words, take over the country. In this way, by astute diplomacy, Leopold acquired his colony; all pretence of internationalism could now safely be dropped. In July 1885, Leopold was proclaimed 'Sovereign of the Congo Independent State'. It was not a Belgian colony—Belgium would still have nothing to do with it—so Leopold, a constitutional monarch at home, became an absolute ruler in the Congo.

Not that anyone was worried; Leopold's avowed aims were so clearly progressive—the establishment of free trade and the suppression of slavery—that his surely would be a benevolent despotism. His rule would mark the beginning of a new era of enlightened colonialism.

Emin Pasha's real name was Edouard Schnitzer. A German by birth, he became one of General Gordon's lieutenants in the Sudan. After the fall of Khartoum and the collapse of Egyptian power in the hinterland, Emin had withdrawn with his Sudanese and Egyptian soldiers and a motley collection of followers to the southern end of the Equatorial Province. There he hoped to remain beyond the Mahdi's reach. But the question was: how long could he hold out in such isolation? Reports of his situation reached the outside world from time to time and they were far from reassuring.

Among those whose interest was aroused by the news of Emin's predicament was William Mackinnon, a Scottish business-man with colonial ambitions. He was that characteristic nine-teenth-century blend of self-made man, pillar of the church and philanthropist; few letters of appeal to him went unanswered. For many years he had been a friend and business associate of King Leopold and he had worked hard to get the British Government to recognise Leopold's International Association. 'The Mackinnon Clan', as Stanley referred to him and his friends, was very useful to the Belgian King; in a country which tended to look on his African activities with a jaundiced eye, it influenced public opinion in his favour. In return, Leopold encouraged a syndicate headed by Mackinnon and James Hutton, President of the

Manchester Chamber of Commerce, to put forward proposals for the construction of a railway into the interior of the Congo on the understanding that it would get the concession if terms could be agreed. Hutton, Mackinnon and Stanley all put a considerable amount of effort into this project but at the last moment, in September 1886, their proposals were rejected and the railway concession went to a newly-formed Belgian company. Stanley wrote gloomily to Mackinnon, 'Every day the King is closing the Congo against the English and seems resolved to make it more and more Belgian.' Mackinnon—and Hutton—remained on good terms with the King, but their collaboration thereafter was formal rather than intimate. Mackinnon reverted to an earlier interest in the commercial possibilities of East Africa. With the Anglo-German agreement of October/November 1886 defining 'spheres of influence', the time was propitious for staking a claim, and that was where Emin Pasha might prove useful. The setting-up of the Emin Pasha Relief Committee, under the chairmanship of Mackinnon, was not therefore an entirely altruistic act. It was immediately followed by the formation of the Imperial British East Africa Company by Mackinnon and his associates.

The British Government of the day was relieved not to have to undertake the task of rescuing Emin. Indeed the Prime Minister, Lord Salisbury, would have gladly washed his hands of all responsibility; when he heard of Emin's plight his initial reaction was to suggest that 'the Germans should be placed in possession of our information. It is really their business if Emin is a German'—this, in spite of the fact that Emin and his garrisons were servants of the Egyptian Government and Egypt was under the tutelage of Britain. The Egyptian Government, in the person of the British Consul-General, Sir Evelyn Baring, was also pleased that someone else was undertaking the evacuation of Emin Pasha (though whether he was to be evacuated or not remained a moot point), but accepted a share of the responsibility and offered to contribute £10,000 towards the cost of the expedition (the Egyptian Government in fact paid £14,000 all told).

As far as Mackinnon was concerned, there was only one possible leader for the expedition and that was Stanley. Stanley himself was anxious to lead the expedition but his position was complicated by the fact that he was not his own master. He was still under contract, at £1,000 a year, to King Leopold. It was a period of intense frustration for the explorer, as the King, although he kept him on the payroll, would not give him any work to do. Stanley felt he no longer enjoyed the King's confidence; and when the Mackinnon syndicate's bid for the Congo railway concession failed, he was bitterly disappointed. As Roger Anstey points out, in his *Britain and the Congo in the Nineteenth Century*, 'For Stanley, September 1886 was a watershed in his relations with Leopold, and the influence of the new, more distant relationship was to be felt within a matter of months. At the close of 1886 Stanley's last African expedition was set on foot. On it, he was required to serve two masters, Leopold and Mackinnon, and Stanley was in no doubt where his first loyalty lay.'

Stanley had to obtain Leopold's consent before he could accept the leadership of the Emin Pasha Relief Expedition and the two men met on 30 December 1886. Before their meeting Leopold had resolved not to let Stanley go; he needed him for his own purposes. But when they met, the King soon saw that it would serve his purposes better if Stanley did go, provided he went via the Congo. This stipulation was not so outrageous as it might appear from a glance at the map. Given that the starting-point of all African expeditions was the island of Zanzibar, the obvious route to the southern Sudan was from the east coast. But, although three alternative routes from the east were under consideration, there were good reasons for eschewing all of them: namely, that the Zanzibari porters would be tempted to desert from any expedition that struck inland from the east coast; and that hostility could be expected, on one route from the Masai people, on another from the Kabaka of Buganda, and on the third— not so much hostility, perhaps, as resentment—from the Germans, whose recently agreed sphere of influence would be transgressed.

Even before his meeting with the King, Stanley had favoured the Congo route for both personal and political reasons. It had long been his personal ambition to explore the area between the Congo and the Nile, and thereby solve the remaining geographical questions in relation to the sources of the Nile and the surrounding terrain. Apart from that, the navigability of the Congo above the long stretch of rapids near the mouth reduced the distance to be marched through unknown country, Stanley estimated, to 322 miles (this estimate was, in fact, wildly inaccurate—the distance was twice as great). Politically, Stanley's scheme accorded so well with Leopold's own idea of opening up a route from the Congo to the Nile—the Nile fascinated Leopold as it had fascinated the explorers who went in search of its source—that the King decided there and then to let Stanley go, with the proviso that his expedition take the Congo route. This would, of course, add considerably to the cost of the undertaking, even though Mackinnon's British India Steamship Company could provide a ship to transport the expedition round the Cape from Zanzibar. Besides, Mackinnon had wanted the expedition to take the east coast route so that Stanley could pave the way for the IBEA Company (as he had once done for Leopold in the Congo) by making treaties in the interior. But if he wanted Stanley to lead the expedition he had no choice but to defer to the King. Leopold sugared the pill with a magnanimous offer of the use of the Congo Free State's flotilla of steamers on the upper river. This offer was readily accepted.

The only way in which the various interests of Leopold, Mackinnon and Stanley could be reconciled was for the expedition to take the Congo route to get to Emin Pasha, but to come back via East Africa. And that was Stanley's plan. In effect, he would serve Leopold on the way out and Mackinnon on the way back.

NOTE: African historians will no doubt take me to task for the loose way I write of 'Arabs' and 'Zanzibaris': the 'Arabs' might more accurately be called Zanzibaris, and the 'Zanzibaris' Africans—since many of these porters who were taken on expeditions originally hailed from the mainland and only got to the island as a result of the slave trade. My excuse for sticking to these outmoded labels is that, as I am quoting extensively from contemporary documents, I am therefore largely constrained to follow contemporary usage. The same applies to the spelling of names. Frequently, though, there are several alternative spellings of a name (Arabic having no vowels). In such cases I have simply—and un-systematically—made my choice and stuck to it. Sometimes I have tried to avoid confusion: for instance, there are two 'Arabs' who are called Selim, Salim, or Salem; for the sake of simplicity I have spelt one one way and the other another. I can only hope that such ingenuousness will be acceptable. Author.

PART ONE

The Story

'Probably under no other circumstances could men become better acquainted with the various phases of each other's character than when campaigning together in the depths of a barbarous country. Under such conditions the true disposition of a comrade soon becomes apparent. A man's courage or tendency towards faint-heartedness are soon betrayed. Living for an uncertain period in a condition of semi-starvation and constant worry proves a man's mettle in the quickest and surest way.

When, added to such physical discomfort and privation, we consider the influence of a malignant climate, which affects the spleen and liver, which racks the frame with burning fever or exhausting dysentery, which dispels sleep and fills the disordered mind with morbid thoughts, and which engenders violent angry passions, it may be understood that no man can act a part; all men must perforce reveal their latent qualities, good and bad.'

HERBERT WARD, *A Voice from the Congo* (1910)

'. . . Indeed the whole story is a very dark one, as dark as any of the many dark stories connected with African travel.'

from *The Diary of A. J. Mounteney Jephson* (1969)

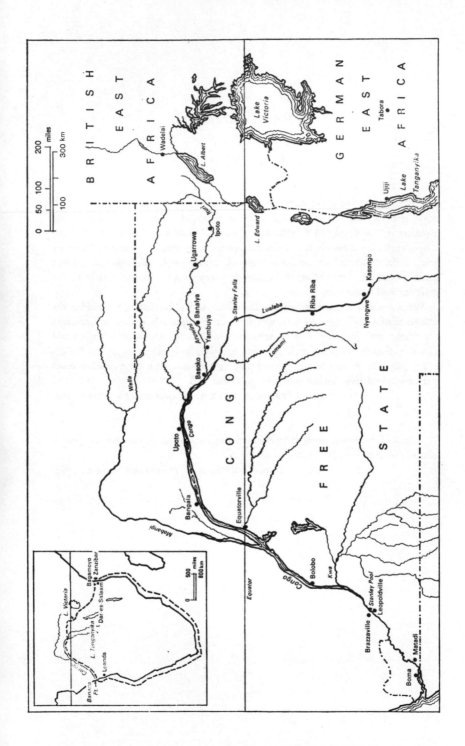

EDMUND MUSGRAVE BARTTELOT, the *Dictionary of National Biography* informs us, was born in 1859, educated at Rugby and Sandhurst, commissioned into the 7th Fusiliers in 1879 and sent out to Bombay. From there he went up to Afghanistan and took part in the defence of Kandahar in 1880. Two years later, when he was home on leave, he volunteered to go to Egypt, where he fought in the battles of Kassassin and Tel-el-Kebir. In 1883 he was again in Egypt, attached to the 1st battalion of the Egyptian army, and went on the (abortive) military expedition up the Nile to the relief of General Gordon. He rose rapidly in rank and, as a brevet-major, was the senior officer accompanying Stanley on the Emin Pasha Relief Expedition, for which he obtained a year's leave from his regiment in January 1887. His rank gave him *de facto* status as second-in-command of the expedition. This meant that he was particularly concerned about his relations with Stanley.

Stanley was already something of a legendary figure in his own lifetime. In the best tradition of heroes his origins were obscure; even his nationality was in doubt. He had come to prominence through his own efforts. By the end of the 1860s he had established himself as a roving reporter on the sensationalist *New York Herald*. Its proprietor, James Gordon Bennett Jr, sent for Stanley one day in Paris and instructed him to 'find Livingstone'. (Or that was Stanley's story: in fact, finding Livingstone came fairly low on a list of assignments which included a trip to India; Stanley did not begin the search for another year.) Nothing but rumours of the great missionary-explorer had reached Europe for some time and nobody knew for certain if he were alive or dead. Stanley, of course, found Livingstone and in the process became well known as an explorer himself. As such, his greatest single exploit was his journey across the African continent from the east coast to the west, in 1874-77, during which he traced the course of the

3

Congo and disproved Livingstone's theory about that great nineteenth-century mystery, the source of the Nile.

For that remarkable journey, Stanley had selected as companions, out of more than a thousand applicants, two brothers from a village in Kent, Frank and Edward Pocock, and a clerk from a London hotel, Frederick Barker. (Two of the three were dead within six months of the start of the expedition. Frank Pocock survived, only to be drowned in the Congo cataracts on the very last stage of the three-year journey.) For the present, quasi-military undertaking, Stanley chose—again, out of hundreds of volunteers —mostly army officers; two civilians who went with him had to pay handsomely for the privilege. This was an altogether more lavish affair than the earlier expedition had been; and Stanley's new companions were mostly of a type that was comparatively unfamiliar to him.

The long sea voyages, first to Zanzibar, where the expedition acquired its porters, and then round the Cape and up to the mouth of the Congo, gave Stanley's officers the opportunity to become acquainted with their famous leader. Barttelot wrote down his impressions in a series of letters to his fiancée, Mabel Godman.

As early as 15 February 1887, while still on board the S.S. *Oriental* heading for Zanzibar, he had an inkling of what might be expected of him in the Congo:

> Stanley hinted to me vaguely this morning that someone would have to be left at Stanley Pool on the Congo, and I strongly suspect that somebody means me. Of course it would be terribly rough on one, still someone must do it . . . Whoever is left at Stanley Pool will join Stanley later on. I am reading all his books through now and I must say I find them very interesting. They are written exactly as he talks himself, straightforward and without much varnish . . . Stanley is very amusing. Fancy he was in the American War Southern side in 1860 and '62 but was taken prisoner in '61 by the Northerners and became a Northerner. [In fact, his third entry into the Civil War was on the Northern side; he joined the Federal Navy in 1864, when the war was nearly over.]

A day later Barttelot was writing, 'Mr Stanley improves decidedly on acquaintance and has been amusing us with stories,

4

chiefly about himself, but he chaffs all of us and keeps everyone alive. I think we shall get on all right, though he is a man who would be easily upset, and when annoyed very nasty.'

At Zanzibar, on 21 February, the expedition collected its porters and embarked on the S.S. *Madura* for the journey to the Congo. After a day or two at sea, a fight broke out between the Zanzibaris and the expedition's Sudanese soldiers. Stanley went in amongst them and, laying about him with a will, soon had things under control. While he applauded this decisive action, Barttelot was beginning to have reservations about Stanley: 'He seems a good sort, of course not a gentleman. His mother keeps a public house at St Asaph in Wales. You never saw such a caution as he looks now with his dyed hair.' (A year and several months later, he was to write to the same correspondent: 'Today we had to open Stanley's boxes and what do you think we found in one, Mrs Allen's Hair Restorer, a large bottle of it—fancy anyone carrying such rubbish across Africa. I don't know whether I told you, that between Zanzibar and the Cape, Stanley's hair changed colour; it grew from a dark mud colour, first to a metallic hue, and then to a pied hue and finally grey, and then he clipped it short. The secret is out.') But the colour of his hair apart, Stanley still impressed Barttelot, particularly in his relations with the Zanzibaris: 'His prestige with these men is something wonderful.'

Barttelot watched his chief closely. He discovered that he was a moody man, and sometimes they did not speak for days. There was growing constraint between the two of them, which Barttelot was naturally anxious to break down. He wrote to Mabel Godman:

Do you remember my telling you that Stanley, on seeing me first in London, impressed on me the necessity of tact and patience with niggers? Well, tonight I asked him if when he said this he knew I lacked those virtues and he said he read it in my face, but also told me it had been confirmed by what I said, and also from what an officer, to whom the only time I had anything to do with I performed a service, told him one night after dinner—[that] I was a perfect fiend with natives. This is not true. I asked Stanley why, knowing all this, he took me. So he said, 'Well, my dear fellow, though I read in your face the

5

want of those two virtues, I saw others in it which more than counterbalanced those two, so I took you and the sequel will show whether I was right.' So I warned him not to be disappointed, although Lord Wolseley, Redvers Buller and others had praised me up, you know. Where I have always done well hitherto has been in those places and times where I have been boss entirely. I am often afraid I may fall short of the mark, for of course and naturally he expects us to be prodigies in the way and amount of work . . . He is a funny chap, Stanley; sometimes I like him fairly well and sometimes quite the reverse.

The officer who had warned Stanley against Barttelot was General Brackenbury, and the occasion for it was an incident during the expedition up the Nile for the relief of Gordon—an incident which Barttelot himself described in his diary for 1884 (when he was 25):

The ship came in on the 24th [September]—150 camels and 300 men. Unfortunately, they were nearly all Aden boys, who are the scum of the earth, and only 16 Somalis . . . There was one scoundrel whom I noticed especially, who seemed to have great power over the Aden boys. I refused to take him at first, but the police-officer who had brought them over from Aden begged me to, as he was such a bad lot.

September 28 we started. Next morning I had some words with the scoundrel, and later in the day he tried to cut a hole in one of the water mussocks. I pulled him away, when he hit me with his weighted stick. I shot him dead.

General Brackenbury no doubt thought the action a little hasty. Certainly this story coloured Stanley's early opinion of Barttelot, which he offered in a letter to Sir Francis de Winton, who was secretary to the Emin Pasha Relief Committee (and knew the Congo well, as he had been Stanley's successor as chief administrator of the Free State). This letter was written towards the end of the voyage round the Cape:

Barttelot is a little too eager and will have to be restrained. He is unsound in discipline, and there is a lurking aggressiveness in him which may lead to open rupture—unless a thorough African fever makes him more amenable. There is plenty of work in him, but you can well understand how lovely this quality would be if it were according to orders. The most valuable man to me would be he who had Barttelot's spirit and go in him, and could come and ask if such and such a work had not better be done. It at once suggests thoughtfulness and willingness, besides proper respect.

While he had reservations about Barttelot, Stanley had nothing but praise for another of his companions—though perhaps his enthusiasm had something to do with the fact that this particular gentleman was one of the two civilians who had each contributed £1,000 out of their own pockets towards the expedition's expenses. 'Jameson,' Stanley wrote to de Winton, 'is still the nice fellow we saw. There is not a grain of change in him—he is sociable and good.'

James Sligo Jameson was born in Alloa in 1856. He was the grandson of that John Jameson of Dublin whose name is synonymous with Irish whisky. His father was a land agent in Scotland and Jameson went first to elementary Scottish schools before going on, in 1868, to the International College at Isleworth, where he read for the army. But in 1877 he decided instead to devote himself to travel and he set off for Borneo, via Ceylon and Singapore. There he amassed a collection of birds, butterflies and beetles, an enduring interest which provided him with an occupation wherever he found himself. And in the next few years he travelled extensively: to South Africa in 1878, and in 1879 up the Limpopo into Matabeleland and Mashonaland, where he hunted lions and rhinoceroses and made his contribution to the knowledge of birds and insects; to the Rockies with his brother on a shooting expedition in 1882; and to Spain and Algeria in 1884. In 1885 he returned home and married Ethel, the daughter of Sir Henry Marion Durand, a soldier.

Sportsman, naturalist and artist, Jameson was a fine example of that common nineteenth-century species, the gentleman-amateur. He was financially independent; he did what he did for the love of the thing; but his ability, enthusiasm and knowledge meant that he was no mere dilettante and ensured that his work had enduring value.

He had been married less than two years, already had a daughter, and when he left England his wife was pregnant again. Jameson obviously felt that he owed her family an explanation for his absence at such a time, and he wrote to his mother-in-law: 'Ever since my childhood I have dreamt of doing some good in this world, and making a name which was more than an idle one. My life has been a more or less selfish one, and now springs up the opportunity of wiping off a little of the long score standing against me. Do not blame me too much . . .'

Jameson's idealism, of course, was not unmixed with baser motives. He enjoyed travel for its own sake and he worked out that his thirty-first birthday, which he would celebrate in August, would be the fifth he had spent 'under canvas' since he had grown up.

Leaving aside Stanley, there was only one white man on the expedition who was older than Jameson and his name was Bonny—William Bonny. In his letter to de Winton, Stanley summed up his feelings about Bonny at the end of the voyage in a single sentence: 'Bonny is Tommy Atkins par excellence, stolid and stodgy with not a single idea in his head, beyond so many months will give him so many pounds pay.' But there was a good deal more to Bonny than Stanley recognised—or was prepared to allow.

Bonny held an equivocal position in the expedition. Though he was a volunteer, unlike the others he was paid for his services, at the rate of £100 per annum. Though he had been in the army, he was not an officer: he had been a sergeant in the Army Hospital Department until, leaving it too late to obtain leave of absence from his unit, he was obliged to purchase his discharge in order to join the expedition. Though he thought of himself as a gentleman and claimed to have a brother who was a consul in Brazil, the others referred to him with that half-affectionate, half-dismissive, but always patronising nickname, Tommy Atkins. While the others enjoyed the luxury of a first class passage out from England, Bonny had to make do with second class accommodation. While the others (apart from Stanley) were still in their twenties, or just turned thirty at most, Bonny was already forty years old.

It is not easy to see why Stanley took him in the first place, unless it was because of his medical experience (Stanley had not then succeeded in recruiting a doctor). Even before the expedition left England, he had shown himself capable of rather odd behaviour. He had been delegated to look after Stanley's African servant, whose name was Baruti, to accompany him to Fenchurch Street station and to take him by train to Tilbury docks, where they were both to embark for Zanzibar. But when they got to the station, Bonny unaccountably took it into his head to visit the Tower of London, leaving Baruti to his own devices. By chance the boy was spotted by Colonel Grant (Speke's erstwhile exploring companion and a member of the Emin Pasha Relief Committee) and returned to Stanley's rooms; but Bonny had done himself no good in the eyes of his employers. According to his own account, he was told by Stanley: 'The whole of the committee are against you and advise me not to take you, but I have decided to take you with me. Your tickets will be here directly.' So Bonny was given a second chance and sent to Southampton to catch the boat he had missed at Tilbury.

[2]

AMONG THE first to greet Stanley on his return to the Congo in 1887 was a trader by the name of Fred Puleston. Puleston had met Stanley once before, in 1883, and had then sat at his feet, content simply to listen to his stories—for Stanley had been his boyhood hero (and remained so to the end of his days). But now he found him less cordial, more reserved than formerly. Stanley seemed totally absorbed in the problems of the moment: the availability of river transport, conditions in the interior, food prospects and 'the temper of the natives'. Puleston and others warned him that the missionaries on the upper river, at Stanley Pool, would more than likely be unwilling to loan him their steamers. This came as no surprise to Stanley: he knew very well how the missionaries regarded him, but he hoped to be able to persuade them to change their minds. After all, where would they have been without him? Was it not he who had obtained for them grants of land on which to build their mission stations?

Even before he arrived in the Congo, Stanley had confessed his doubts to de Winton. 'My thoughts at leisure moments,' he wrote, 'are fixed as you might imagine on the steam transport on the Upper Congo. Will the King or his officers and others play me a trick? We shall see. I shall know no happiness until I am on terra firma on the Upper Congo. Those miserable Baptists—have they made up their minds to lend me the *Peace*?'

The *Peace* was a steamer belonging to the Baptist Missionary Society which had been donated by one Robert Arthington, who was known as 'the miser of Leeds'. Before leaving England, Stanley had written to Arthington to request the loan of the steamer, but he did not really expect it to be granted.

Puleston, like other traders, had little time for missionaries, whose favourite 'indoor sport', as he put it, was writing letters to *The Times* or the *Manchester Guardian*. He suggested to Captain Nelson, one of Stanley's officers, that they simply steal the *Peace* from the Baptists and then, when they had quite finished with it, scuttle it.

But Puleston was not enjoying Stanley's company as much as he had anticipated; his loyalty was stretched to the limit. 'To be perfectly frank,' he admitted many years later, 'he was decidedly grouchy.' Puleston and his friends did what they could to cheer him, but they got little in return for their efforts. Only once, when Stanley had loaded his men and goods on to the steamers that were to transport them up the lower river to Matadi, did he unbend sufficiently to talk about anything other than the expedition. Puleston reminded him of their previous meeting in the old days of the *Association Internationale Africaine,* as the Congo Free State was then called, and said how great a change he saw in him since those days. 'The old AIA,' Stanley replied, 'was the happiest time of my life, and the opening of the Lower Congo was the most interesting. But this . . .'

He was now confronted with such a hazardous undertaking that even he had moments of doubt. Ahead of him lay a journey right across Africa, part of it through the unexplored Ituri forest, a terrain that promised to be anything but hospitable. He had nearly a thousand loads: goods, ammunition, stores of all kinds, even a boat in sections, which had to be transported over thousands of miles; and he was responsible for some 800 people. As if that were not enough, rumour had it that there was a serious scarcity of food in the region of Stanley Pool. This meant that the expedition, after an exhausting 200-mile march through the hilly country which separated the upper from the lower river, would not be able to rest and recuperate without precipitating a famine in the area. Then again, he had nagging doubts about the number of steamers that would be available to him on the upper river: would he be able to transport the entire expedition in one go, or would he have to make more than one journey and thus lose valuable time as well as risk starvation for his own people and the natives alike? And what about his officers, who were young and mostly untried in African conditions—conditions which, as he knew better than anyone, could undermine the strongest constitution in next to no time? Small wonder that he rounded on Puleston and his fellow traders, so comfortably established on the coast, and spoke to them sarcastically.

'I am surprised,' he said, 'you gentlemen do not invite my men ashore and ask them to point out their last resting-place.'

What he was referring to was an initiation rite practised by Europeans in the Congo. Their way of welcoming a new arrival was to take him out to the local graveyard and invite him to select the spot where he wished to be buried. Most took it in good part, but some took the next boat back to Europe.

When the expedition reached Matadi, at the lower end of the cataracts, all the goods and equipment had to be unloaded from the river steamers and re-packed in loads not exceeding 64 pounds. These had to be carried the 200 miles up to Stanley Pool. Later there would be a railway, but in 1887 every article had to be carried on the heads of native porters. With the help of a missionary named Ingham, who was acting as advance agent for the expedition, Stanley tried to sort out the fearful tangle of men and goods; and this irksome task, which had to be done in stifling heat, did not improve his temper.

So when Barttelot arrived at Matadi on a Portuguese gunboat in the cool of the evening, rather later than he had been expected, it was obvious even to an onlooker that there was some constraint between Stanley and him. Puleston wrote of Barttelot:

This was our first meeting, and he certainly made a favourable impression. Well built, erect, of military carriage, with square, determined chin, blue eyes, altogether Barttelot had the look of a man accustomed to command, but impatient of restraint. I don't think he and Stanley agreed very well, for their natures were too much alike, strong and quite domineering, and in Barttelot's case there was not much patience or forbearance . . .

We all went in to dinner. Stanley was still irritable. Things were in an awful mess. Barttelot was stiff . . . As soon as dinner was over, Stanley went to his room.

The next morning the expedition began in earnest. Everyone, including Stanley, seemed more cheerful as they set out in a long line from the barren, rocky Matadi—'so named because it is nothing but rock'—towards the interior. But Puleston and his friends, who remained behind, 'spoke in a pessimistic spirit of the outcome, because for some unaccountable reason the start was not auspicious'.

Once the march was under way, the officers saw another side of Stanley. While on board ship, he had lectured them on the need for tolerance and restraint towards their men and discouraged more than a token use of force—'it has been usual with me to be greatly forbearing, allowing three pardons for one punishment'—but the moment he set foot in Africa he completely ignored his own advice. 'I did not hit anybody for a long time,' Barttelot wrote, 'but I found that Stanley did, right and left, and that it was really the only plan to get these Zanzibaris on. Stanley expected us to hit the men, though he always took their part when they complained. We have been nothing but slave-drivers since we started, and the trouble I have had to get the Sudanese along was something dreadful.'

It was the Sudanese who caused the first row between Stanley and Barttelot. They finished their rations several days early and Stanley was furious. He went out and told them he would shoot the first man who disobeyed his orders again. Barttelot, whose responsibility the Sudanese were, but who was not with them at the time, went in later to see Stanley and apologise for the trouble they had caused. But Stanley was still fuming. He blamed Barttelot for it and threatened to blast his reputation as an army officer if the Sudanese revolted and had to be shot down.

'As how?' Barttelot asked him.

Stanley said it would be in every newspaper, that General Brackenbury would get to hear of it, and he 'had the ear of Wolseley' (future Commander-in-Chief of the army).

Barttelot was loftily impervious to such a threat. The son of a baronet and long-standing Tory MP for West Sussex, he had nothing but the traditional upper class contempt for newspapers and for those who made their living by writing for them. (In so far as Stanley was exempt from this judgment, it was because Barttelot regarded him as an explorer rather than a journalist.) Barttelot could trace his family back to the Norman Conquest; the family estate of Stopham, outside Pulborough, had been theirs for generations. How could such a man either need or fear newspaper publicity? When he was at home he hunted alongside Lord Leconfield; his was a world in which reputation still rested on family connections and personal contact. He could even afford a measure of contempt for a high-ranking army officer. 'Thank

God,' he told Stanley, 'my reputation with Lord Wolseley doesn't rest with what General Brackenbury thinks or says.'

To Stanley, whose whole life had been a struggle to escape the stigma of illegitimacy and the workhouse—to acquire a name where none had existed—such arrogance was intolerable. With his black followers he could play the stern but loving father, a mixture of brutality and quixotic generosity, but any relationship approaching equality was impossible for him. 'I have had no friend on any expedition, no one who could possibly be my companion, on an equal footing, except while with Livingstone,' he would write in his autobiography. But his relationship with Livingstone had scarcely been one of equality. It had worked because each had a need of the other and had been able to cast him in a role that was mutually satisfying. Thus Livingstone could be the father Stanley had never known, and Stanley the kind of son and heir Livingstone would really have liked. Stanley had need of a hero and Livingstone filled the bill to perfection; but Stanley also wanted to *be* a hero and have others regard him in the way he regarded Livingstone. The irony is that there were those among his officers who were perfectly ready to make him a hero, if only he had given them a chance.

ONE SUCH was Herbert Ward, who was the only volunteer to be taken on *after* the expedition arrived in the Congo. Tired of the Congo, Ward had been on his way home when he met an old friend, the missionary Ingham, at Matadi and learnt of Stanley's impending return. He knew nothing of Emin Pasha, but he was galvanised by the name of Stanley. He immediately wrote Stanley a letter offering his services and, without waiting for his arrival, turned back and set about recruiting the porters whom Ingham told him Stanley would need to transport the expedition's goods up to Stanley Pool. He knew that with Stanley, actions spoke louder than words.

Ward was only twenty-four years old, but he had already packed a good deal of travel and adventure into his life. He had left school at the age of fifteen in defiance of his parents' wishes. He went out to New Zealand, and over the next three years travelled extensively in New Zealand and Australia. He was in turn kauri-gum digger, coal and gold miner, stock-rider, circus performer and sailmaker. He worked his passage back to England via San Francisco and Cape Horn as an able-bodied seaman. Next, he went off to Borneo as a cadet in the British North Borneo Company. There he spent several months in the interior, living among the Dyaks, until a bout of malaria left him so weak that he had to return once more to England.

He met Stanley for the first time in 1884. The intermediary was Joseph Hatton, a novelist and the father of a friend of Ward's who had died in a shooting accident in North Borneo. Ward was attempting to write a book about his travels and he had been sharing with his friend Alfred Harmsworth (later Lord Northcliffe) first a cottage in Hampstead and then, when their combined resources dwindled almost to nothing, a single room in Lavender Sweep, Clapham. Partly no doubt to escape this poverty, but more out of an habitual restlessness and eagerness for adventure, Ward went along to Grafton Street to see Stanley, who was then recruiting officers for the newly established Congo Free State.

At first, Ward had been ill at ease in the great man's presence. Stanley's solemn manner and his penetrating gaze were more than a little disconcerting; and Ward was conscious all the time that he was being tested.

'People die there,' Stanley said of the Congo.

Ward spoke of his experience of Borneo and the fact that he had survived a fever there. Stanley was amused.

'Well, after all,' he said, 'the Congo is a sanatorium compared to Borneo, and you seem suited for the life. If, however, I decide to send you, I should of course require some testimonials, as you would occupy positions of great trust and responsibility.'

Ward was at a loss to know what to produce until a happy inspiration led him to fish out of his pocket his sailor's discharge, a crumpled scrap of paper which he handed to Stanley. Stanley was perfectly satisfied with this; he himself had shipped before the mast in his younger days and knew all about living on salt-pork and ship's biscuits. This gave him an immediate sense of kinship with Ward, whom he went on to describe in an enthusiastic letter of recommendation to the King of the Belgians as 'a Clive, a Gordon', adding that he showed more promise than any of the 600 volunteers he had previously interviewed.

Stanley's recommendation meant that Ward was soon offered a contract. The terms of service were appalling: 'I was warned that if at any time I fell ill, I must do so at my own risk and expense, and it was almost implied that if I died in the service of the State, such conduct would be considered most reprehensible . . . In fact the whole [contract] was so constructed that those who for a miserable pittance volunteered service in a deadly climate received little or no consideration for the risks they ran.' Yet Ward was so eager to go out that he signed the contract there and then, committing himself to a period of three years in the Congo.

He served fifteen months on the lower Congo and a further six months at Bangala on the upper river, but then through no fault of his own was replaced by a Belgian officer. He was one of several victims of the policy of 'Belgianisation', through which Leopold tightened his grip on the Congo Free State after the Berlin

Conference of 1885. Ward resigned from the service of the State and, with Stanley's support, got himself taken on by the one semi-foreign company still allowed to operate in the Congo—the Sanford Exploring Expedition. This had been founded by Leopold's friend, General Sanford, who was for many years American Minister in Brussels. Two other British pioneers in the Congo—'Stanley's men', as they were called—found refuge in this company, and both were close friends of Ward's: E. J. Glave and Roger Casement.

After two and a half years in the Congo, Ward had had enough. He felt, as he put it, 'a longing for glimpses of the outside world other than those afforded me by newspapers whose latest intelligence was six months old'. And he was making his way to the coast with a view to getting a passage on the first homeward-bound steamer when he heard the news of Stanley and his latest expedition.

He collected together some 400 porters and marched them towards Matadi. But he had not taken them far when, coming over the top of a hill, he was confronted with the entire expedition strung out in a line before him. It was an impressive sight: Stanley, mounted on a mule and wearing his celebrated African costume—peaked cap with air vents and a piece of cloth at the back to keep the sun off his neck, frogged jacket, knickerbockers and boots—preceded by a tall Sudanese soldier in a dark blue greatcoat and hood, carrying the flag of the yacht of James Gordon Bennett, proprietor of the *New York Herald* (Stanley's former employer), and followed by his Somali servants, Zanzibari porters and Sudanese soldiers, all distinctively clad and fresh looking, as they had only been on the march a day or two.

When Stanley saw Ward, he dismounted and with an expansive gesture invited him to sit down, though there was nowhere to sit but the ground. He then flourished a silver cigar case, which was a present from the Prince of Wales, and got down to business. He quizzed Ward about the steamers at the Pool, how many there were, their condition and so on. Only then did he say that if Ward could clear out the thousand loads he'd been forced to leave at Matadi and bring them up to Stanley Pool by the end of April, he would 'take him along'.

That gave Ward a month. He hurried on to Matadi and

succeeded in sending off the thousand loads in the first week of April. He himself left at the end of the week. It was a miserable journey through the cataract region; it rained heavily and he and his men had to cross swollen rivers and deep swamps. By the time they reached Manyanga—halfway between Matadi and Leopold-ville—they were a pretty bedraggled lot. There he joined forces with an old friend, John Rose Troup, who had also served in the Congo. On the advice of Sir Francis de Winton, Stanley had selected Troup specially to supervise the transportation of the expedition's many loads. To that end he had travelled direct to the Congo, while Stanley and the others had gone the long way round, via Suez, Zanzibar and the Cape. (So neither Troup nor Ward knew any of the other officers.)

'Methodical in his habits and conscientious to a degree,' Ward wrote of Troup, 'he was just the man for the job.' His father was a General who had made his name in India, and Troup himself had passed the army entrance exams, though he never took up his commission. He had travelled around, toyed with the idea of becoming a journalist, and then enlisted in the service of the Congo State, where he became something of a protégé of Sir Francis de Winton. Throughout the expedition he wrote regular letters to his erstwhile chief.

Ward and Troup stayed for a week at Manyanga to allow stragglers to catch up and get all the loads together. Then they marched to Stanley Pool. It was still raining heavily and their spirits, low enough already, were further depressed by the sights that daily greeted their eyes. All along the path lay the dead and dying—evidence of the merciless haste with which Stanley had driven his men. The officers did what they could for those who were still alive; the dead they buried.

Before they reached the Pool, they ran into an officer of the State who had been sent by Stanley to intercept the mail and confiscate any letters addressed to the two missions at Stanley Pool—the Baptist Missionary Society and the American Baptist Missionary Union—which looked official, and might therefore contain instructions to the missionaries not to loan their steamers to Stanley. Ward wrote, 'This struck me as a very crooked proceeding.' A day or two later, Ward and Troup met the head of the ABMU, Mr Billington, who had just left the Pool in high dudgeon. He told them that he had refused to let the expedition use his steamer, the *Henry Reed*, but that Stanley had taken charge of it by the simple expedient of placing a guard on it—and another at the mission station. Ward thought such high-handed action would create a controversy when it was reported in Europe.

But Stanley really had no choice. Leopold's promise of 'his whole flotilla of steamers' was revealed as the sham Stanley had always feared it might turn out to be—amounting to no more than a single steamer, the *Stanley*, and a whale boat. And the expedition could not remain at Stanley Pool without causing a famine in the area. So Stanley began by trying to negotiate with the missionaries. The BMS, recognising that their steamer, the *Peace*, would be requisitioned if they refused to hand it over voluntarily, lent it with good grace (Stanley having intercepted the inevitable letter of refusal from their head office in London). But the ABMU held out longer, with Mr Billington considering the matter 'prayer-fully'—or playing for time. One of the two officers sent by Stanley to see Billington complained that they had to sit and listen to 'a lot of pious cant for an hour but always with the same result—a refusal'. He, at least, applauded Stanley's decision to seize the steamer.

There was, of course, another side to the question. It was all very well for Stanley to appeal to the missionaries' better nature by emphasising that it was an English expedition and that its aim was an essentially humane one: namely, to rescue Emin Pasha and his people from the fate that General Gordon had met at the hands of the Mahdi and his dervishes. It was all very well for him to point out to them that for the sake of their own people they should lend him their steamers—otherwise they would find themselves facing starvation. The missionaries had to consider what effect it would have on the natives, seeing their steamers full of armed and excitable Zanzibaris—not to mention the man whom Stanley, 'on behalf of His Majesty the King of the Belgians and Sovereign of the Congo State', had appointed Governor of the Stanley Falls district. This man was practically the devil incarnate; he represented everything the missionaries abominated. To be responsible for providing the means to convey him to his post was something they would indeed have to consider 'prayerfully'.

4

HAMED BIN MOHAMMED el Marjebi, known to the world as
Tippu-Tib, was the most notorious of the Central African slave-
raiders. Though he was an Arab from Zanzibar, his features were
more negroid than Arab. But he wore the distinctive dress, a long
and spotless white robe, that marked out the Arabs—or so-called
Arabs—in Africa. By the time he was appointed Governor of
Stanley Falls district he was about fifty years old and his beard was
flecked with grey.

He had begun his career in the manner of many Zanzibari
Arabs seeking riches, by raising enough money to equip a caravan
for the purpose of trade in the interior of Africa. He took with
him on his first journey 400 porters loaded with cloth and beads,
which he hoped to exchange for ivory and slaves. He also had
100 fighting men in case he should need to use force to gain his
ends.

On his first journey into the interior Tippu arrived at a village
called Ruemba, to the south-west of Lake Tanganyika, and
entered into negotiations with the chief there, whose name was
Nsama. Nsama was known to have large quantities of ivory, but
he had also acquired something of a reputation for murdering
Arab traders and making off with their goods. Tippu-Tib was
making so little progress with this chief that after a time he
decided to move on. His stock of cloth and beads, which the
covetous chief kept demanding in the form of presents, was rapidly
dwindling. But at that moment—so the story goes—Tippu
discovered a plot to murder him and that gave him the excuse, if
he needed one, to take the offensive. Although his men were
outnumbered they had guns, whereas the natives only had spears;
so the fighting, though fierce, was brief, and the outcome never in
doubt. The men of the village were massacred, the women and
children were taken as slaves and the village itself was burnt.
There are various accounts of what happened to Nsama: some say

he was beheaded on the spot; others that he was spared after he had handed over his accumulated wealth to Tippu-Tib.

Was it on this occasion or on another, later journey that Tippu was ambushed while out walking unarmed, and wounded in the thigh? Accounts differ but the story is much the same: one of his women, who was close by preparing food or drawing water, heard his cries and rushed to his tent to fetch him a gun. He then killed one of his assailants and the others ran off. This was the signal for a general massacre such as the one that took place at Nsama's village. It makes little difference whether or not it was this occasion, since the pattern was always the same. And Tippu-Tib, penetrating further and further into the interior, grew rich in slaves and ivory until he was known and feared throughout the land.

He did not always need to use force. Often his reputation went before him and he got what he wanted without a fight; once, approaching the Manyema country, he picked up a story which he was able to turn to good account with the credulous natives. Again, there is more than one version of this story but the point is the same. There was a war between two neighbouring tribes and either the chief's two sisters were taken into slavery and never heard of again, or it was the chief himself and his wife who secretly left their country one night and never returned. Whatever the facts of the case, Tippu-Tib successfully posed as the long-lost heir and thus swiftly and peaceably made himself the reigning sovereign of thirty or forty thousand people.

There is also uncertainty about the origin of his nickname, Tippu-Tib. Livingstone, who met him in 1869 and received help from him, referred to him in his journals as 'Tipo Tipo' and noted what Susi had told him, that when Tippu stood over the spoil taken from Nsama, he said, 'Now I am Tipo Tipo, the gatherer together of wealth.' Others attribute the nickname to a nervous twitching of his eyelids, but the most commonly accepted explanation is that the name was bestowed upon him by the natives of the districts he attacked, because the noise of his guns, all blazing away at the same time, sounded in their ears like 'tip u tip, tip u tip.'

During his travels between Central Africa and the coast opposite Zanzibar, Tippu-Tib met and helped many European explorers, not only Livingstone, but also Cameron, Wissman, Dr Junker and, of course, Stanley. All were impressed by his dignity and his gentlemanly manner—'personal virtues,' Herbert Ward wrote, 'which contrasted strangely with his professional depravity.' It is also recorded that he was strict in his religous observances; he was a Muslim, of course.

Stanley met him at Kasongo in October 1876 on his famous journey across the 'Dark Continent' when, taking up where Livingstone had left off, he traced the length of the river Congo down to the sea. 'After regarding him for a few minutes,' Stanley wrote (he was always trying to out-stare the chiefs and others he met on his travels, and he was quick to notice that nervous twitching of the eyelids which characterised Tippu-Tib), 'I came to the conclusion that this Arab was a remarkable man—the most remarkable man I had met among Arabs, Wa-Swahili, and half-castes in Africa.

'He was neat in his person; his clothes were of spotless white; his fez cap brand new; his waist was incircled by a rich dowlé; his dagger was splendid with rich filagree work; and his *tout ensemble* was that of an Arab gentleman in very comfortable circum-stances.'

Stanley thought him 'a picture of energy and strength' and was impressed by his large following of young Arabs and Africans who were clearly so full of admiration for their chief.

Tippu-Tib, for his part, remembered a conversation he had with Stanley the morning after the latter's arrival. Stanley showed him a gun and said, 'With this gun you can fire 15 shots at a time.'

Tippu-Tib had never seen or heard of such a thing.

'From one barrel?' he asked.

'They come out of one barrel,' Stanley replied.

Tippu decided Stanley was lying, so he said, 'On the Lomami is a bow on which you place 20 arrows, and when you shoot it off the whole 20 fly at once, and every arrow strikes a man.'

Stanley got up without a word, went outside and immediately fired off twelve rounds, greatly to the astonishment of the Arab leader. It was his turn to be impressed.

Stanley proceeded to draw up an agreement with Tippu-Tib that he should accompany him some distance down the Congo, with 400 men, in return for 5,000 dollars. In the event they did not get very far before Tippu decided he had had enough. The going was extremely difficult, through the dense undergrowth of the forest, and his men were being decimated by smallpox. Stanley claimed that the courage of his escort was exhausted and maintained that he released Tippu from his contract, after Tippu had used his influence to prevent the Zanzibari porters deserting from the expedition. Tippu's version was that the men had mutinied and would have turned back more than once if he had not, with great difficulty, managed to persuade them to go on with Stanley. The difference is one of emphasis. But Tippu-Tib also averred that Stanley, in gratitude, had promised him all sorts of presents if the expedition succeeded and he returned to Europe. It was a grudge Tippu bore against Stanley that he had never received a single one of those presents.

Shortly after this encounter Tippu-Tib returned to Zanzibar, fighting more battles and picking up more slaves and ivory on the way. He stayed a year in Zanzibar, then re-entered Africa with another large force and headed west. This time, following where Stanley had blazed the trail, his destination was the region of Stanley Falls, which the Arabs called Zingiti. Once he had established himself there, he succeeded in tyrannising the whole of the surrounding countryside with his bands of Manyema mercenaries. It was a heavily populated area and the native villages, small and unorganised, always at war with their neighbours, fell easy victims to the plundering Arabs. Local quarrels between one tribe and another always worked to the advantage of the Arabs, who took sides and decided the outcome with their superior forces and weapons. The natives of the region were cannibals, and those who fought with the Arabs were rewarded with the corpses of their enemies; they had a feast and the Arabs made off with the ivory. Over the years in which they had been left to live their own lives and fight their own battles, these natives had accumulated great stores of elephant tusks, so that the whole region was for the Arabs, as one writer described it, 'a veritable Eldorado'.

It was not only the missionaries who were surprised to find Stanley giving Tippu-Tib free passage to the very headquarters from which he conducted his nefarious trade. Many of the State officials, too, were puzzled; and they pronounced it a very short-sighted policy to make him Governor of Stanley Falls. This was one poacher, they felt, who should never have been made game-keeper. They simply did not believe in his conversion.

Neither, of course, did Stanley. It was merely a matter of convenience. In approaching the Equatorial province from the west, he was taking a risk; he had to go through country dominated by the Arabs. And relations between the Arabs and the infant Congo Free State had reached their nadir. Less than a year before, the Arabs had attacked the Stanley Falls station and driven out the State's representative, an Englishman called Deane. Deane had been sent there in the first place to keep the peace between the Arabs and the natives, but he was quite powerless; he had guns but no manpower. If he sided with the Arabs, he had to turn a blind eye to their depredations; if he defended the natives, he earned the Arabs' enmity.

The quarrel flared up over a woman. She had been badly beaten by the Arabs and came to Deane for protection. The Arabs demanded her return; Deane refused: 'As an Englishman I will not, and as an officer of the State I cannot, give her up.' He offered them money instead, but they would not take money. Most probably the woman was simply a pretext; the attack would have happened anyway. Without the restraining influence of Tippu-Tib—he alone, among the Arabs, recognised the futility of fighting the Europeans, and he had gone to Zanzibar—the Arabs were anxious for a trial of strength.

Deane resisted for several days. But eventually he was forced to abandon his island station and blow up the guns and ammunition. He took to the forest with his few remaining followers and was rescued by a steamer a month later—too weak even to stand. He had been reduced to grubbing for roots and even caterpillars. But he survived the ordeal and, after a brief interlude, returned to the Congo as a big-game hunter.

Tippu-Tib was still in Zanzibar when Stanley arrived there at the beginning of 1887. He made no secret of his intention to prevent the expedition going through his country to reach Emin. When Stanley sent for him, he arrived in a belligerent mood. He brought with him a Krupp shell which had been sent to him from the Falls, and he represented himself as the injured party.

'This is what your people gave me as presents at Zingiti

[Stanley Falls] after you left,' he said. 'This is how they showed the friendship of the white man for the Arab.'

Stanley was conciliatory. He played down the seriousness of the dispute, dismissing it as an unfortunate misunderstanding attributable to the hot-headedness of the young people on both sides. He had not come, as Tippu-Tib perhaps feared, to avenge the white man's defeat at Stanley Falls, but for quite another purpose. The King of the Belgians, he said, desired peace with the Arabs and to that end he was prepared to make Tippu-Tib his official representative at Stanley Falls with a monthly salary of £30. In return, Tippu-Tib was to hoist the flag of the Free State at the very place where his people had so recently torn it down, and to prevent both the Arabs and the natives from engaging in the slave-trade. Yet at the same time he was to be free to 'carry on his legitimate private trade in any direction.'

Since Tippu-Tib's private trade, 'legitimate' or otherwise, depended on the taking and bartering of slaves for ivory, it is difficult to see how these conflicting demands, both solemnly recorded in the agreement signed by Stanley and Tippu-Tib, could be reconciled. But it looked reasonable on paper, and it was the piece of paper which would be read in Europe where the issue of slavery still aroused such passions.

It was further agreed, after some haggling, that Tippu-Tib should provide the expedition with 600 carriers from among his Manyema followers, at the rate of £6 per head for the journey from Stanley Falls to Lake Albert and back. And Stanley undertook to give Tippu-Tib and his entourage of 96, including his priest and his 18 wives, free passage round the Cape to the Congo and up the river to Stanley Falls. In fact, Tippu-Tib would have preferred to have gone to the Falls by his usual overland route, but Stanley was in a hurry and gave him no choice.

[5]

WHEN THE expedition left Stanley Pool in the steamers it had acquired by fair means and foul, Stanley singled out Ward, his newest recruit, for the honour of travelling with him on board the *Peace*. This riled some of the other officers. Barttelot, who had already left the Pool and was doing the next leg of the journey on foot, was particularly scathing when he heard that, in addition, Troup had been left behind at Leopoldville in charge of the loads which could not be accommodated on the first trip upriver. 'A beastly shame,' he wrote in his diary, 'as Troup has done more good work besides being the first chosen; and Ward at the best is only a loafer. But Stanley regards no man's rights nor merits and has no sense of justice. He is intensely selfish and shows his inferior breeding at every turn.'

The contemptuous dismissal of Ward is surprising in view of the favourable opinion Stanley had of him. But that was just the trouble. If Stanley held him in high esteem, that alone would prejudice Barttelot against him. And prejudice it was, as Barttelot had not yet met either Ward or Troup.

Ward, of course, was flattered that he was the one selected to accompany Stanley. He wrote about him to a friend in terms little short of idolatry:

I have got on remarkably well with HMS and have had about half-a-dozen very pleasant and complimentary letters from him. He is a curious man though, and about as harsh and rough, sometimes, as any Western State desperado, but when things are all square he is a most admirable man, and although he has his drawbacks, in being inconsiderate and stern, I like him, and would follow him to any part of any country, at any time, and be proud to be with him. There's a great fascination about him, and he has his soft side, if only you knew where to find it.

But Ward looked all set to become Stanley's Lieutenant, in charge of his No. 1 Company of Zanzibaris, all hand-picked men; whereas Barttelot learned from Stanley that he was to remain at Bolobo, which was the next stop upriver, with 125 of the weakest men (who, it was hoped, would recover their strength during the enforced rest) until the *Stanley* had made the round trip to Stanley Falls and back, picked up Troup and the remaining loads and started upriver for the second time. Even then he would not be going forward with Stanley, but would be left behind once again in command of a second column consisting of himself, Troup and their men. They would occupy an entrenched camp prepared for them by Stanley before he forged ahead to meet Emin. After that it would depend on Tippu-Tib. If he turned up with his 600 men, Barttelot would be free to follow Stanley to Wadelai; otherwise he might have to wait for Stanley's return.

When Stanley outlined his plans, Barttelot could scarcely contain himself—especially when he heard that William Bonny was also detailed to remain at Bolobo:

> This sounds very well, but my stay at Bolobo in Bonny's enlightened society would probably be of four months' duration and unless I obtain a distinct assurance of aid from Tippu-Tib and promise of proceeding to Wadelai I would go home, for Stanley's mere word is as nothing, he has no honour and can lie as well as most men and with utter unscrupulousness, as long as he obtains his object. His object at present is personal dislike to me and hatred of the Sudanese and his treatment of Troup is most unfair. However he is to give me a letter of instructions at Bolobo. Should they not be what I desire and if he fails to answer certain questions and comply with certain requests I go home.

Barttelot's diary for this period is filled with hatred, both for Stanley and for his own men: it is littered with references (deleted in the published version) to the 'loutish' Sudanese, the 'brutish' Sudanese and their 'nigger noise'.

During the march from Matadi to Leopoldville, Bonny had been highly critical of the way Barttelot handled the Sudanese, whose disorderliness created such problems. 'I here say that up to the present time,' he wrote in his diary, 'the Major is not the proper man for them. He will bully at one time and pander to them at another. My belief is that the "Major" is not a disciplinarian but should be at college or some place where he can lark.' It was his opinion that Barttelot was really afraid of the Sudanese, and he wondered why a man who was 'fearfully officious but utterly useless except for cheek' should be made second-in-command of the expedition. He concluded that it must be because he was 'the son of his father—it cannot be on account of his ability because he has none.'

By contrast, Bonny was in awe of his leader. He wrote, 'Stanley treats me with awful contempt in everything I do up to the present.' And it must have been a relief to turn his attention back to Barttelot (whose 'cheekiness' to Stanley he no doubt secretly envied). He went on obsessively about how Barttelot was 'no use himself but would make believe that it was others that were no use and he the big man'.

Barttelot, of course, was still very much an army officer, and Bonny resented the fact that he treated *him* as though *he* were still an NCO. To begin with, at least, there was no love lost between them.

On 14 May, when Barttelot reached Bolobo, his mutinous spirit was soothed somewhat by the news that Stanley had changed his mind. Under pressure from his officers, Stanley had decided to take Barttelot with him to Stanley Falls and in his place leave Ward at Bolobo. Stanley told Ward that it was essential to have somebody in charge at Bolobo who knew the country and could speak the language. But that was not the real reason, as Ward well knew.

So Ward remained with Bonny at Bolobo. Writing for publication during Bonny's lifetime, he described Bonny as a 'valuable assistant', who was 'plucky in spirit and methodical in principle, with ideas bounded by considerations of rigid discipline'. Yet Ward had reason to be grateful to Bonny, whose 'enlightened society' Barttelot had so dreaded. When he was knocked down by a particularly rebellious and undisciplined Zanzibari and was completely at his mercy, Bonny stepped in and felled the man with his musket. Bonny's only comment on the incident was: 'This had been brewing for a long time, Ward had treated them so badly and without a cause.'

Bonny was quite as critical of Ward at Bolobo as he had been of Barttelot on the march to Leopoldville. On 25 May he wrote, 'The men are getting very troublesome through Ward continually interfering with them when there is no occasion for it. He continues knocking them about and swearing at them instead of leaving them alone. I am convinced that this man is not up to much but he appears to be in great favour with Stanley.' Scarcely a day passed without some jibe from Bonny. His diary is a record of constant aggravation. The next day he is writing, 'Ward and I disputed about what *mitakos* [brass rods used as currency] each of us were allowed,' and this is followed by a torrent of abuse, ending: 'He says that he has been in correspondence with Stanley in London, that Stanley used to ask him to send him espionage accounts of the affairs of the Congo'—and in different writing (added later?): 'He is an awful liar.'

No matter who his companion might be, he revealed himself to Bonny as the coward, bully, liar, hypocrite or thief he really was. Bonny saw through all men; and though he hated some more than others, none of them entirely escaped his vituperation.

6

BY THE end of May the main body of the expedition had reached Bangala, about halfway between Stanley Pool and Stanley Falls. Since the loss of the Falls station this was the last of the stations the Free State held. Here Barttelot received orders from Stanley to escort Tippu-Tib and his party to the Falls in the *Henry Reed*. He was to take 40 of the Sudanese with him, as Stanley was frightened that if the Zanzibaris went they might desert at the Falls, preferring service with the Arabs alongside their own kind to the more arduous life of the expedition. After he had seen Tippu-Tib safely to the Falls, Barttelot was to make his way back to the Aruwini river and up to a place called Yambuya—the site of the fortified camp he was to command—where Stanley would be waiting for him.

This gave Barttelot an opportunity to get to know the man he would have to rely on for the 600 carriers the expedition needed to convey loads up to Lake Albert. His first impression had been favourable. At the end of April he had written to his fiancée, from Leopoldville, 'Tippu-Tib who accompanies us the whole way is a great pal of mine and he seems a good old chap. I hope he will turn out so.' Now he had more reason than ever for hoping so. If Tippu-Tib failed to fulfil his side of the contract and provide 600 men, Barttelot would be unable to march his column out of Yambuya and follow Stanley. He could be delayed for months. So it was vital that he should establish a good understanding with the Arab leader.

It was not long before Barttelot got some insight into how the Arabs and natives regarded one another. On 10 June, Tippu-Tib ordered a halt at a village so that his people might trade with the natives. He went through some kind of ritual peace-making and the trading began. While it was going on Barttelot went for a walk through the village, alone and unarmed. Suddenly all hell broke loose: there was shouting and screaming and as Barttelot hurried towards the noise, 20 of Tippu's men dashed past him in the other direction. Two of them were wounded. Next came a whole crowd of natives, waving their spears and knives, but the odd thing was that they made no attempt to attack Barttelot, though he was unarmed. Indeed they went out of their way to avoid him, running into the grass on either side of the path where he was standing. He then met three of his own Sudanese who persuaded him to return with them to the steamer. On their way they picked up one of Tippu's men who had been stabbed in the back and carried him on board. There they found that six of Tippu's men and one of his women had been wounded, as well as one of the Zanzibari crew of the steamer.

The new Governor of Stanley Falls determined that such audacity on the part of the natives should not go unpunished, and he marched on the village with Barttelot and his Sudanese in attendance. But the village was now deserted. The wretched inhabitants, knowing what to expect, had disappeared into the bush and Tippu-Tib had to content himself with razing the village to the ground.

News spread quickly in Central Africa. The ubiquitous drums beat out the rhythm of war and by the time the steamer came to the next village the natives were already assembled on the bank. Tippu-Tib was all for putting ashore; but Barttelot said no. Tippu then ordered the Sudanese to open fire; but once again Barttelot intervened, countermanding the order. He explained that Stanley had given him orders on no account to provoke the natives unnecessarily; they had already punished one village and that was enough. He could not disobey Stanley.

Tippu was furious. Since Barttelot refused to help him, he said, he would do nothing more for the expedition. It was a nasty moment. But Barttelot, by insisting that he was only carrying out Stanley's orders, felt he had succeeded in diverting the Arab's anger.

They were now in Tippu's own country. They had passed the junction of the Congo and the Aruwini and were within 100 miles of the Falls. Unaware of the results of Stanley's diplomacy, natives and Arabs alike mistook the purpose of the steamer's visit, thinking it had been sent by the State to avenge Deane and the burning of the Falls station. The natives clustered round it in their canoes looking for protection from Tippu's people whose raids had left them homeless, while the Arabs themselves opened fire on it, since they had no way of knowing that their leader was on board. Tippu, however, soon made himself known both to his own men and to the natives—whom he promised to protect in his new capacity as governor of the district. From this point on, his was a triumphal progress. He was greeted enthusiastically at the Arab settlements and his people's pleasure at his sudden return was only equalled by their wonder at the means of it.

Yet his authority did not go unquestioned, even among the Arabs. He was without doubt the biggest and most influential chief, but there were others; and not all of them felt obliged to give him their allegiance—especially after he had made a compact with the Europeans. His political shrewdness would be misunderstood by these and given a less than flattering interpretation. Foremost among his 'enemies', as Tippu-Tib described them in a letter to the acting British Consul-General in Zanzibar, Frederic Holmwood, was one Said bin Habib. He was an independent slave trader of some substance. He had crossed Africa some twenty years before and married a Portuguese African woman at Loanda; he had even been mentioned in one of Livingstone's books.

Tippu-Tib complained that Said bin Habib and his followers had 'spoiled the river'—by which he meant, their indiscriminate raids had depopulated the area. Tippu himself was anxious to get the conquered villagers to return to their homes and lead useful lives. He maintained that if it came to a fight he could beat Said bin Habib, but he wanted to avoid that. Therefore he got Barttelot to write a letter for him to the King of the Belgians requesting that His Majesty send two white officers and 30 or 40 armed men as an outward and visible sign of State support. Perhaps he did not altogether trust Barttelot, because he also urged Consul Holmwood to write on his behalf. But the message was the same. If he was to be undisputed chief of the Falls, he argued, he desperately needed the European presence: officers, men and, if possible, a boat as well.

While the Arabs drank coffee and talked endlessly among themselves, Barttelot wrote letters home and took in his new surroundings, which included some fairly bizarre sights: '16 June

—I saw about 20 slaves in a chain—men and women—at Yarukombe. I also saw some yesterday at Ukanga.'

The next day they reached the Falls, which Barttelot described as 'very like a cataract on the Nile, except there is more vegetation'. He was impressed by the sheer volume of water there, but he was rather less impressed by some of the people he met for the first time: Tippu-Tib's cousin Nzige, for instance, he thought looked 'very like one of those Jew Arabs who come on board to sell ostrich-feathers'. It was at the Falls that he had a final palaver with Tippu-Tib which did not bode too well for the future. Stanley had promised that if Tippu-Tib provided 600 carriers for the expedition, he would supply them with ammunition; but this ammunition had been left behind at Bolobo and could not be handed over for another month or two—not until the steamer bringing up the remaining loads arrived.

As Barttelot understood it, Stanley had explained the situation to Tippu-Tib and asked him to provide the ammunition on the understanding that he would be repaid later. But Tippu now chose to make an issue of it. Barttelot thought it was probably because of the stand he had taken in refusing to help Tippu subdue the natives. He believed he had succeeded in diverting Tippu's anger on to Stanley, but now it seemed he had succeeded only too well: Tippu was accusing Stanley of breaking faith with him over the gunpowder. A far more likely explanation, however, is Tippu's own, which was that when he got to Stanley Falls he found that gunpowder was in great demand (and short supply) and the price was exorbitant. He knew that Stanley drove a hard bargain and was therefore unwilling to buy it at a price which he might not be able to recoup.

All that Barttelot was able to extract from him was a 'half promise' that he would provide 200 men, with ammunition, as soon as he could. But this was enough for Barttelot. He reckoned that with 200 men he would be able to 'cut on' after Stanley as soon as Troup and Ward came up—provided, of course, Stanley would give him his head (as he himself, who 'dearly loved a horse', would have put it).

33

7

STANLEY, MEANWHILE, had reached Yambuya without mishap.

On the way up the river the war drums rattled and boomed. The natives danced on the banks, brandishing spears and bows, and when the fleet of steamers and little boats had gone past without offering a fight, they stuck out their backsides and slapped them in a gesture of contempt which was reminiscent of the London 'cad'. But that was all. When their bluff was called they instantly transformed themselves into avid traders and would sell anything they possessed. The women went naked and Thomas Parke, the medical officer, observed that in general 'the higher up the river we found ourselves, the higher the dress reached until now it has, at last, culminated in absolute nudity'. Jameson saw this as a physical manifestation of a moral condition: 'The people here are the genuine savage, without a vestige of civilisation.'

Jameson had a special reason for taking an interest in his surroundings. During the expedition he and Major Barttelot had become such firm friends that when Stanley asked Barttelot which of the officers he would like to remain with him at Yambuya as his second-in-command, Barttelot had no hesitation in asking for Jameson. Troup, Ward and Bonny would join them later.

Jameson had found common cause with Barttelot in his opposition to Stanley. He, too, had suffered as a result of Stanley's arbitrary administration of justice. Once, for instance, on the march to Leopoldville, he had reported the loss of one of his company's ammunition boxes to Stanley. Stanley had ordered the chief who had been responsible for receiving the loads in camp to identify all those who had brought in their loads. This left one man whom he could not remember having seen. Stanley decided this man must be the culprit, and—in spite of Jameson's protestations that the man was one of his best carriers—gave him 100 lashes. Several times during the beating he stopped to ask where the box was, and each time the man swore that *his* box was in camp. Jameson was disgusted. Stanley, he wrote, 'then chained and padlocked the chiefs all together, and accused me of losing three boxes of ammunition (which I flatly denied), and told me that in '77 it would have been death, and if it happened again we must part. If this sort of thing is to go on, and he speaks to me again as he did today before the men, I should not be sorry if we did part, for I certainly will not keep my temper again.'

But Jameson kept his temper, and as he steamed up the Aruwini towards Yambuya he was simultaneously attracted and repelled by what he saw around him. At one moment he would remember it was 'Cup-day at Ascot' and be filled with nostalgia, wondering uneasily how many of his friends would spare a thought for absent ones such as himself. But the next instant he would thrill with curiosity about these strange-looking savages who were reputed to be cannibals. He could readily believe it. He had already heard a few stories. One of the Belgians at Bangala had told him about three Hausa soldiers the natives had captured. They had tied them to trees and crammed them with food until they were fat enough to eat; but one of them, being a scrawny old fellow, did not respond to this treatment and remained unappetising. So he survived his colleagues and, at the third attempt, made his escape.

The natives on the Aruwini filed their teeth to a sharp point—the better to eat human flesh with, no doubt. They sold necklaces and other choice ornaments made out of the teeth of their victims. They had huge ears sticking straight out from their heads, though from a distance it was impossible to tell if they were real or not. The officers were moved to question whether the different methods of self-adornment practised in different parts of the country had not something to do with the kinds of wild animal that predominated in the particular area: lower down there had been quantities of buffalo and there the natives had tied their hair in bunches which resembled buffalo's horns; here it was elephants, hence the enormous ears. That was one theory. Jameson, when they got close enough to see, noted how the effect was achieved. 'The curious appearance of their ears,' he wrote, 'is due to tufts of dry coloured grasses, bunches of teeth, and all sorts of things stuck into the holes bored all along their edges.'

These natives were anything but friendly. They shook their spears and shields, they yelled and shouted insults and illustrated with unmistakable gestures how they would cut the throat of anyone who tried to land. Jameson thought it was 'a bad look-out for our chances of trading for food at the entrenched camp'. During the months ahead he and his future companions would have to rely on the neighbouring tribes for provisions.

Yambuya itself was a disappointment. Jameson had expected a large waterfall or series of waterfalls at this, the highest navigable reach of the river, but in fact the rapids were nothing more spectacular than a few lines of broken water. The inhabitants of the large village on the south side of the river were unwilling to let the expedition land, so Stanley was forced to land on the other bank. But he had no intention of staying there. The next morning there was a palaver with the natives. Stanley argued that the presence of the expedition would protect them from Arab marauders, but there was no argument that could induce them to abandon their homes to an invader, be he Arab or white. Stanley described what followed in a letter to William Mackinnon:

> We had been nearly two hours at this work of negotiating, and the natives, being addicted to palavers, would not have minded very much had the palavers lasted a week. We therefore signalled to the *Stanley* to appear with the troops. A few minutes later, at a second signal, both steamers [the *Peace* was the other] set up a hideous steam whistling, under the protection of which the troops disembarked, and in a few seconds we were in possession of an empty village. There was no occasion to fire a shot, for the natives had disappeared as completely as the vapour of the steam whistling had dissolved.

The expedition had arrived. With only this token show of force, Stanley had acquired the site he wanted for a base. He now set about fortifying it, making a proper encampment that could be defended against either Arabs or natives. Except on the north side, where there was an almost sheer drop of 40 feet into the river, Stanley planned to dig a large ditch which would surround the camp like a moat. Inside this ditch he would build his stockade, or 'boma' as it was called locally. The village, which was thus to be enclosed, consisted of peculiar cone-shaped huts with low doors and long sloping roofs made of overlapping palm leaves. The officers had not come across these before, though they had read about them in Stanley's books. They thought they resembled nothing so much as 'overgrown beehives'. The men settled into the huts and the officers pitched their tents. Outside the camp, Stanley insisted that they clear the bush for 150 yards in all directions to prevent the natives from creeping up unobserved and making a surprise attack. He was leaving nothing to chance. As he told Jameson, when he called the officers into his tent on the evening of 16 June, should anything happen to the stores he was leaving behind, the expedition would be at an end. He would not leave Yambuya, he added, until he was convinced that the camp was unassailable.

He had summoned his officers to tell them his plans. He would wait seven days for Tippu-Tib and his men, and while he was waiting he would supervise the construction of the entrenched camp. Then he would march. His intention was to make contact with Emin, hand over to him the ammunition he would need to defend himself and then return by the route he had taken going up. That way he would be sure of meeting the rear column if it managed to move; if not, he would be back at Yambuya in October or November. He was leaving Barttelot and Jameson in charge of the entrenched camp. He explained to the assembled officers that while he thought Barttelot was 'not sufficiently forbearing', he was sure that Jameson's experience of Africa would 'correct his impetuosity'.

Stanley was worried about Barttelot, about his capacity to deal with Tippu-Tib and the Arabs, not to mention the Africans. When there was no sign of him on 20 June, the day he was expected to arrive, Stanley's doubts turned to alarm. He imagined all sorts of things: that Tippu-Tib had seized the *Henry Reed;* that the Sudanese had mutinied, or worse, that Barttelot had had a row with the natives and *they* had captured the steamer. He put all his fears on paper in a letter of instructions which he gave to Lt. Stairs, an officer in the Royal Engineers, whom he was about to send to look for Barttelot when Barttelot himself turned up.

On 24 June Barttelot received his final orders from Stanley, also in the form of a letter of instructions. He was given the option of marching, if he felt able to do so without having to discard too many of the expedition's valuable stores, or remaining at Yambuya until Stanley's return in November. Here are some of the key passages from this long-winded document:

Pending the arrival of our men and goods, it behoves you to be very alert and wary in the command of this stockaded camp. Though the camp is favourably situated and naturally strong, a brave enemy would find it no difficult task to capture if the commander is lax in discipline, vigour, and energy. Therefore I feel sure that I have made a wise choice in selecting you to guard our interests here during our absence . . .

The interests now entrusted to you are of vital importance to this Expedition. The men you will eventually have under you consist of more than an entire third of the Expedition. The goods that will be brought up are the currency needed for transit through the regions beyond the Lakes; there will be a vast store of ammunition and provisions, which are of equal importance to us. The loss of these men and goods would be certain ruin to us, and the Advance Force itself would need to solicit relief in its turn. Therefore, weighing this matter well, I hope you will spare no pains to maintain order and discipline in your camp, and make your defences complete, and keep them in such a condition that however brave an enemy may be he can make no impression on them . . . For remember, it is not the natives alone who may wish to assail you, but the Arabs and their followers may, through some cause or other, quarrel with you and assail your camp . . .

It may happen, should Tippu-Tib have sent the full number of adults promised by him to me, viz. 600 men (able to carry loads), and the *Stanley* has arrived safely with the 125 men left by me at Bolobo, that you will feel yourself sufficiently competent to march the column, with all the goods brought up by the *Stanley*, and those left by me at Yambuya, along the road pursued by me. In that event, which would be very desirable, you will follow closely our route, and before many days we shall most assuredly meet . . . It may happen also that, though Tippu-Tib has sent some men, he has not sent enough to carry the goods with your own force. In that case you will of course use your discretion as to what goods you can dispense with to enable you to march ... If you still cannot march, then it would be better to make two marches of six miles twice over, if you prefer marching to staying for our arrival, than throw too many things away ...

In the ordinary duties of the defence, and the conduct of the camp or of the march, there is only one chief, which is yourself; but, should any vital step be proposed to be taken, I beg you will take the voice of Mr Jameson also. And when Messrs Troup and Ward are here, pray admit them to your confidence, and let them speak freely their opinions ...

Your treatment of the natives, I suggest, should depend entirely upon their conduct to you. Suffer them to return to the neighbouring villages in peace, and if you can in any manner by moderation, small gifts occasionally of brass rods, etc., hasten an amicable intercourse, I should recommend you doing so ...

The one eventuality for which Stanley had made no provision at all in this letter of instructions was if Tippu-Tib failed to send *any* men. What if none came and Barttelot had only the men Stanley was now leaving with him and those due to arrive with Troup and Ward from Bolobo? Most of these were being left behind because they were sick already. Was he still to try and follow Stanley, with many more loads and considerably fewer men than Stanley himself was taking, and by so doing risk losing many of the stores on which Stanley placed such a premium? On this point Stanley was strangely silent.

Meanwhile, Stairs had shown Barttelot *his* letter of instructions (which Stanley had written when he feared Barttelot was missing), and repeated to him what Stanley had said when he handed him the letter, that if any one of his officers got into danger through foolhardiness or want of proper caution he would not lift a finger to help him. Barttelot was furious. He went in to see Stanley and told him bluntly that he had read his letter to Stairs and that his suspicions were absurd. He reminded Stanley that he had allowed him a margin of two days; he had kept within that margin, so why the panic? How could Stanley possibly imagine that the Sudanese might mutiny? It was absurd; they were doing well under his command. And it was just as absurd to suspect him of having a row with the natives when he had so much food on board that he did not need to have any dealings with them. As for Tippu-Tib, was it not Stanley himself who said that he would as soon trust Tippu-Tib as he would any white man?

'Yes,' Stanley replied, 'but I would only trust a white man to a certain point and no further, as my letter of instructions showed.'

Barttelot said, 'Yes, that is the worst of it. Trust me all in all or not at all.'

Stanley was angry too. He was angry with Stairs for showing his letter to Barttelot; he was probably angry with himself for having written it in the first place and he was certainly angry with Barttelot for bringing the matter up again. On top of that, Barttelot had been the bearer of bad news from Tippu-Tib: he had told Stanley that Tippu thought he had broken faith with him over the ammunition. Stanley's first reaction had been petulant; he had told Barttelot he did not want Tippu-Tib's aid, he could manage perfectly well without the men. He had not meant it, of course, but Barttelot always managed to get on his nerves. He would keep nagging at him. At this moment Stanley must have heartily wished he had taken General Brackenbury's advice and had nothing to do with the young major.

As for Barttelot, when the row with Stanley was over he poured out his feelings in a letter to his brother-in-law, Major Sclater. He told him all that had happened on the journey up and went on:

> This has been a doleful letter, but I write to you because I think one of the family should know how we are situated. I have never been on such a mournful, cheerless trip as this. The harder we worked, the glummer Stanley looked. After a long march, no smile from him or word of any sort, except to say 'You have lost a box,' or some sneer of that sort. As for the Zanzibaris, they are the most loathsome brutes I have ever met, lazy, impertinent, filthy and such liars, nearly as big as Stanley himself—for he often gives orders and when carried out gets furious and swears he never gave them and so forth.

The only saving grace, as far as Barttelot was concerned, was his friendship with Jameson.

8

FOR THE next few days Yambuya was the centre of unwonted activity. The officers hurriedly finished their letters home before the departure of the steamers; for most of them it was the last opportunity they would have to send any mail for many months. There was work to be done on the fortification of the camp, and loads had to be repacked and provisions distributed to the men going with Stanley.

In the midst of all this the natives began to reappear in ones and twos and make friendly overtures. Recognising a *fait accompli*, they had now settled on the other side of the river. They brought a few plantains and the odd stringy chicken as peace offerings; and after a day or two the chief himself came over to seal the treaty in the traditional manner, by going through the ceremony of blood-brotherhood. A few people on either side assembled to witness this ceremony, which the chief performed with Barttelot. Each had to make a little incision in the other's arm and cover the wound thus made with salt. They then licked the blood off each other's arms and rubbed their wounds together so that their blood should mingle. Afterwards a chicken was killed and its blood sprinkled over the people gathered around. The chief kept its head and its body was given to Barttelot, who found the whole performance 'an exceedingly nasty one'. Jameson, who did not have to go through it, was more concerned with what effect it might have. He hoped it would induce the natives to bring food to the camp; otherwise the situation could rapidly become desperate.

To Jameson's great disappointment there was no game in the immediate area, neither flesh nor fowl, and the natives had removed every goat and chicken from all the villages within reach of the camp. The only thing they could not take with them was the manioc growing in plantations around the camp. This manioc (cassava) was their staple diet, a root vegetable which could be made into a kind of bread. As long as it had been thoroughly soaked in water it was nutritious, but if it was eaten raw or cooked unsoaked it could be poisonous, as the Zanzibaris learned to their cost. The first thing the chief requested, once the ceremony of blood-brotherhood was over, was permission for his people to collect manioc from the plantations near the camp; but Barttelot would not hear of this unless the chief first brought a present of a goat and some chickens. This way he hoped to establish a regular trade.

The two officers' own rations for six months were extremely meagre. Each had $2\frac{1}{2}$ pounds of coffee, $1\frac{1}{2}$ pounds of tea, 4 tins of condensed milk, 3 small tins of butter, $1\frac{1}{2}$ tins of sardines, $1\frac{1}{2}$ tins of sausages and 4 pots of Liebig's extract of beef. For emergencies there were some sacks of rice and a few biscuits, most of which were already mouldy.

Stanley departed on 28 June with four officers (Captains Parke and Nelson, Lt. Stairs and A. J. Mounteney Jephson—who, like Jameson, was a civilian and paid £1,000 to join the expedition) and some 380 picked men. Barttelot and Jameson watched them go with envy. Theirs was the glamorous job, blazing a trail through country that had yet to be explored. It would certainly be dangerous, but that was all part of the adventure—and it was in a spirit of adventure that all the young officers had volunteered to come in the first place. However important the work of the rear column might be in the overall effort—however dangerous it too might be—it still lacked glamour.

Stanley's last words to Barttelot were, 'Good-bye, Major; shall find you here in October, when I return.'

The advance column set out in high spirits, but the two officers left behind were disconsolate. For two or three months at least—perhaps for as many as six—they were doomed to a life of inactivity. For Barttelot, who could not bear to be still for more than a moment, it was sheer anathema. Unlike Jameson he had no interest whatsoever in his surroundings. He was no naturalist; the extraordinary number of butterflies to be found at Yambuya, nearly all of them different from ones they had seen on the Congo, were just butterflies to him. He made no collections of wild life; he had no talent for drawing, no interest in writing (though he did write letters and keep up his diary in his laconic fashion) and no curiosity about the men he had under him. His whole mind was concentrated on the problems of his command, and discipline had top priority.

Most days began with the sound of flogging. Barttelot and Jameson took it in turns to be duty officer for the night, getting up every two hours to visit the sentries and check their alertness. If they caught a man sleeping on duty, he automatically received 25 lashes the next morning. The men, seeing no reason for it, groaned at the severity of the discipline; but Barttelot did not dare relax it for fear of an attack. Stanley had impressed upon him the need for constant vigilance.

Until the remainder of the rear column came up from Bolobo, they were only a small force of 130 men, made up mostly of Zanzibaris but with 45 Sudanese and 5 Somalis. They were a miserable and demoralised party from the start. Stanley had taken all the best men with him and left the sick and useless; more than a third of those who remained were ill to begin with and deaths occurred in the camp every few days. He had also left behind the worst headman, whose name was Munichandi. Barttelot complained that not only had Munichandi no authority over the men but he was also 'laziness personified'. For this expedition the recruiting of porters in Zanzibar had been hurried and slapdash, left in the hands of agents. As a result, many of these porters were in fact slaves and lacked the zest for life which they would need to survive the months ahead. Barttelot attempted to instil in them a sense of danger and turn them into a military unit, but their apathy was profound. So the floggings continued. Jameson found it sickening but saw no help for it. If only the men would show a little more spirit.

Camp life at Yambuya settled into a routine. Barttelot and Jameson got up every morning at 5 a.m. and roused the men so that they were at work by 5.45. Breakfast for the officers was at 6, after which they worked through till 11.30 a.m. There followed a long break for lunch in the heat of the day and then work again from 1.30 to 5.30 p.m. Dinner was at 6.30 and the two officers would talk until about 9, when they went round to check up on the sentries, and then to bed.

They enjoyed their after-dinner conversations most of all. The talk of home and old times cheered them both, and each reflected that life at Yambuya would be intolerable without the other. Jameson was flattered that Barttelot had especially asked for him to stay, pleading with Stanley to leave him; it helped to stifle the disappointment he still felt at not being with the vanguard.

Their immediate worry was food. They had hoped the business of blood-brotherhood would establish a pattern of trading, with the natives bringing food to the camp, but this had not happened. Jameson made long excursions in the neighbourhood looking for food. Sometimes he and his men would suddenly come upon a village, only to find it quite deserted—not a man or goat or even a chicken in sight. Yet the odd thing was that the fires were still smoking and the village had evidently been full of life only minutes before their arrival. How did the natives always know they were coming? It was a question that teased Jameson as he returned to the camp empty-handed.

Something had to be done if they were not to starve. The villagers came over the river in their canoes and were once again asking to be allowed to gather manioc from near the camp. Once again Barttelot told them they must bring food first—two goats he demanded this time. Nothing happened; no one came. But Barttelot and Jameson now had a plan. They suspected the natives would come for the manioc whether or not they had permission, so they prepared a little surprise for them. On 10 July Jameson took 25 of the Sudanese and they went down to the river . . .

The path took a sudden turn down to the water's edge, and there lay a large canoe with only one man in it; he tried to push off but we made a dash at it, seized the end, and he jumped overboard. He made a great noise, and I hid my men on the path close to the canoe. Presently down came a woman with a load of manioc, looking about her on every side, as she had evidently heard the noise. We let her come quite close, then made a dash, and caught her. We tied her up and waited, when along came another woman with a baby. We caught her too, but she screamed fearfully, and I thought she would bring a perfect hornets' nest about us; but the noise of the rapids drowned her voice. In the meantime there were now five men and two boys standing up to their necks in the water, as we had got between them and the canoe. The Sudanese officer advanced to the edge of the water, and, pointing his gun at one of the boys, he swore he would shoot him if he did not come out. He came out, and we promptly collared him, tied the two women together, and went off at the double for camp.

Barttelot was delighted with the success of the scheme. The day's catch of two women and a baby represented food—not that the officers had suddenly 'gone native', turned cannibal or anything of that sort, but because the women could be ransomed for food of a more acceptable kind. The boy they had captured Barttelot let go, telling him to go to his village and inform the chief that his women would only be released in return for goats and fowls.

One of the women managed to escape while bathing in the river but the other, with her baby, fetched a good price. She was bartered for 'two goats, nine fowls, and some fish, with a promise that they will trade'.

The promise of trade, however, was no more than a conciliatory gesture. Three days later, on 20 July, Jameson wrote, 'One miserable canoe, with some stale fish for sale, was the only sign of trade today.' And the next day: 'I see no chance of getting any more, for the natives do not trade, or offer to, in the least; as a last resource we must catch some more of their women.'

In spite of his concern about food Jameson still found time to look around. There was a colony of black weaver-birds for instance that nested in the palm trees above his hut and he watched them at work, intrigued by their method of construction. The weaver-bird would gather leaves from the palms and then tear them into thin strips which it incorporated into the fabric of the nest in a most skilful way. Holding one end of a strip against the side of the nest with one foot, the bird used its beak and its other foot to push the other end in through a hole in the side, then pull it out again through another hole and so on, until the nest came to resemble an intricate piece of basketwork—hence its name.

Jameson spent all his spare time in this way, observing natural phenomena, skinning little birds and animals, attending to his collections, drawing and writing. He was never idle. Sometimes he reproached himself for being such a poor companion to

Barttelot who, having no use for leisure, was often at a loose end.

Conditions were far from ideal. The weather was often stiflingly hot and when it rained, it poured down. Thunderstorms were common and Jameson found that his hut leaked prodigiously. Then there were the vermin, ranging from quantities of rats down to a particular sort of small black beetle which got into the tin box where Jameson kept his collection of bird-skins and did considerable damage before he realised they were there.

There was no news of Tippu-Tib and little prospect, it seemed, of further trade with the natives. But then, at the beginning of August, came a rumour that a party of Tippu-Tib's men were coming down the river in canoes. This puzzled the officers, who were expecting them to come from the opposite direction. They came to the conclusion that these men were not Tippu-Tib's but a body of Arab marauders who were camped some distance upriver; the noise of heavy gunfire left no doubt as to what they were up to. As far as the rear column was concerned, the proximity of these Arab freebooters had the salutary effect of bringing back the natives, who could distinguish the lesser from the greater evil. They now looked to the camp for protection and brought provisions for sale as evidence of a renewed wish to be friends.

Among the natives who came to the camp was the husband of the woman who had been ransomed. Jameson was surprised to find that 'he seems to bear us no ill-will for having taken his wife and child, but was as merry as possible'.

[9]

AT 11.30 in the morning of 14 August a shout went up as the S.S. *Stanley* was sighted coming round a bend in the Aruwini. Jameson was hard put to think of anything that had ever given him such a thrill as this sudden but long-awaited appearance of the steamer. As short of food as he and Barttelot were, this hunger was as nothing compared to the hunger they felt for news from home, and the *Stanley* brought up their letters as well as the contingent of officers and men from Bolobo. These letters, and the arrival of three more white men, cheered them up no end.

The newcomers, for their part, were impressed by what they saw. John Rose Troup wrote home:

It is a capital place for a camp—not very high from the water, nearly a small sheer precipice. The whole of the place is stockaded round, no man being allowed out without leave. A wide, deep trench has been dug all round; Sudanese sentries at the river gate, as well as the side one. From the latter a good view can be had of the Rapids, all the ground having been cleared. There are two raised platforms or watch towers, and it would take a good deal of manoeuvring for either natives or Arabs to knock us out of it.

Though all the officers had been with the expedition for several months, they had not all been together, so Barttelot and Jameson hardly knew Troup and Ward. Barttelot in fact had never seen Troup though, as he wrote to his fiancée, 'by all accounts he is an excellent fellow'. Ward he described merely as 'a most energetic fellow'.

First impressions were on the whole favourable, though Ward and Barttelot were out of sympathy from the very beginning. Barttelot was prejudiced against Ward because Stanley had favoured him; and Ward found Barttelot too autocratic, too much the British officer for his taste. He contrasted his own relaxed approach to adventure with Barttelot's soldierly concern with discipline and the job in hand.

Ward wrote later:

He was a stranger to African manners and speech, with the ever-present suspicion of everyone and everything which this disadvantage must always excite. I had an acquaintance with two or three of the languages, and that knowledge of native methods which could only be acquired by residence amongst the people. As a consequence of all this, the black people with whom he was brought into contact were to Barttelot an unknown quantity, and the contempt and disdain natural to the highly strung officer who believed nothing was equal to the British soldier, gained full and unfortunate sway. He had been used to the plain and upright dealings of the white man, and, if trickery, such trickery as he could understand. He was completely at sea when dealing with the black whose word is so frequently a lie.

Troup put it more bluntly. He said of Barttelot:

It did not take me long to discover that he had an intense hatred of anything in the shape of a black man, for he made no disguise of this, but frequently mentioned the fact. His hatred was so marked that I was seized with great misgivings concerning his future dealings with them, more particularly when he would have to handle Tippu-Tib's men.

Yet Ward, though he did not like Barttelot, could recognise his good qualities and how, in different circumstances, he could have made an excellent companion.

He had a fund of stories and a wealth of humour, so that he appeared at his best as a *raconteur*. His affection for his father was unbounded, and the man would have been a cold spirit indeed who would have failed to respond with an admiring thought, as he rang the pleasant changes of reference to the 'dear old Guv'nor'. He was British, too, to the finger tips in the matter of his tastes. He dearly loved a horse, and it was amusing to us to note sometimes how horseflesh was such a frequent standard of reference, in the discussions of human ills, and remedies. His talk was a breath from the country lanes and pleasant fields; his stories constantly those of the hunting-field.

One thing Ward shared with Barttelot was friendship for Jameson. Ward and Jameson were drawn to one another from the start by the similarity of their interests; both were inveterate travellers, keen naturalists and amateur artists, and both were civilians. Ward wrote:

In many ways Jameson was the perfect antithesis of Barttelot. While the latter was full of energy, burning with zeal, and mercurial even to hot-headedness, never two minutes quiet, walking up and down to let off steam and burning with desire to be up and doing; Jameson was quiet to a degree, extremely modest and unassuming, with a most refined expression of countenance, and a voice which, in its low-pitched pleasing tones, spoke the true spirit of the man. Barttelot, with his square-jawed, firmly moulded face, in which there was no shiftiness and no desire to hide, reminded you of the straight daring rider across country; Jameson, with his soft winsome features and musical intonation, drew your thoughts away to the quiet of the library, and the seclusion of the student. Yet there was no keener sportsman than he. His face gave you the idea of delicacy, but the limbs of the man were hard and muscular, and courage and determination shone from out his clear and fearless eye . . . Always bright and pleasant, cheering us in our hours of despair, he who had been bred in the lap of luxury taught us lessons in the way of roughing it, meeting inconveniences with a laugh, and suffering with a joke. He, in truth, was one of nature's noblemen, for never in the course of all our friendship did I hear him say a bitter word of a single soul.

Jameson, the only one of the officers to be married, was certainly the most popular among them. The camp was a gloomier place when he was absent.

The rear column was now at full strength. There were the five officers (for Bonny, as a white man, counted as an officer) and 246 men, of whom 200 were Zanzibaris, 44 Sudanese and 2 Somalis. Seven men had died in camp since Stanley's departure. Barttelot had pitched his tent in the middle of the men's quarters; the others lived in huts, Troup and Bonny for the moment sharing a large one which contained the stores for which Troup was responsible. Jameson also occupied a large hut with the ammunition and personal baggage Stanley had left in his charge. Ward had a smaller hut to himself. His duties included the messing arrangements, while Bonny was made responsible for buying food from the natives.

Food, as ever, was a problem. Ward had an argument with Barttelot over the provisions for Europeans. Quite naturally he thought that he, Troup and Bonny should be issued with the same supplies as Barttelot and Jameson had been allowed by Stanley. But at first, to Ward's astonishment, Barttelot refused. He said that Stanley had left no instructions. Later, with misgivings, he relented to the extent of providing them with rations for three— but not six—months. He recognised that they had every right to these provisions, but he wanted to avoid opening food boxes which Stanley might expect to be delivered intact.

Meals, such as they were, were taken in Jameson's hut. Fish or meat of any sort was a luxury; for the most part the officers lived on a staple diet of rice, plantains and tea. The men had the run of the manioc plantations, but as it was not what they were used to they often made the mistake of eating the roots raw, so that they suffered from food poisoning as well as fever and dysentery. The manioc leaves they made into a sort of spinach mixed with palm oil—when they could get palm oil. To begin with they were given one *mitako* per week.

Among the officers there was a certain amount of haggling over their responsibilities. Troup, for instance, had expected to take over No. 1 Company of Zanzibaris, which Jameson had been looking after for him. Jameson was not to have had a company, according to Stanley's instructions, but Troup was informed by Barttelot that as Jameson wished to keep his company, he would be given responsibility for half of the men from Bolobo instead. Troup did not like this decision, but there was nothing he could do about it.

The day after the arrival of the Bolobo contingent, and while the *Stanley* was still at Yambuya, the officers were disturbed by a commotion on the opposite bank. They heard shots and ran out to see what was happening, Jameson grabbing his binoculars. On the other side, the natives were making for the river as fast as they could and smoke hung in the air above their village. There was no doubt whom they were fleeing from—only the Arabs had guns. Presently some of these natives arrived at the camp. They said they had been attacked by Tippu-Tib's men and begged the white men to go over and tell the Arabs not to fight them. Barttelot, who wanted to find out if these were indeed Tippu-Tib's men, sent over Ward and Bonny. But they arrived too late. The Arabs had gone. They had killed two men and captured four women.

This incident gave rise to discussion among the officers about the likelihood of Tippu-Tib ever providing them with men for the march. Troup gave his private opinion in a letter he was writing home:

> Between ourselves, I am very much inclined to think that Tippu-Tib either has not been able to get his men to come or else never intended to send them. We have to consider that all round here they have been raiding on the poor natives for years, and, for all we know, might try and have a shot at us here. It is a great temptation to them, no doubt, knowing the large quantities of guns, powder, and ammunition we have, not to be able to have a try for it. It will be an awful sell if we have to wait until Stanley comes back; not only that, but it would be almost fatal to the expedition.

Jameson summed up the prevailing mood of isolation and helplessness when he wrote in his diary on 17 August, the day the *Stanley* finally departed, 'We are now fairly cut off from the world. We have almost given up hope of Tippu-Tib's men, and are already talking about how we shall employ our time until November.'

10

THE DAY the steamer left, another deputation of natives came over to try to persuade the officers to intercede with the Arabs on their behalf. Barttelot decided to send four Zanzibaris up to the Arab camp, but he took the precaution of keeping one of the natives as a hostage. The following day at noon the chief Arabs arrived with some of their Manyema followers. When Barttelot asked them exactly who they were, they explained that they belonged to Tippu-Tib but had not been sent by him. He had, however, sent the 600 men but somehow or other they had overshot the mark, missed Yambuya and, coming upon the trees blazed by Stanley, assumed the expedition had gone on without them. And so they had dispersed. That was the story the Arabs told and their 'boss chief', as Barttelot referred to him— Abdullah Korona by name—offered to take a letter to Tippu-Tib or escort one of the officers to Stanley Falls if they wished to see him about it.

Barttelot, who was not well himself, decided that Jameson should be the one to go to Stanley Falls, and Ward should accompany him as witness. Abdullah promised to return with an escort party in two days' time. As it turned out, it was four days before they saw him again.

In the meantime Bonny went over to the village the natives had already rebuilt on the other side of the river to bargain with them for food. They were delighted that a white man should actually come and pay them a visit. So Bonny had to go through some sort of bloodless variation of the blood-brotherhood ceremony before the negotiations could begin. This involved cutting a roll of palm-leaves in half, dipping each half in water and sprinkling the bystanders. Afterwards he returned in triumph with six fowls, causing Barttelot to note in his diary: 'My opinion as to Bonny has considerably altered; though slow he is straight and brave, and I believe down below on one or two occasions he has shown tact, common-sense and firmness. I use him chiefly for the natives and as a food provider, but what work he has to do he does well.'

Barttelot wrote out instructions for Jameson and Ward on their visit to Stanley Falls. Ward was to return first with news of whatever had transpired with Tippu-Tib, and Jameson was to follow as soon as he could. Barttelot also composed a letter to Tippu-Tib, in which he asked him to send the men again and explained the mistake they had made; he told Tippu that the gunpowder had now arrived, so that the agreement made with Stanley at Zanzibar still held good. Troup helped Barttelot with this letter and they checked the Arabic version by having the interpreter read it back to them in English.

Then Jameson and Ward set out for the Falls with Abdullah and some 30 of his men. They were five days on the march. It was an uncomfortable journey through bush and swamp and they had almost nothing to eat. They arrived at Stanley Falls exhausted and famished; but Tippu-Tib gave them such a courteous welcome and so much food that they soon revived.

Tippu-Tib's explanation for the failure of his men to reach Yambuya was that he had not expected to have to go so far up the Aruwini: Stanley had led him to understand that the camp would be at Basoko, near the junction of the Congo and the Aruwini. What had happened, he told them, was that he had started from the Falls with 500 men in a fleet of canoes, paddled by Washenzis (the Arab word for the natives, or conquered people), and got as far as the Aruwini without mishap; but there they had run into trouble. He had sent some of his men to a village for food, and though the natives had run away at their approach, they ambushed them on their way back to the river and killed four of them. Naturally Tippu-Tib had to punish the natives. He attacked their village immediately and burned it down the following morning— by which time the paddlers in the canoes had had enough and refused to go any further.

In the letter he wrote to Consul Holmwood in Zanzibar, Tippu-Tib implied that Stanley was to blame—for not providing the powder he had promised to supply:

When the people of Usuku [Aruwini] see [us] they want to fight; every day they stabbed my people with spears, and as I

53

had not sufficient gunpowder I was not able to fight. The powder which I had I was to take to Mr Stanley. Then I went on until I reached the place where Mr Stanley was [supposed to be]. On my first journey 100 people of mine got drunk and fell asleep at night, when the Washenzis attacked them suddenly and killed four of them. I fought with them, and burnt their place, and nearly exhausted my powder, and Mr Stanley was far from me. He had promised to await me at this place. The Washenzis who accompanied me were all sick. Then I returned.

In his autobiography, Tippu-Tib tells a rather different tale. There he claims he got together his 500 men and gave them to one Ali bin Mohammed to take up the Aruwini. He does recollect that gunpowder was 'extremely scarce', and goes on: 'I myself had a little and gave some to Ali bin Mohammed who went off . . . up the Usuku. The river was running swiftly and they were strung out in line. Amongst the villages of the locals there were some very large ones. They went a distance of four days up river by dug-out; on the fifth, they came in to the village where my men under Selim Mohammed had been killed. They fought until the powder ran out and then returned.'

Whatever the truth of the matter—whether or not Tippu-Tib went himself—there can be no doubt that he sent the men, 500 of them; and there can be very little doubt about what happened *en route*: that they were diverted into settling an old score with some native warriors who had once got the better of them. Once the powder was gone they could not risk further encounters with hostile natives, so they turned back.

According to what he told Jameson and Ward, Tippu-Tib then sent small parties overland to try and find the camp. Indeed, Abdullah's was one of them—which made it rather extraordinary that Abdullah had made no attempt to contact the rear column before they had sent emissaries to him. He had been in the area some time and must have known very well they were there; the arrival of a steamer was not an everyday event on the Aruwini and the camp itself, with its prominent fortifications, was hardly invisible. But the officers were so overwhelmed by Tippu-Tib's friendliness and promises of immediate action that they did not like to cross-examine him too closely. What he promised, though, was vague: he would collect as many men as he could and bring them to the camp, but he feared he would not be able to gather as large a number as the original force, since the men who made up that force were now scattered all over the country.

By chance Jameson and Ward had come to Stanley Falls during an Arab holiday and the next day Tippu-Tib took them on a conducted tour of the place. They crossed the river to the island just below the Falls where the old Free State station had been and examined the Krupp guns which Deane had made famous. They went to another island, above the Falls, to watch a wrestling match between two village champions which, though it ended in uproar, did little damage to either stalwart. Then they were taken to see a tree which was considered something of a marvel. It had been lying on the ground so long, its branches being lopped for firewood, that it came as a great surprise to the Arabs when one day it had suddenly sprung upright again. Ward and Jameson were unimpressed; since the roots of the tree had never been cut it was only natural that, lightened of its branches, it should spring up again. But other things they saw did impress them, as Jameson acknowledged. 'The Arabs are wonderful civilisers,' he wrote; 'they grow quantities of rice, sweet potatoes, onions, guava trees, mangoes, paw-paws, and pomegranates. A blacksmith's shop is one of the sights here. One very good law made by them to encourage trade is, that no natives living near the water are allowed to cut firewood, and no natives from inland are allowed to catch fish, thus the dwellers by the river buy their firewood with fish.'

Another day, spent in the company of such a civilised Arab as Selim Mohammed—'Tippu-Tib's nephew, one of the nicest of all the Arabs, a gentleman every inch, down to the soles of his feet', he had travelled all the way from Zanzibar with the expedition— put Jameson in a mellow mood. As he sat with Ward on the rocks by the river and they smoked their pipes and watched the setting sun, he was moved to reflect how easily one might grow fond of such a spot . . . 'there is a mixture of wildness and quiet about it which is really charming.'* Yet there were constant reminders of

* It is interesting to compare this with Joseph Conrad's reaction to the same place. Conrad was there three years later, in 1890, and he describes the experience in a late essay entitled, 'Geography and Some Explorers'. He explains how,
[continued overleaf

the recent hostilities between Arab and white man: for instance, one of the Arabs produced some tins of Crosse and Blackwell's Liebig and asked what it was, pointing out at the same time that they used it as an ointment for sores on their legs. Jameson was tactful enough to refrain from asking how they had come by these tins.

In general, he was struck by the way the Arabs and natives of Stanley Falls lived together, 'in the most perfect harmony', he thought. 'You will meet an Arab strolling along hand in hand with one of the native chiefs, and if a canoe is wanted, it is ready in a moment, the chiefs themselves paddling it.' True, the Arabs were in festive mood, but their relationship with these natives they had already subjugated—as opposed to those they went out to raid and plunder—seemed a model of peaceful co-existence.

Jameson, however, had trouble with one or two of his own men; in particular, a Zanzibari interpreter by the name of Bartholomew,

------

as a boy, he had greatly admired Dr Livingstone and one day, in a spirit of bravado, he had announced to his schoolfellows that when he grew up he would go to the then unexplored heart of Africa. Eighteen years later, when he was almost at the end of his career as a sailor, he found himself captain of a river steamer which was ordered to Stanley Falls to relieve a sick agent of the Free State.

'Everything was dark under the stars,' Conrad recalls. 'Every other white man on board was asleep. I was glad to be alone on deck, smoking the pipe of peace after an anxious day. The subdued thundering mutter of the Stanley Falls hung in the heavy night air of the last navigable reach of the Upper Congo, while no more than ten miles away, in Raschid's camp just above the Falls, the yet unbroken power of the Congo Arabs slumbered uneasily. Their day was over. Away in the middle of the stream, on a little island nestling all black in the foam of the broken water, a solitary little light glimmered feebly, and I said to myself with awe, "This is the very spot of my boyish boast."

'A great melancholy descended on me. Yes, this was the very spot. But there was no shadowy friend to stand by my side in the night of the enormous wilderness, no great haunting memory, but only the unholy recollection of a prosaic newspaper "stunt" and the distasteful knowledge of the vilest scramble for loot that ever disfigured the history of human conscience and geographical exploration. What an end to the idealized realities of a boy's daydreams! I wondered what I was doing there, for indeed it was only an unforeseen episode, hard to believe in now, in my seaman's life. Still, the fact remains that I have smoked a pipe of peace at midnight in the very heart of the African continent, and felt very lonely there.'

who had been stealing brass rods. 'This is one of those beautiful boys brought up at a Mission,' he commented, 'and I must say that I have always found they beat any savage at lying and thieving!'.

When he discovered that the *mitakos* were not the only things missing, but that a quantity of cloth had gone as well, Jameson got Tippu-Tib to put both Bartholomew and an accomplice of his called Msa in chains. He feared they would try and escape during the march back to Yambuya—which they did, two days later. They broke their chains and escaped during the night. Jameson made out an inventory of all the missing items. It read: '57 *mitakos*, one piece of cloth, one axe, one knife, a pair of scissors, and a table napkin.'

Jameson told Ward to go on with Abdullah and his men; he himself stayed in the hope that Bartholomew and Msa would be speedily recaptured. With him were Selim Mohammed and his retinue, which included Tippu-Tib's interpreter, Salem Masoudi; they too were going to Yambuya. After a couple of days, when there was still no sign of the offenders, they gave up waiting and followed the others. Once again food was scarce and Jameson often went to sleep hungry. It was a frustrating journey, but before it was over they heard that Tippu-Tib's men were out in force looking for Bartholomew and Msa. They were bound to catch them soon.

At midday on 12 September, when Jameson marched into the camp at Yambuya, he heard that Ward had collapsed on his return four days earlier. He was suffering from a severe attack of dysentery which would keep him out of action for six weeks. At times it was touch and go whether he would survive. But the day before, Barttelot had written in his diary, 'Ward a little better,' adding parenthetically: 'he ain't much of a chap'.

11

ABDULLAH HAD returned with Ward; Selim Mohammed arrived with Jameson and set up camp within a stone's throw of the rear column. At first it made no difference. Bonny had established a brisk trade with the natives by the time-honoured method of capturing their women and exchanging them for fish and fowls. As an indication of the growing intimacy between the officers and these natives, their chief suddenly acquires a name—Ngungu, or as Barttelot wrote it, 'Ingungo': 'Ingungo brought us heaps of splendid fish, and we gave him back one woman.'

It all seemed to be going spendidly when, without any warning, Abdullah attacked the native village twice within the space of two days. The first time the officers muttered among themselves. 'Very unfair,' Jameson commented, 'as he promised us to leave them in peace.' 'Beastly shame after their promise to us,' wrote Troup, 'and we have given them presents so they should not molest the natives whilst we are here.' But the second time they went and protested to Selim Mohammed. Part of their indignation arose from the fact that they could do nothing but look on helplessly while the natives struggled to escape their tormentors. Jameson called it 'a most pitiable sight', and went on:

> A number of natives were swimming in the water, others [were] in canoes trying to pick them up, whilst the Arabs, who had surprised them in the village, were firing into them from the bank. A good many who had not [had] time to escape in the canoes had jumped into the water, and hidden under the overhanging scrub. I saw the Arabs peering down into it, and noticed one man fire, upon which a poor native could be seen splashing about, but a second shot finished him and he sank. Three were deliberately shot in this manner.

Ngungu came into the camp later that day and told the officers that nine of his men had been killed. They suggested he return to their side of the river and rebuild his village close to the camp so as to come under their protection; but he would not commit himself. He and his people had had bitter experience of whites and Arabs alike and he trusted neither.

Even Barttelot was horrified. 'Poor chaps!' he wrote. 'The Arabs have treated them very badly; the scene yesterday was disgraceful. They shot the poor fellows in the water.' His protest to Selim Mohammed drew an apology from Abdullah—along with the excuse that the attacks had been made in retaliation for the killing of one of his men. But the damage was done and the natives were now homeless.

Barttelot found himself in the same dilemma as Deane had been in when he was the State's representative at Stanley Falls: he wanted to protect the natives, but he had to keep on good terms with the Arabs. Should he be over-zealous on behalf of the natives he would only alienate the Arabs, whose help was vital if he were to have any hope of following Stanley.

The arrival of Selim Mohammed and his men had complicated the position considerably. Their precise function at Yambuya was a matter for speculation among the officers. Their presence could be taken either as an earnest of Tippu-Tib's intention to provide the carriers for the expedition, or as a standing threat to the security of the rear column. The proximity of the two camps caused all kinds of friction. Barttelot was afraid that his Zanzibaris would desert *en masse*. The Arabs' easy-going, freebooting way of life could hardly fail to appeal to men subjected to the disciplined drudgery of camp life with its regular floggings and ever-increasing sickness. A bid for freedom would surely be preferable to almost certain death. In the graveyard outside the camp there were already fifteen graves. Floggings were so frequent that the officers did not always bother to note them down—Troup, for instance: 'I forgot to mention that four Sudanese were flogged last week for having been mixed up in the stealing of an axe and selling it to the natives.'

Jameson had been full of optimism when he came back from the Falls. He had been sure that Tippu-Tib would provide the men, or enough for them to make a start, and quickly. Selim Mohammed agreed; he thought they would arrive in ten days. But after a few days back in camp, even Jameson, who tried so hard to keep everyone else's spirits up, succumbed to the general malaise. 'This weary waiting,' he confided in his diary, 'month after month, is perfectly sickening, and takes all the spirit and interest in the Expedition clean out of it.' And again: 'I am beginning to long for an active life again. I would rather a thousand times go through all sorts of hardships than lead this miserable existence—doing nothing and living upon what we can get in ransom for the few native women we can catch!'

By this time he was beginning to doubt that the men would come. As yet there was no sign of them. He was upset, too, when he discovered that two tortoises he had brought back from the Falls had been stolen. He had intended to skin them and take home their shells—'one to be made into a box for my wife's dressing-table (as all her brushes etc. are of tortoiseshell), the other to be made into a cigarcase on rollers, to pass round the table after dinner: so it is a great disappointment to me.'

Now these pleasant luxuries would never materialise, and all because of a disturbance one night among a group of hungry Sudanese soldiers. It had to be the Sudanese as the Zanzibaris would never touch such *unclean* things. When one of them finally confessed, he was flogged in front of all the men.

Other and more severe floggings followed. The two Zanzibaris who had escaped on the way back from the Falls, Bartholomew and Msa, were brought in by some of Tippu-Tib's men. Barttelot had them chained and padlocked in the guardroom while he considered how best to punish them. In the end, Bartholomew received 150 lashes in front of everyone, and Msa 100. All the time he was being flogged, Bartholomew howled, 'I die today, I die today.' But he survived and escaped a second time, along with Msa. Both were eventually recaptured and Barttelot left it to the other officers to decide on a further punishment. They opted for flogging by three to one. The one dissenting voice was Jameson's; he was sick of flogging and proposed that the prisoners be made to work each day in chains. But he was overruled: the sentence was a further 150 lashes each. 'Msa took his 150 lashes,' Jameson wrote, 'Bartholomew only 75, as he is still tender from his last flogging.' *

* Ward's friend, E. J. Glave (*see* Aftermath), describes a Congo flogging and the instrument commonly used to inflict it thus:

'The *chicotte* of raw hippo hide, especially a new one, trimmed like a corkscrew,

Towards the end of September Selim Mohammed broke the news that Tippu-Tib had so far been unable to collect the men for the expedition, and said that he would have come to tell the officers himself but that he was ashamed. His men had heard about the size and weight of the loads to be carried and refused to have anything to do with them. He had written to his son, Sefu, at Kasongo to ask him to send the men, but that was a month's journey away and Stanley was due to return before any men could be expected from as far away as Kasongo. By way of a sop Tippu-Tib sent 40 men, free of charge, who could be used as carriers should Barttelot decide to start after Stanley with his own men and a limited number of loads. But that was out of the question; there were far too many loads. As Jameson wrote: 'We shall simply have to sit down for another two or three months, and exist.'

Troup, in his disappointment, was inclined to doubt that Tippu-Tib had ever sent the first lot of men. He simply could not believe that they had got so close and then turned tail because four or five of them had been killed and the paddlers were tired.

Barttelot determined to go to Stanley Falls himself, with Troup for company, 'partly for pleasure, partly for business', as he explained in a letter to his fiancée. He wanted a change and hoped to buy food, but he also wanted to see Tippu-Tib and find out the truth from him, 'which is a difficult matter with the Oriental'. On 28 September, he wrote cryptically in his diary, 'Selim Mohammed is puzzled because I am going to the Falls. It may be our position is one of more danger than I think for; I shall fight it out.'

Before he left for the Falls, however, Barttelot had to investigate a rumour that Stanley was on his way back. It was difficult to verify as the rumour originated with Ngungu, who had been

---

with edges like knife-blades, and as hard as wood, is a terrible weapon, and a few blows bring blood; not more than 25 blows should be given unless the offence is very serious. Though we persuade ourselves that the African's skin is very tough, it needs an extraordinary constitution to withstand the terrible punishment of 100 blows; generally the victim is in a state of insensibility after 25 or 30 blows. At the first blow he yells abominably; then quiets down, and is a mere groaning, quivering body till the operation is over, when the culprit stumbles away, often with gashes which will endure a lifetime . . . I conscientiously believe that a man who receives 100 blows is often nearly killed, and has his spirit broken for life.'

hounded to such an extent that he had become extremely elusive. Jameson and Troup had to go some distance up the river to find him.

'How are the mighty fallen!' Jameson wrote. 'It is really sad to see the shelter, for it cannot be called a hut, that this chief now lives in, or rather sleeps in, since the Arabs attacked his village and killed a lot of his men. It is built just below the rapids, in the forest at the edge of the water, and consists of a few leaves placed across a couple of horizontal poles. He lives all the daytime in his canoe, the few wives left to him accompanying him.'

The more they investigated the rumour, the less likely it seemed to the officers that Stanley was coming. But it did seem likely that there were deserters from the advance column in the area, and they would have news of Stanley. All the indications were that they had gone to Abdullah's camp. So Barttelot and Jameson decided to pay Abdullah a surprise visit. They set off long before dawn one morning and arrived at Abdullah's at 9 a.m. But they found no deserters. The Arabs denied all knowledge of them and Stanley. They said the natives were always telling them stories about Tippu-Tib being only a day or two away, and they had learnt to discount such tales. Barttelot and Jameson were forced to concede that there was no evidence to support Ngungu's story. They returned to the camp not much the wiser, though the day's journey got them thinking about the larger issue of the Arab presence in the area. They had noticed how the Arabs were making 'a regular station' of their village, while at the same time they were destroying all the other villages around.

As Jameson observed, Tippu-Tib had a very tough job ahead of him if he really intended—as Jameson believed he did—to carry out his mandate from the King of the Belgians and put a stop to slavery in his territories:

Ivory is really the wealth of the country, and captured native men, and especially women, mean ivory, those of them not ransomed by their friends remaining slaves. In Abdullah's village we saw one gang of women working with ropes round their necks, and all fastened together, who bore on their bodies the unmistakable marks of pretty severe floggings. As the Arabs do not shoot elephants themselves, and hunt nothing but

62

men and women, it is their only means of becoming rich and obtaining ivory. Once put a stop to this trade, and their only reason for remaining in the country ceases. I cannot believe that any effectual change will take place for a very long time, no matter how much Tippu-Tib himself may desire it.

If Jameson was inclined to give Tippu-Tib the benefit of the doubt in the matter of slavery, he was not blind to his political and territorial ambitions. He noticed a phenomenon that others before him had noticed: that the immediate effect of Stanley's explorations was to open up new areas for Arab exploitation. The Arabs themselves had as little enthusiasm for exploration as they had for hunting elephants, but they were not averse to taking advantage of other pathfinders:

The Arabs seem to be making stations right along the route Mr Stanley went to the Lake; they will soon have a very large force up there. It looks as if Tippu-Tib were largely increasing his territory, so that, in case of any disagreement with the Congo Free State, he will be more powerful than ever. Selim swears that he has entered into an arrangement with the Free State to settle the Congo right down to Bangala, making stations at all the principal native towns. If he once does this, the State will find him a very nasty customer to dislodge, should they ever wish to do so.

It was not lost on Jameson that while Tippu-Tib pleaded that he was unable to get men to carry the expedition's loads, he had no trouble in finding men to go after slaves and ivory. The work, of course, was more to the liking of the Manyema, who were fighters, not beasts of burden, by habit and inclination. Yet Tippu-Tib was reputed to have such authority over them that he might justifiably have been expected to exercise it to overcome inclination—if only in order to be able to say that he at least had carried out *his* side of the bargain with Stanley.

12

FOR A while Jameson was the only fit white man in camp. Barttelot and Troup had gone to the Falls; Ward was still sick and now Bonny went down with a fever. This meant that Jameson had to do the rounds of the sentries six nights in a row. It was a difficult time. The Arabs were putting up the price of fish by trading with cloth and axe-heads, so that the natives would only sell the very smallest fish for *mitakos*; the weather had turned nasty and during a particularly heavy thunderstorm four captured native women made their escape; and the death-toll in camp had risen to 21.

In the evenings Jameson would often sit with Ward in his hut. One night their conversation was interrupted when a rat came scurrying out from under Ward's bed:

Ward said he thought there was a snake after it, and sat up; he had hardly done so, when a large snake glided up beside his pillow. He sprang out of bed, and got on to the top of a box in the middle of the room, whilst I procured a stick. The snake fell on to the ground before I could hit it, and came out from under the bed straight at my legs. A well-directed blow broke its head, however, just as it raised it to strike. It proved to be a long black snake about five feet in length, and a really poisonous one, very much resembling the common black cobra. Its belly was pale yellow, with beautiful tints of opal on it.

Jameson picked up the dead body of the snake and slung it over the crossbeam of Ward's hut, intending to remove it in the morning. But Ward woke up during the night. He had completely forgotten about the snake, and when he saw its body glistening in the moonlight he was paralysed with fright: he could neither cry out nor move. He just lay there for what seemed like hours, gazing at the venomous reptile and waiting for it to drop from the beam and slither across the floor.

The rats were something of a plague. Jameson caught six of them in a single night and remarked that it did not seem to have reduced their number at all. Every night now there was thunder and lightning and the rain beat down on the huts, rotting the roofs so that they gave off a most unpleasant smell.

Jameson got a letter from Barttelot in which he learned that indeed there must have been several deserters at Abdullah's village the time they visited it. Tippu-Tib had just handed over five of them and told Barttelot there were another five still at Abdullah's. So Ngungu's story was at least partly true, and the Arabs had been lying when they denied all knowledge of Stanley's men. The news of Stanley himself was inconclusive: clearly he had not got on as well as he would have liked—it was a difficult journey, food was scarce, a number of his men had died and there had been fighting—but apparently the officers were well and the advance continued. Barttelot, who was anxious that his Zanzibaris should not take their cue from Stanley's and desert, instructed Jameson to take away their arms—if possible, without arousing their suspicions.

Jameson took all their rifles away, saying they were not properly cleaned or cared for; in future they would be looked after by an officer and only issued for picket duty. He also sent a party of Sudanese to Abdullah's village, but they found only one deserter. A few days later another, who was wounded, hobbled into camp. But the men did succeed in retrieving six rifles and a quantity of ammunition.

In Barttelot's absence there was a more cheerful atmosphere in the camp. The men threw off their lethargy and made a couple of drums for a dance they held one afternoon. They also had a free fight with sticks. Never mind the odd black eye, Jameson for one was 'glad to see a brighter tone amongst the men'.

Not Bonny, though; he thoroughly disapproved of Jameson's leniency. When Jameson refused to punish two of the men he reported for some offence, Bonny wrote: 'I think this man is afraid of losing popularity with the men or with Stanley.' He would punish the men himself from now on. Someone had to keep order, as the men were 'going from one advantage to another through Jameson's lax treatment'.

Jameson was also fraternising with the Arabs, which Barttelot had always discouraged. He spent a lot of time with Selim

65

Mohammed, who told him, for instance, that all the natives from Bangala up to the Falls, both on the Congo itself and on its tributaries, were cannibals. Jameson asked him which they preferred to eat, black or white, and Selim at once replied, 'White'. That was because they thought the white man was 'all fat' and wondered what he ate that made him so 'fat'. They simply would not accept that the white man's colour was natural.

Barttelot returned from the Falls early in November. Evidently the trip to Stanley Falls marked some kind of watershed in his relationship with Troup. Barttelot was quick and impetuous; he was such a fast walker that he had earned the nickname 'Kapeppo', or whirlwind, among the men. Troup was just the opposite: cautious and slow and inclined to be something of an old maid. He had been unable to keep up with Barttelot on the march out and was always having to stop to attend to his boots or his feet; and he irritated Barttelot still further by constantly questioning his sense of direction. So much so that on the return journey Barttelot went on ahead and left Troup to find his own way through the forest. To add to his troubles, Troup had a flock of goats to shepherd back to Yambuya. Some days later, when the officers were enjoying their after-dinner pipes, they heard shots in the distance and surmised that Troup must be in some sort of difficulty. Jameson set off immediately with some Sudanese and half an hour later came upon Troup, his men and goats, all floundering in a cane-swamp; they were hopelessly lost. As Jameson described it, 'the air was blue all about the swamp with the bad language that had been used in many tongues'. He managed to extricate them all and guided them back to the camp.

Now it was Selim's turn to go to the Falls. The idea was that he would go on from there to Kasongo to take charge of the 600 men Tippu-Tib was trying to raise there. Not that Tippu-Tib had given Barttelot much encouragement on that score: he had told Barttelot that his son Sefu was engaged in fighting at Kasongo and would not be able to spare any men before December. And Barttelot had written to his fiancée: 'I have done all I can now till Stanley puts in an appearance, and, failing that, I shall not take any decided step till February; it will be weary waiting, but it must be gone through with . . .'

Barttelot and Troup both felt very seedy on their return to

camp. But then came news to lift their drooping spirits—
'Glorious news if it only turns out to be true!' Jameson wrote. It
was that Stanley himself was coming down the river and would
arrive in three days' time. But it turned out be as false as the
earlier rumour had been. This time it was a case of mistaken
identity: a party of Arabs whose leaders had a very pale skin had
gone up the river some time before and now they were returning.

Barttelot threw off his fever in a matter of days, but Troup's
condition worsened and Jameson, too, went down with jaundice.
Troup's birthday was on 17 November but, as neither he nor
Jameson was in any state to celebrate it, the feast they had planned
had to be postponed.

With Selim Mohammed gone, the Arabs took steps to prevent
the natives trading directly with the camp. They aimed to control
the trade themselves; they would buy fish from the natives, come
to the camp and offer to sell it at double the original price. After
a fruitless palaver with these Arabs, Barttelot decided to send
Ward (who was still not fully recovered) to the Falls to make a
formal complaint to Tippu-Tib.

Ward left on 19 November with instructions to explain the
facts of the case to Tippu-Tib, and ask him either to remove his
men to a greater distance from the camp or to send a headman
with sufficient authority to prevent further interference in the
trade between the natives and the rear column.

Ward's journey was to prove unnecessary. A few days after he
left, all but ten of Tippu-Tib's men cleared out, going to 'make
war' near the mouth of the Aruwini, and Ngungu promised to start
bringing in fish again. He told Bonny that the Arabs had threatened
to shoot him if he traded with the camp while they were there.

During all the comings and goings between Yambuya and
Stanley Falls, Bonny had not been idle. Apart from his efforts to
maintain good relations with the natives so that they went on
bringing in food, by the middle of November he had built himself
a house and started work on a mess-house and a house for Barttelot.
For safety, Barttelot had now moved out of the men's camp and
into the strongly fortified inner sanctum. Bonny's efforts, Troup
wrote, 'to improve the sanitary conditions of the camp and the
comfort of both men and officers were most praiseworthy'.

Now that Ward was away at the Falls, and Troup and Jameson

were both sick in bed, Barttelot was thrown back on what he had once described as 'Bonny's enlightened society'. But over the months his attitude towards Bonny had modified—as this series of entries in his diary shows:

November 24. Bonny and I talked about our probable action in the event of Stanley doing certain things. I expressed myself openly . . .

November 29. I went for a walk with Bonny, who told me Ward had told him Tippu-Tib hated me, but gave me no reason for it. Of course followers follow suit.

Wednesday, November 30. I resumed conversation of last night with Bonny, and he told me John Henry had told him that Tippu-Tib's men hated me. Assad Farran told me Selim Mohammed hated me, and only stayed here to get what presents he could out of us . . . [John Henry and Assad Farran were both interpreters, one a Zanzibari, the other a Syrian who came with the Sudanese; neither was particularly trustworthy, though Bonny, who spoke no African languages, was in the habit of taking copious notes of their stories.]

According to Bonny's confused account, Barttelot said Tippu-Tib . . .

must be unlike most Orientals if he dislikes with one hand and accepts presents with the other. 'He certainly returned my revolver, but he received a bale of cloth from me which Troup advised me to give.' I said that, 'If Troup advised you to give the cloth he makes a different statement to other members of the expedition. He, Troup, said that you had a row with him about keeping his accounts, that you said to him that they were not correct but, added Troup, "I suppose he wants to economise after throwing bales of cloth about as he likes, that he is afraid of Stanley." ' Barttelot was surprised and said, 'I will ask Troup in your presence tomorrow if he did not advise me to give Tib a bale of cloth. I can't understand why Troup and Ward are working against me, for Ward is trying to foster it. I cannot trust one of them.'

Perhaps it was after this confrontation with Troup that Barttelot wrote in his diary, 'Troup better, but I think his illness has left him weak in the head.' Certainly, Bonny did all he could to inflame Barttelot's dislike of Troup and Ward; playing Iago to Barttelot's Othello, he lost no opportunity to fuel his suspicions.

30 November was Bonny's forty-first birthday. Barttelot put it in that day's orders that he was to take over the medicine-chest from Jameson, and that in future he would examine the sick every morning. Troup commented, 'We were all under the impression that according to Stanley's letter of instructions to Barttelot, Jameson was to see to them, but the cry has always been that there are no suitable medicines.'

30 November was also the day Ward got back from the Falls. He had arrived there only to discover that Tippu-Tib had left for Kasongo five days earlier. But he had prevailed upon Selim Mohammed, who had not gone with his uncle after all, to return to Yambuya; Ward was not to know that in the meantime the Arabs had gone off to fight their wars and left the rear column in peace. He brought back with him from the Falls 40 eggs, which he gave to Troup (Jameson could not touch them) to help build up his strength.

He had not been back more than a couple of days when half a goat was stolen from his hut. Jameson called the robbery 'the most daring they have yet attempted'. An agglomeration of bones was discovered close to the Sudanese quarters and suspicion fell on one Burgari Mohammed, in whose hut a quantity of meat was unearthed. Burgari suffered the usual public flogging, which Jameson witnessed: 'The Sudanese are wonderfully plucky in bearing pain, for although he received 150 strokes, which cut him up very much, he never uttered a sound.' But even then it was not over for Burgari Mohammed. As he had tried to implicate another man, he was not only fined nine months' pay but also sentenced to another flogging, to be administered when he had recovered sufficiently from the first one.

By the beginning of December, 30 people had died in camp and the death rate was increasing almost daily. Bonny's sick parades attracted a large and miserable crowd of Zanzibaris and Sudanese, all suffering from festering sores of one kind or another. Their condition was truly pitiable; numbers of them were just wasting away. Jameson contrasted their plight with that of the natives, who were—momentarily, at least—enjoying their freedom from

Arab oppression: 'The natives on the other side of the river had quite a gala afternoon, canoe-racing, manoeuvring, dancing, singing, and tomtoming to any extent. One of my men died today. Several of the men in camp are only walking skeletons, and the marvel is how they exist or move at all. One man, who walks with a rather active upright motion, is a horrible sight, having nothing but loose folds of skin over his bones.'

In the middle of the month parties of Tippu-Tib's men arrived to await Selim Mohammed's return. One lot had orders to build him a house. The officers groaned at the thought. Jameson: 'It is a great nuisance, as we get on so much better without him and his men.' Troup: 'I am sorry they are coming back; our men are much better without them.' And sure enough, no sooner had they arrived than there was trouble. They captured Ngungu and put him in chains, demanding that his people come across and build their village on the near side of the river. They wanted them to hold a regular market as did the 'Washenzis' in other Arab-dominated villages.

The reason the Arabs were so unwelcome now was that the officers expected nothing but trouble from them; they no longer had any hopes of marching after Stanley. Their thoughts were concentrated on Stanley's return. By his own reckoning he was to have been back in November. It was December already and, after the earlier false alarms, there was not even so much as a rumour of his approach. It was very frustrating for the officers he had left behind. Scarcely a day passed when they did not think of him and worry over where he might be and why they had heard nothing from him. He even invaded their sleep at night. Jameson wrote on 17 December:

Troup, the Major, and I all dreamt of Stanley's return the night before last. Troup dreamt that he came back by himself, without any of the other white officers, and when asked where they were he quite calmly remarked that he did not know, and evidently did not care, merely saying that they had each chosen their own road, and he knew nothing about them. The Major dreamt that he arrived at camp looking jolly and well; that William [Hoffman], his servant, came inside our boma, when the Major at once ordered him out, and proceeded himself to

Mr Stanley's tent, and found him with a lawyer, upon which he at once remarked, 'Oh, you are for the Crown, I won't say anything'; and the dream ended. I dreamt that we saw a number of canoes coming down the river in a long line, and in one of them a large white umbrella, and I at once saw that it was Mr Stanley, at which moment I awoke.

Jameson had now been at Yambuya six months, and the prospect of getting away from the place was more remote than ever. 'Our days are divided,' he wrote, 'by breakfast, lunch and dinner, which, in their turn, are regulated by the sun, as there is only one watch that goes—Troup's—and that only goes by fits and starts. It is very like life at sea, the same deadly monotony, only broken by intervals of eating.'

On Christmas Eve they killed a goat, and Barttelot recorded in his diary, 'It is a year since I first met Stanley.'

13

CHRISTMAS CAME, and the officers had little cause for cele-
bration: no news of Stanley, no men from Tippu-Tib; their own
men dying off at a depressing rate and they themselves prone to
debilitating sickness. But Troup and Jameson had both recovered
from their recent ailments and all the officers were united in their
determination to make this one day, at least, memorable.

On Christmas Eve Jameson and Ward had sat up half the
night, 'engaged', as Troup put it, 'in a joint conspiracy' to
provide the others with Christmas cards. For Barttelot, Jameson
drew a picture of a huntsman with horse and dog, and the caption
read: 'I wunner when Mas'r Edmund ull be cummin home
again.' Troup's was a watercolour sketch, or rather two in one. The
upper half represented him in the Slough of Despond—in the
middle of a thicket of trees, surrounded by struggling, baa-ing
goats in all sorts of absurd positions, his own attitude expressing
the most abject despair. But below that was another picture which
showed him dressed in a cashmere coat (Stanley's parting gift),
reclining in the camp's one easy chair, a kettle and a cup of tea
beside him, and looking, in spite of his exhausted air, 'the very
picture of comfort'. In the background were the expedition's
precious stores—a sombre reminder of the reason for their having
to remain at Yambuya in the first place.

Bonny's card was also divided in two. One half featured a
lonely, pregnant woman, sad at Bonny's absence, while the other
had him out shooting with caps that were too large. Bonny liked
to go out shooting: it was a gentlemanly activity, the pleasures of
which he had only recently discovered—since he came out to the
Congo, in fact—so he was not properly equipped for it. His
interest in women, naturally, was of longer duration. It was a moot
point whether or not he had a wife at home; he was later to
suggest that he had been duped into a bigamous liaison just before
he left England—though the bigamy, needless to say, was not

his. On the journey up to Yambuya Bonny had noticed that 'all the State officers keep black women, and some of them have families by them'.* And since his arrival he had, as he readily admitted, 'tried on several occasions to get a woman from the natives but have failed. They do not care to let you have their women and seem very fond of them.' But he would keep on trying.

There were presents, too. Jameson seems to have done particularly well: Ward gave him a bar of soap, and Troup, noticing that his pipe was burnt out, gave him a new one which he had come across among his private possessions. Troup also gave Ward and Bonny a pound of coffee each. All these gifts were luxuries.

But the greatest luxury of all was food. After months of bare subsistence, Christmas was to be a feast day. All the officers chipped in with such delicacies as remained in their possession. Barttelot and Jameson together contributed a tin of flour and a tin of jam; Ward gave a tin of flour and Troup provided not only a ham, but a bottle of prunes, a tin of marmalade, a bottle of pickles and some English mustard as well.

Breakfast consisted of fish, cold goat and the ham which Troup had given. As Ward carved this ham and handed it round, the others went in for an elaborate pantomime of politeness, pretending to refuse or at best reluctantly to accept the proffered slices.

'My dear fellow,' Barttelot said, 'that is quite enough for me.'

'Don't give me too much, Ward,' said Jameson.

'Perhaps—yes, really, another slice, a thin slice, would be acceptable.'

In their eagerness to make the most of the occasion, they turned anything and everything to account—even the scraps of year-old newspapers which had been used for wrapping stores. They smoothed them out and read them in the hope that they would provide some moments of distraction. They were not

* Fred Puleston defends 'the almost universal custom of the white man keeping a harem' in *African Drums*: 'Practically every European had one; some men had three "lights of the harem," some two, and others were content with one. These women are a decided help in combating . . . loneliness. Although they are black savages, and often cannibals, in a very short time their feminine helpmate characteristics and qualities, in addition to sex matters, come to the top . . . I do not hesitate to say that they kept a good many men straight—both mentally and physically—who would otherwise have gone to the devil.'

disappointed. The advertisement columns were full of suggestive material: a maid who wanted a situation, a widow seeking another partner in her life's journey, a plea addressed to one 'Lil' whose 'Reggie' was still waiting for her outside St James's Park station, and some quack's announcement of his particular nostrum. What would not Bonny give for some of that? And that widow—perhaps she was still young and pretty, with a taste for African adventurers. But whom would she choose? Not old Jameson; he was booked already. What about Troup? . . . So it went on. And the men outside, who had been given a holiday and two *mitakos* each, they too caught the spirit of the occasion, and the whole camp had an unusually festive air about it.

'For lunch,' Jameson recalled, 'we had a meat pudding, consisting of five eggs, parrots' (species unknown, but good), two small doves, and a chicken (same size), ham finely chopped up, suet and mutton (Christmas name for goat), onions, pickles, and a little Worcester sauce; the whole enveloped in a blanket of dough and boiled. This pudding was certainly one of the best I have ever eaten anywhere.'

At the end of the meal Jameson exclaimed, by way of an impromptu grace, 'Thank God for my good lunch,' to which the others responded with a hearty 'Amen'. It was to Ward, in fact, that most of the credit was due. He had spent the entire morning cooking the lunch and in the process had had to put up with some heavy ribbing from Troup, whose contribution to the Christmas spirit was a relentless facetiousness. Eventually Ward drove him out of his hut, saying, 'I'll never finish this if you stay bothering me with your jokes, so you just get!'

In the afternoon they sat around a big wooden drum, kicking their heels, smoking and swapping stories. Barttelot talked mainly of England, and in particular of the hunting-fields of his native Sussex; the others yarned about their times in Borneo or the Transvaal, their service in Zululand and the Sudan. Yet in the end Christmas made them thoughtful. After all the talk of their travels and their deeds in strange lands they were left with an overwhelming nostalgia—for Christmas at home, traditionally celebrated, among relations and friends. This was what drew them together: shared memories and shared longings and a sudden revulsion from an alien way of life which had imperceptibly become theirs too.

The menu for dinner might have been written by Troup—and probably was:

Goat Soup, à l'Africaine
Grilled Goat Steak, à la Yambuya
Roly-Poly Pudding, à la Ward
Tea, noir
Cognac, une liqueur à chacun.

The last item was very special. Stanley had left Barttelot and Jameson a couple of bottles of brandy when he went and there was a tiny amount left at the bottom of each bottle, just enough to provide everyone with a few drops. (There were also two unopened cases of brandy, but these were to remain unopened; they had to be delivered intact.) The toast was 'Absent Friends' and the officers drank in silence as they thought not so much of friends at home now, but of Stanley and their colleagues in the advance column. They began to wonder uneasily if they would ever see them again.

After the toasts, the songs. Bonny had a fine tenor voice and he led the singing. They sang comic and sentimental songs, but because it was Christmas the most popular numbers were those that reminded them of home. Outside, around the camp fires, the men were also singing. Perhaps their songs too reflected a longing to be elsewhere. 'Poor fellows,' Troup wrote, 'they had no romance of chivalry, no expectation of fame, no dream of doing good to poor beleaguered fellow-creatures, to keep up their drooping spirits during those weary days of waiting!'

The officers sat up late, talking and smoking; they were reluctant to end the day. But their conversation grew desultory now as each withdrew into himself a little. In the larger silence of the night they listened to the voices of the men singing and the sounds of the rushing river until at last there was nothing for it but to knock out their pipes, do the rounds of the sentries and go to bed. Christmas, à la Yambuya, was over.

14

AFTER CHRISTMAS things went on much as before. The Arabs reported that Ngungu, whom they had released, refused to come over and build a village or hold a market. So the scuffles between Arabs and natives resumed. The Arabs shot the natives and the natives stabbed the Arabs and in some cases—according to the Arabs—'made soup' of them. Canoes changed hands, backwards and forwards, and the occasional mutilated body floated down the river to get stuck on the rocks or caught in the overhanging branches. Both sides tried to enlist the white man's aid and the officers did what they could to prevent hostilities. But it was hopeless. The natives had their sympathy but the alliance with Tippu-Tib, their need of his men and the precariousness of their own situation, as well as Stanley's written instructions, all dictated a policy of neutrality.

In camp the men continued to die off—in Jameson's graphic phrase—'like rotten sheep'. There were two young Zanzibari boys who shared a hut; both had been ill since Stanley's departure. Their names were Khamis and Abadi. On 28 December, Khamis died and that evening Jameson remarked to Barttelot, 'You will see that Abadi will die almost immediately, for I have always noticed that where there are two people together, who have both been ill for a long time, when one dies the other is almost sure to follow.' Abadi died the next day. He was the fortieth to die in the camp.

On the last day of 1887 Jameson looked back over the past six months at Yambuya with disgust. He described them as 'the most miserable and useless I have ever spent anywhere', and went on: 'Had it not been for the odd little bits of collecting and drawing, which filled up a lot of my time, I think I should certainly have become an idiot here.' Not one of the officers could summon up the interest or enthusiasm to sit up until midnight to see the New Year in.

Barttelot did have a plan though. Back in October he had said to

Troup, while they were at the Falls together, that if they had heard nothing and Stanley had not returned by the beginning of February, he would be forced to assume that something had happened to the advance column and he would go up and look for Stanley—taking Jameson and Troup with him. Now, at the beginning of January, he broached the subject with Troup again, saying he would take two officers and 100 Zanzibaris and Sudanese and carry only ammunition in the way of loads. He was quite convinced that some sort of disaster had overtaken the advance column and told Troup that he did not expect ever to see Stanley back. But he was interested to know what Troup thought.

Troup told him—at length. He said that in spite of Stanley's long absence he could not see any reason for assuming there had been a disaster. It was much more likely that what the deserters had reported was true, that Stanley had had to face considerable difficulties: rough country, hostile natives, and trouble in getting his own men to stay with him and carry the loads. It had probably taken him twice as long as he had expected to reach the Lake, and once there he would have to make camp and then contact Emin and make the necessary arrangements with him—all of which would take time—before he could think of returning. Then there was the journey back. All told, it could easily account for his six-month absence and Troup saw no reason to doubt his eventual return.

He opposed Barttelot's scheme from every point of view. Such a small force as he intended taking could not possibly do any good, even if Stanley were in trouble, unless of course he happened to be short of ammunition—a most unlikely contingency, in Troup's opinion. He could just see Stanley when Barttelot turned up without the loads. His first question would be, 'Well, Major, where are my loads?' And when Barttelot told him they had been left behind and explained why he had come, he could imagine what Stanley would say next. 'Well,' he would say, 'now you have found me, what do you propose to do?' No, Barttelot had his written instructions from Stanley and these, Troup thought, were perfectly clear: 'He was to follow on with all the officers, men, and stores *when* he had the carriers promised by Tippu-Tib, and in the event of Tippu-Tib sending only a part of the requisite number, a list was given of loads which he might not dispense with.'

Barttelot listened to what Troup had to say and then told him he would call a council the next weekend to get the opinion of the other officers. But no council was held and this lulled Troup into supposing that 'the wild-goose chase to go and look for Stanley' had been abandoned. Then Barttelot sprang another surprise on him. It was in the afternoon and they were walking up and down their 'promenade' together when Barttelot casually mentioned something about an unsigned piece of paper Stanley had given him, which, he said, contained instructions on how to transport the vital loads should Tippu-Tib provide no men at all. The Zanzibaris would have to make something like twelve journeys backwards and forwards, over a similar number of days, between one camp and the next to move all the loads; and the whole process would have to be repeated at each stage of the march.

Troup was frankly incredulous: 'This is what I understood Barttelot to say the paper contained; but I have not seen it and this is the first time I have heard that Stanley made such a suggestion. It was not in accord with the general written instructions.'* He thought it was a 'perfectly insane' idea, and pointed out to Barttelot that if they had followed this suggestion they would not have got very far before they met Stanley coming back, had he kept his time; and since he had not, they would still have been on their way up if they had had any men at all left by now. But Barttelot was growing impatient of argument; he told Troup he was sure that Stanley would blame him for failing to bring up the loads and would try and damage his reputation at home. This thought was becoming an obsession with him.

Selim Mohammed returned on 9 January. Barttelot recorded the event in his diary and added tersely, 'We did not get much news out of him.' The others gave a fuller account of the Arab's return. Selim told them he had not heard from Tippu-Tib but he understood that the men could be expected shortly. They would be coming down the river to Stanley Falls in canoes, in parties of 50 or 60 at a time. Ward thought this strange as they had often

* Stanley's own account of his conversation with Barttelot before leaving Yambuya supports Barttelot's allegation. 'We then proceeded to make some calculations with pencil and paper,' he wrote, 'upon the basis of the Major's promise that he would move from Yambuya with his own men within a day or two of the *Stanley*'s arrival . . . The calculations, based as they were on unknown quantities, were most wild . . . The paper was given to him as a memorandum.'

Major E. M. Barttelot

J. S. Jameson

Herbert Ward

J. Rose Troup

William Bonny

H. M. Stanley

Tippu-Tib

The Emin Pasha Relief Committee, with William Mackinnon standing centre
and Sir Francis de Winton seated on his right

The steamers *Stanley* and *A.I.A.* on the Aruwini river

Interview of Barttelot and Jameson with Tippu-Tib at Stanley Falls
(from a sketch by Ward)

Arabs raiding a native village opposite Yambuya
(from a sketch by Ward)

Tippu-Tib's fleet of canoes on the Congo river

Jameson's Christmas card to
Barttelot, 1887

A Congo Warrior by Herbert
Ward. In later years Ward
became well-known as a
sculptor, primarily of African
subjects

Four of 'Stanley's men' - pioneers in the Congo.
From left to right, E. J. Glave, Alfred Parminter, Herbert Ward and
Roger Casement

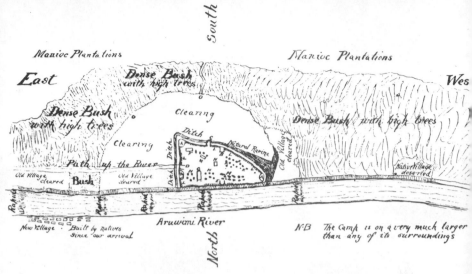

South

Manioc Plantations   Manioc Plantations

East   Dense Bush   Wes
with high trees

Dense Bush   Clearing   Dense Bush with high trees
with high trees

Clearing   Ditch   Natural Ravine

Path up the River   Native Village
deserted

Old Village cleared   Bush   Old Village cleared

New Village . Built by Natives   N.B   The Camp is on a very much larger
Since our arrival   than any of its surroundings

Aruwimi River

North

Jameson's plan of Yambuya entrenched camp

Beehive huts in Yambuya camp

Stanley giving final instructions to Barttelot on his departure from
Yambuya, 28 June 1887 (from a sketch by Ward)

travelled 500 or more at a time in the past. But Selim explained that it was because the river was low and they had to use small canoes to negotiate the rapids safely.

Barttelot was sick of Arab prevarication; he wanted a straight answer. So he sent for Selim Mohammed the day after his arrival and asked him point-blank if the men were really coming or not. Jameson was there as witness:

> Selim answered that he could not read Tippu's heart, but he believed we should get the men, and that Tippu himself would return to Stanley Falls on the fifteenth of next month, when he expected to have 200 men there from Kasongo. It was very difficult, he added, to get the men to carry loads, so they were told that they were required here to fight the natives. The Major asked him why, in the first place, we did not get the men who were on the Lomami River. He said (as Farran translated it) there were murmurs amongst them, which I suppose simply meant that they flatly refused to carry loads. The Major then asked if there was any personal feeling of dislike to himself in the matter, and Selim said there was none. I am afraid that if we do get the men from Tippu-Tib, once they discover that they have been taken in, we shall be unable to do anything with them.

Barttelot's only comment was, 'I had a long palaver with Selim Mohammed . . . but I could get nothing out of him.'

There could hardly be a greater stylistic contrast than between the diaries of these two friends, Barttelot and Jameson, at this juncture. Barttelot, always laconic, practically dries up. He obviously felt obliged to write something, however rudimentary, nearly every day, in the same way that he felt obliged to shave.*

* He wrote to his father in March, 'My boots and socks still hang out, and I still shave, but that is all.' Ward remembered that he used to keep his moustache carefully trimmed and was in the habit of saying, 'I hate to see a man with a long moustache, it gets entangled in the teeth.'
As well as shaving and writing his diary, Barttelot would read his Bible daily; and he recorded in his diary that he read, at different times, Pepys, Shakespeare and Longfellow.
Jameson, in a letter to his wife (also written in March), claimed to have learnt almost the whole of Edwin Arnold's *Light of Asia* by heart: . . . 'there is something of real comfort in the many beautiful truths contained in it.' He even

[continued overleaf

But his restlessness, pent-up energy and frustration show only in occasional flashes of irritation; for the rest it is a record of consummate boredom, as this fairly typical sequence of entries demonstrates:

January 19. We have been ten months in this country. Rain yesterday and to-day. Mursah Topji, a Sudanese, died.

Tuesday, January 24. Selim Mohammed came into camp and told Jameson some news.

Friday, January 27. We lead the usual life day after day. Rain this morning and most days.

Saturday, January 28. Seven months since Stanley left.

Sunday, January 29. Very hot, the thermometer registering 136 degrees in the sun at 2 p.m. We had slight rain in the evening. I issued a supply of tea and we killed a goat.

January 30 and 31. Bought eight fowls.

Here is Jameson's entry for 31 January, in which he describes his own typical day (and being a generalised description it is one of the less vivid of his entries):

This morning I shot a pair of finches, of which I have only seen one specimen before, and that was one I shot on our arrival

---

wrote an imitation of the poem and called it, *My Justification* or *The Light of Equatorial Africa*. It must be admitted that it is not very distinguished as poetry, but its sentiments are impeccable and it ends thus:

> If one, then, being rich and fortunate,
> Young, dowered with health and ease, from birth designed
> To live, if he would live, just as he chose—
> If one not tired with life's long day, but glad
> I' the freshness of the morning, one not cloyed
> With love's delicious feasts, but hungry still—
> If one not worn and wrinkled, sadly sage,
> But joyous in the glory and the grace
> Of living here below, with loving wife,
> A little child, and many many friends—
> If such a one, having so much to leave,
> Left all, going forth to do some work
> He felt was noble, and he fitted for,
> Surely, at last, far off, sometime, somewhere,
> His recompense would come, and he would meet
> His death with no regrets for deeds not done!

here, the skin of which was destroyed by beetles. This evening I shot a beautiful small warbler. I find that every minute of the day I have something to do. First thing in the morning parade men and tell them off to their work, then breakfast, followed by a stroll with the gun as long as it is cool. Most likely a new bird is shot, when he has to be drawn, painted, and skinned; then perhaps a boy will come in with a new beetle or a curious insect, which is subject to the same fate; then, before the sun goes down another ramble with the gun. Through it all, one cannot help feeling how utterly one is left out of all the real work we came to do, and the sense of keen disappointment crops up at all times.

Jameson was no less disappointed in their situation than Barttelot; it was just that he reacted differently. If Barttelot at times suggests the schoolboy forced to keep a diary against his will—who can find nothing in his daily life worth the effort of recording, whose mind goes blank at the sight of an empty page—then Jameson is a man of sensibility. In contrast to Barttelot's complete indifference to his surroundings, Jameson is marvellously interested in things. He was, of course, a naturalist and his diary is full of natural history notes, detailed observations of the animals, birds and insects which people brought in to show him, or he went out and shot. But he was just as interested in people and enjoyed to the full any break in the deadly routine of the camp—for instance, when an Arab chief called Nasibu came to visit:

He told us that some of the Lights of his Harem had never seen white men, and had expressed the wish to come down and visit us, especially a woman who came from Upi. We told him we were quite willing to be inspected, and shortly after his departure a man came down in charge of four black Venuses, evidently in their Sunday best. Two of their names were translated as 'Sugar-stick' and 'Finish Everything'. When asked to be seated, they all sat down in a body on my poor camp-bed; but luckily, just as it was going smash, they got up and dispersed. The lady from Upi was certainly the best-looking of the lot, but the gilt of civilisation sat very lightly upon her. We presented each with a few *mitakos*, and they went away evidently much pleased with their visit.

But a couple of nights later:

A most unpleasant accident happened to me . . . I was in the midst of pleasant dreams, when, with a crash, my bed broke down, and I fell with my head and shoulders on to the ground, and my feet in the air. I put my hands out to see what on earth had happened, when they met with the mosquito curtain, which I found all round me, and at once commenced to struggle with. Luckily I realised what had happened before I had torn the curtain too badly, and I fixed the whole thing up somehow, but for the rest of the night had to sleep with my heels in the air, and my head almost on the ground. It is a curious thing what an amount of thought goes through one's brain in a second of time when one is asleep. I remember perfectly well that my last dreaming thoughts were of being in a chair which kept tilting over backwards, and yet, from the manner in which the bed was broken, it must have happened instantaneously. One thing is certain, however: the next time we receive the Lights of anyone's Harem, they will not sit on my bed!

If the evidence of Jameson's own diary were not enough to establish the excellence of his character and disposition, there is the independent judgment of his fellow officers. Barttelot scarcely ever referred to him without some flattering epithet, and Herbert Ward, who celebrated his twenty-fifth birthday on 11 January, spent as much of his time with him as he possibly could. These two, Ward and Jameson, would often go out together sketching and botanising, and their friendship matured and deepened during this period—so much so that Ward was moved to give his friend this unsolicited testimonial in his diary: 'Jameson is an awfully good fellow, energetic, amusing, very clever in many ways, and has exceedingly good taste. He is one of the best fellows I ever met, or am likely to meet. His kind attention to me during my attack of dysentery probably saved my life. I shall always remember that.'

Ward provided a certain light relief when he turned his hand to caricature and made a comic sketch from memory of Stanley and his officers in the advance column. Like Jameson, he made use of his talents to fight off boredom. He was a gifted artist; he was also an excellent linguist, and he used this opportunity to improve his knowledge of Swahili. In the process, he drew closer to Selim Mohammed, who was also something of a linguist, speaking not only Swahili and Arabic, but also 'Hindostani, Malagasy (Madagascar), and about six different native dialects, or rather languages, which are in use between the east coast of Mombassa and this part of the country.'

Selim had assured the officers, when he first returned, that he would make treaties and live at peace with the natives, but only a fortnight later he made a dawn raid on a village a mile down on the other side of the river and killed four natives, including the chief. His men captured 27 women and two boys, as well as three canoes. That evening, as a placatory gesture perhaps, he sent down his band to play and sing to the officers during their dinner.

A week later, on the evening of 3 February, songs of a very different kind emanated from the Arab camp. The Arabs, Ward wrote, were 'chanting their melancholy war-song' in preparation for another raid, this time on the unfortunate Ngungu just across the river. The next day was Jameson's wedding anniversary: he had been married just three years. He was woken on this occasion by the sound of Arab guns, and he dashed out of his hut to see what was happening. But he found he could see next to nothing as there was such a thick mist over the river. There were the odd flashes from the Arab guns as they picked off the natives who were floundering in the river; and a thick pall of smoke and flames rose out of the mist as, once again, Ngungu's village burned. A number of natives escaped in their canoes up the river, but there were still 'plenty of dead bodies', according to Ward, 'for the fish in the Aruwini'. When the Arabs returned they brought with them the head of a dead man which they gave to Ward and Jameson to make sketches of; then Jameson skinned and preserved it with a view to taking it home with him later.

The Arabs, with the inestimable advantage of guns over spears and knives, had no trouble in routing the natives; but they suffered a surprising reverse when they tried to intercept the fleeing canoes a little way up the river. Ten of them were killed and then, before they could be revenged, the natives gave them the slip under the cover of darkness. All Selim Mohammed found, when he went to investigate, was a string of dead men's fingers tied to the scrub on the river bank, and a lot of dead men's flesh in cooking pots; the fires were still burning. Evidently the natives had gorged themselves and then had to leave in a hurry.

Oddly enough, in view of the officers' professed desire to protect the natives and Ngungu especially (Ward had written: 'Poor Ngungu! I shall be sorry if he is killed, for I never saw a finer type of savage—powerfully built, full of pluck, and a decided air of command about him'), Barttelot lent Selim Mohammed a Remington rifle and 100 rounds of ammunition with which to pursue him. Perhaps Selim had succeeded in convincing Barttelot—as he convinced Jameson—that he was only making war with the natives because Ngungu had 'broken faith' with him by not returning a number of guns he had captured in earlier skirmishes. Alternatively, it may have been a token of renewed friendship between Barttelot and Selim after a period of coolness between the two leaders.

Two days before, Selim had come into the camp to see Barttelot, and had given him some news. Troup wrote in his diary:

By what I can gather from Barttelot's conversation with me afterwards, Selim has not received any letter himself from Tippu-Tib, but expects one in a few days! But he has been told that Tippu-Tib will be here about the fifth day of the next moon, which should be the sixteenth of this month, with about 250 men; and that he (Selim) is going to build a house at the back of our camp for him. Selim stated to Barttelot that there is a road from Stanley Falls right up to Lake Albert, that is to the Unyoro end, and that they have Arabs right along it. He says it is a better road than the one Stanley took, and that it would take about three months to reach the lake by this route. This is like everything else connected with Tippu-Tib's people— rumours, contradictions; statements, contradictions; keeping back news, then springing something quite new, at different periods. There have often been rumours that they had a road to the Lake, direct from the Falls, but no definite statement has been made before by Selim to this effect. Barttelot talks about going to the Falls to meet Tippu-Tib, if he can get Selim Mohammed to accompany him.

What Barttelot withheld from Troup for the moment was that he and Jameson had a new plan. Jameson wrote on the same day:

> The Major and I have talked matters over together, and have decided, in case we hear of Mr Stanley having either met with disaster or being hemmed in, that we will personally sign a guarantee for £5,000, which we will give to Tippu-Tib upon his signing an agreement to give us sufficient men to go up to the Lake, and see what has really happened; that is, if he will not do it for less, or if he will not give us enough men to move the loads now. If we have to do this, we shall only take food and ammunition, and go simply to fight our way through if necessary.

It was not until ten days later, just before he left for the Falls with Jameson and Selim Mohammed, that Barttelot told the others how he and Jameson were prepared to offer Tippu-Tib an extra £5,000 for the men if all else failed. All the officers except Troup agreed that Stanley's prolonged absence justified their taking steps to find out where he was and what had happened to him. Barttelot went so far as to say—more than once, according to Troup—'that he thinks Stanley has been killed, and never expects to see him again'. Troup took the opposite view, that nothing had happened to him, no disaster had occurred; that he was merely delayed. The journey there and back had taken much longer than he had anticipated, that was all. But he *was* puzzled by the lack of news; he too thought it strange that no messenger had been sent to tell them the position.

It was part of Barttelot's plan to send all the loads over to Stanley Falls and leave them there in the care of a white man, who would also be responsible for the sick. Troup disapproved of that too. He felt the white man would be powerless if Tippu-Tib decided to 'play false'. But he had nothing better to suggest, only that they should wait for Stanley who, he fervently hoped, would not be much longer delayed. In the end he equivocated, 'Whilst I do not like the idea either of leaving loads at Stanley Falls, or of our going up without them I cannot well vote against getting men as a last resource to go up and obtain some intelligence as to the whereabouts of Stanley's column . . . I should most reluctantly go with such a column.'

Jameson, though he supported Barttelot, was also uncertain what they should do. He summed up their dilemma thus: 'Make a move of some kind we must; but it is useless to do so unless we are in a position to be of real help to Stanley.'

The officers felt that the longer they stayed at Yambuya, the less chance they had ever of marching. They had to make a concerted effort to get out or they would *all* die of inanition. There were now 50 graves outside the camp and in addition, Ward wrote:

> There are 30 men who are simply skin and bones, unable to walk, and to see the poor dying wretches, their great hollow eyes staring at vacancy, sitting naked on the dusty ground, propped up by their elbows, with drooping heads, gradually dying, it is a hard sight. Poor devils! they do not seem to care an atom about death; in fact they seem apparently to look forward to it as a relief to their sufferings. They are nearly all slaves. They have lived hard, worked hard, and now are dying hard—it's hard luck indeed.

Yet there was no relaxation of discipline in the camp. The Sudanese soldier who had stolen the goat's meat from Ward's hut, Burgari Mohammed, was still being punished for his offence; he was forced to march up and down in the sun every day—and now it was hotter than ever—wearing heavy chains. At last he could stand it no longer and contrived to escape with his guard's gun and twelve rounds of ammunition. The officers did not relish the thought of him prowling round the camp with a loaded rifle, and he was soon recaptured. Whereupon he was tried for desertion.

Jameson and Troup argued that Burgari should be punished by flogging, as the Zanzibari deserters had been. But Barttelot, Ward and Bonny were for the death penalty. They maintained that as the Sudanese were engaged as soldiers, not porters, they came under military discipline. This was a case of desertion in an enemy's country, and the deserter should be shot. It would also serve as a warning to others. Jameson felt that 'a little leniency to such a poor wretch would not be flung away', but he and Troup were outvoted and Burgari Mohammed was sentenced to be shot.

The entire camp was on parade to witness the execution. Jameson described it:

He was tied up to the flogging post on the road outside the camp, and eight Sudanese formed the firing party. Death was instantaneous, one bullet going right through the backbone, and another through the heart. He took the whole thing quite coolly, without the sign of a tremble, or an utterance of any kind, and waited quietly with his head slightly bent for the signal to fire.

The date was 10 February. The next day another man died and the total of deaths in camp rose to 53—and that did not include Burgari Mohammed.

15

SELIM MOHAMMED agreed to accompany Barttelot to the
Falls, but he was unenthusiastic about the trip; he said it might
be another month or more before Tippu-Tib got back from
Kasongo. Jameson wondered if it would not have been wiser to
have waited at least until they had news that Tippu-Tib had
actually left Kasongo. Although he looked forward to a change of
scenery, he could not help thinking that a month at Stanley Falls
might be too long, 'knowing all the time that we are unwelcome
guests'.

But Barttelot would not hear of any further delay; so they left
on 14 February—Barttelot, Jameson, Selim Mohammed, the
interpreter Assad Farran and a small number of carriers. (They
had no way of knowing it, of course, but the five white men who
had been together so long at Yambuya would never again be all in
the same place at one time; from now on they would be more
scattered than heretofore.) That evening Ward wrote in his diary,
'We are very quiet now. Sorry Jameson's gone.'

Barttelot left Troup in charge of the camp with instructions to
strengthen the *boma*, to keep the Sudanese under the 'strictest
supervision' and never to leave less than two white officers in the
camp at any one time. For a few days after Barttelot and Jameson
had gone, Bonny busied himself teaching the Zanzibaris how to
use rifles. They were porters, not soldiers, and many of them were
afraid to fire a rifle. It was plain they would not be much use in an
emergency. On the first day out, only one bullet out of 100 was on
target. What they really needed was food, not rifle practice—food
and proper medical attention. Ward wrote:

Poor wretches! They lie out in the sun on the dusty ground,
most of them with only a narrow strip of dirty cloth a couple of
inches broad. There they lie all the lifelong day, staring at
vacancy, perfectly aware that they will never live to leave this

camp. It was a truly pitiable sight, a few days ago, to see an emaciated skeleton crawl, with the aid of a stick, after a corpse that was being carried on a pole for interment. He staggered along, poor chap, and squatted down alongside the newly-made grave, watching the proceedings with large round sunken eyes, knowing it was only a matter of a few days and he himself would be laid in the sod. He told me in a husky hollow voice, 'Amekwa rafiki angu' ('He was my friend'). One poor fellow in particular—he is a mere mass of bones—persists in doing his work, and every morning he staggers into camp. He has been told to lie up, and his manioc shall be provided for him, but he refuses. He said to me in reply to my expression of sympathy on observing how thin he was, 'Only a short time more, Master!' Death is written in plain letters on many faces in this camp. Almost as many lives will be lost over this philanthropic mission as there are lives to save of Emin's people.

On 24 February, 70 men arrived and announced that 80 more would be coming the next day. They said they had passed Barttelot and Jameson on the Congo. Troup got very excited: 'After eight months' waiting some men have come at last! This, they say, is the first contingent of a lot more coming from Kasongo. If this is the case, there will be no necessity for Barttelot to propose the extra money scheme for men *not* to carry loads.'

The following day more men did arrive and Troup felt justified in sending messengers with a letter to Barttelot telling him of their arrival. After all, he reasoned, Barttelot might well have passed them on the Congo without having the faintest idea where they were going. Troup was greatly relieved at the thought that there might be no need to leave the loads at the Falls or make a new bargain with Tippu-Tib. But when he turned his attention to more immediate issues, he was very annoyed to discover that Barttelot had given Bonny instructions about buying canoes without reference to him. He was now in command of the camp and he had always had charge of the treasury, so all such orders should have come through him; and this particular order had not even been written down. Bonny wrote, 'Troup thinks it interferes with his temporary charge of the camp. This is foolish. If he is in temporary charge of the camp, I am in charge of the whole of the

Zanzibaris . . . After the manner of his behaviour I feel that his charge has affected his head. I would not give him charge of a WC. I told him so.' This, no doubt, accounted for the 'animated wrangle' which Ward overheard as he was writing his diary that evening, and for the 'frigid air of indifference' Troup and Bonny maintained towards each other throughout the next day.

Selim Mohammed did not stay long at the Falls. When he returned he brought a letter from Barttelot to Troup (which crossed Troup's letter). It was clear from this letter that Barttelot knew of the men sent to Yambuya but did not share Troup's elation at the sight of them. He was now talking of 'getting 500 or more fighting men in excess of the 600 carriers'. Troup was exasperated, but no more than Barttelot was when he received Troup's 'idiotic letter'. When he replied to it, three days later, Barttelot made no attempt to conceal his feelings.

'Dear Troup,' he wrote, 'We got your letter March 2 at midnight, and we both thought, "News of Stanley at last," or a mutiny in the camp, or some other very serious matter. But we were agreeably disappointed at finding nothing of importance in it . . .' (Barttelot was not in the habit of using such a subtle figure of speech as the oxymoron, so his use of it here gives the measure of his exasperation.)

If Bonny's account can be trusted, it seems the officers took advantage of Barttelot's absence to introduce a little female companionship to soften the rigours of camp life. Bonny himself took the initiative. On 3 March he at last succeeded in buying a slave woman. She had been captured by the Arabs in a raid some weeks earlier, and Bonny paid Abdullah six pieces of handkerchief for her. 'She is a cannibal I think,' he wrote, 'but not being able to talk to her I cannot ascertain for the present. She can speak a few words of Kiswahili. She readily told me her name is Subitaki and asked me to give her something to eat. She does not take it amiss being thrown among white men for the first time and within half an hour after arriving commenced to cook food for herself.' Bonny thought she was probably eighteen or twenty years old and added—improbably—that his 'real object' in buying her was to get information about Stanley, whose march had taken him through the region she came from. He hoped also 'to gain an insight into the native character'.

Troup and Ward, apparently, were not slow to follow his example. By 7 March Troup had also got a woman for six pieces of handkerchief, and Ward in exchange for a pair of long boots. Bonny wrote of his own acquisition: 'My woman has become quite useful and said she hopes I will not let the Arabs have her again. She would like to go back to her village, but I cannot send her for the Arabs would take her again. They occupy the village.'

To begin with, all went well. Bonny noted cheerfully, 'Our cannibal concubines are quite at home and appear quite happy.' But then, when the officers woke up on the morning of 11 March, they found their concubines had bolted. As the women had slept in different huts, they concluded the escape must have been planned in advance. But they did not all succeed in getting away; Bonny was too quick for one of them—unfortunately, not his own. 'I heard a slight noise and was just in time to catch Troup's woman. I called Troup. When he tied her up, she then began to make a sort of refrain something after this style—"Ho-yo-yo-yo-yo, ho-yo-yo-yo, mama mama mama, ho-yo-yo-yo" etc. Mine and Ward's have got away . . .'

Two days later he wrote: 'I heard that our two runaway cannibal women had been seen about two and a half days off in the bush still going upcountry. I am glad and hope they will get safe home. Fancy, Uncle Tom's Eliza is nothing to this affair. Here are three women captured, made to carry heavy loads, beaten and sold for twelve pieces of handkerchief and a pair of boots, travelling days where even if caught people of their own colour would keep them as slaves or eat them as enemies. I laugh and admire their pluck but Ward moans over the loss of his boots.' According to Bonny, Troup's woman, too, eventually made her escape.

If Bonny is telling the truth (and this is by no means certain: in compressing his account I have given it a consistency lacking in the original), then it would not be surprising if the men, too, had tried to get hold of women. And indeed this was the moment when Selim Mohammed complained to Ward that the Zanzibaris were making a nuisance of themselves with his Manyema women. Fortunately, Ward had become so proficient at Swahili that he was now able to act as interpreter. But no sooner had he relayed this information to Troup than the headman Munichandi was caught *in flagrante delicto*, tied up and brought before the officers. The Manyema who had caught him claimed that Munichandi had tried to bribe him with cloth to keep quiet, so Troup ordered Munichandi to hand over the cloth he had promised the man. The difficulty was that the Manyemas encouraged the Zanzibaris; they could easily have prevented any interference with their women had they felt so inclined, but they let it happen so as to frighten the Zanzibaris into parting with a little cloth or a few *mitakos*.

Troup thought the 'woman palaver' had been 'amicably settled'. But a little while later the Manyema returned, forced his way past the sentry and announced his intention of shooting Munichandi. Troup sent him packing, but there was more trouble at the gate when he came back a second time with some of his friends. This time the Sudanese kept him out. Troup sent Ward to remind Selim of the Standing Order which forbade his men entry into the camp without the permission of an officer. If they persisted, he was told, they would be shot.

In spite of this warning they were there again the next morning, hustling and provoking the sentry; they even knocked the rifle out of his hands. When Ward went to remonstrate with Selim once more, Selim suggested the officers themselves punish the offender. Troup refused to do this, thinking it was a trap. So the man got off with an admonition, and the officers tried to improve relations with Selim's men by placing a Zanzibari alongside the Sudanese sentry to act as interpreter. After that, things quietened down.

16

BY 24 MARCH, 67 people had died in camp. The day was dull and wet and there had been a heavy thunderstorm in the morning. At about 4 p.m. Barttelot staggered into the camp. 'They thought I was a ghost,' he wrote. 'I weighed about 8 st. 10 lbs., I suppose.' He told Troup that both he and Jameson had been very sick at the Falls; he said the food was bad and he suspected the Arabs of trying to poison him. He certainly looked ill—'a bad grey colour', according to Ward.

In the end Barttelot had tired of waiting for Tippu-Tib to return and he had sent Jameson to Kasongo 'to try and run him to earth', as he characteristically put it. If Tippu-Tib would provide all the men they needed, Barttelot was prepared to convert all the loads into half-loads—so there would be no cause for complaint on that score. Jameson was going to try and get 1,000 men in all, and he had been authorised by Barttelot to make the best terms he could, with the two of them guaranteeing the extra money involved if that would satisfy Tippu-Tib.

At the same time Barttelot decided to cable a report of the situation to William Mackinnon, the Chairman of the Emin Pasha Relief Committee in London, and ask for his advice. This was no simple matter, of course; it meant someone going all the way down to the coast—a journey of some 3,000 miles there and back. It would take time and it would be dangerous. The question was, who should go? Barttelot wrote in his diary, 'Had words with Jameson about Ward, concerning his carrying the message, I saying he was not to be trusted.' Jameson stuck up for his friend and Barttelot himself must have known in his heart of hearts that Ward was the only one capable of undertaking such a journey. After a conversation with Barttelot a month earlier, Bonny, who was privy to everyone's secrets, had noted: 'He thought that he would take Ward if he went upcountry because Jameson wished it, and leave Troup in charge of the stores. He would only die if he came, Troup was not strong.' So Ward it was who was detailed to carry the message.

Troup thoroughly disapproved of Barttelot's scheme; he wrote, 'It is a long way to send for very little benefit to the Expedition.' Ward did not know what to think; he was stunned by the suddenness of it all. He was to start for the coast in five days' time. 'I expect to have a pretty hard job,' he wrote, 'to pass some of those populous places like Monungeri, Upoto, Mobeka, etc., but we shall have to make them smell powder, or else be cooked and eaten. This is all very startling news; and I do not know whether it is a step in the right direction or not.'

This is the text of the cable he was to send:

No news of Stanley since writing last October. Tippu-Tib went Kasongo November sixteenth, but up to March has only got us two hundred and fifty men; more are coming, but in uncertain numbers and at uncertain times. Presuming Stanley in trouble, absurd for me to start with less numbers than he did, I carrying more loads, and minus 'Maxim' gun; therefore have sent Jameson Kasongo to hasten Tippu in regard to remainder of originally promised six hundred men, and to obtain from him as many fighting men as possible up to four hundred; to make most advantageous terms he can as regards service and payment of men, he and I guaranteeing money in name of Expedition. Jameson will return about May fourteenth, but earliest date to start will be June first. When I start, propose leaving officer with all loads not absolutely wanted at Stanley Falls. Ward carries this message. Please obtain wire from King Belgians to Administrator 'Free State', to place carriers at his disposal, and have steamer in readiness to convey him Yambuya. If men come before his arrival, start without him. He should return about July first. Wire advice and opinion. Officers all well, Ward awaits reply. BARTTELOT.

While Troup and Ward puzzled over this latest development, Bonny had the ear of Barttelot; and he found plenty to tell him about the conduct of the camp during his absence. On 25 March, Barttelot wrote in his diary the first of a series of cryptic entries reminiscent of those of the previous November when Jameson had been ill and Bonny had first insinuated himself into the Major's confidence. 'I was prostrate,' he wrote, 'and Troup took that opportunity to play me false.'

Troup himself wrote, 'Barttelot is very ill; after luncheon he had to turn in, with strong symptoms of fever. I went in to see him; he seemed much upset.'

As the lower reaches of the Aruwini were populated with warlike natives who would not readily give right of way to a couple of unprotected canoes, Ward was to start his journey from below Stanley Falls; he would face dangers enough on the Congo without courting unnecessary ones on the Aruwini. Barttelot was most anxious to see him off, but he was in no state to march across country to the Congo. So Troup volunteered to go with Ward in his place. Ward would begin his journey at Raschid's camp on the Lomami—Raschid was Tippu-Tib's nephew and, after Tippu himself, the most important Arab chief in the region of Stanley Falls—and Troup could take advantage of this visit to Raschid to buy goats for the camp. Barttelot agreed to this.

The next day, Troup wrote:

Barttelot slightly better, insisted on getting up; he was very excited, and it did him no good. Later in the day he spoke in the course of conversation about the necessity of leaving a white officer at Stanley Falls, in the event of there not being sufficient carriers provided to take up all the loads, and he did not wish to leave Bonny. Bearing in mind that I had been informed by Bonny that Barttelot wished to leave me, but hardly liked to ask it, I had thought the matter over from the point of view of the benefit of the Expedition, and I came to the conclusion that it would be best if I should offer to remain. Of course I knew by Barttelot's remarks that, counting Bonny out, I was the only one he had to leave, so I told him I would stay in charge of the loads. Barttelot informed me that I had taken a great load [sic] off his mind.

Yet all Barttelot wrote that day was: 'I find they have been playing the mischief since I have been away.' He busied himself writing innumerable letters. He accepted Troup's help in composing the ones he sent to Congo State officials on Ward's behalf; his own efforts went into the letters he wrote home and were concentrated on self-justification.

Without Jameson to support him, Barttelot felt utterly isolated. The strain was telling on him; he was physically weakened and he saw himself threatened on all sides. He was beginning to doubt that he would survive his present ordeal and he poured out his feelings in a letter to his beloved brother-in-law, Major Harry Sclater:

. . . Stanley should never have left without his whole force, nor without Tippu-Tib's men. Of course, if he returns all the blame will be mine; should I be alive, however, I can defend myself: if dead, please let Mackinnon read this letter. Many, many times have I averted war with the Arabs by eating simple dirt; and I can tell you it is not pleasant for me. By constant and petty annoyances and insolences they forced Deane into a row, and burnt the Falls Station, September 1886, and they have all got their eye on the spoil at Yambuya. I never allow a single Arab into camp without my leave, or even sale and barter to go on. Jameson is a dear good chap, you would like him very much, true, honest and brave; the others I don't think much of. Don't show this letter to anybody but keep it, I may want it some day . . . Ward takes our mail down. I don't think he is either true or very brave, but I cannot send Bonny or Troup, as they would be more than useless and Ward knows the language of the natives and the people in the State for he was in it himself once, and he is undoubtedly a good walker . . . Good-bye, dear old Harry, and God bless you! I hope I will see you once again on this earth.

And all the time Bonny was feeding his feverish brain with suspicions and innuendos, so that Barttelot wrote—and under-lined—in his diary on 27 March, '*I am much upset at what I find.*'

Ward, observing his overwrought state without understanding half the provocation, was unusually sympathetic: 'Poor Barttelot is almost beside himself with his fever, weakness, and the preparation of letters for me.'

The others, too, made use of Ward; they all wrote letters home now that there was an opportunity to post them. Bonny wrote a letter to a Miss E. Thomas of Bristol (whom he describes elsewhere as his 'agent'), instructing her to write to the Secretary of the

Emin Pasha Relief Committee in London on his behalf, which she did in June:

> Sir, I received a letter the 15th of this month from Mr Bonny, dated Aruwini Falls, 16 March 1888, in which he desires me to write informing you that if a woman should call at the office, or write claiming to be his wife, will you please not recognise her. But only my address which he left with you.
>
> Mr Bonny went through the ceremony of marriage with her, but he discovered just on the eve of leaving England that on her part it was a bigamous marriage, she having married before and her husband still living.
>
> He obtained proofs by seeing the certificate at Somerset House tracing the man, etc. He also charged her with it, but had no time to prosecute.

Troup wrote to Sir Francis de Winton, giving his side of the argument with Barttelot:

> ... I grant that nine months is a long time to be in a camp waiting for men who never turn up; and all the trouble and anxiety caused by the Arabs has been most tiresome to say the least of it. We have had to put up with a deal of it and it has required great patience and forbearance, but I think we must have a little more patience. Barttelot looks at it from the point of view that something has happened to Stanley, that he won't return and I can't get it out of his head. He is also in an upset state of mind and thinks he will be blamed for not having gone up after Mr Stanley.

Troup told de Winton that he had agreed to remain behind with the loads:

> You will, I am sure, understand that my reason for volunteering to stop at the Falls, should there be any necessity for leaving a white man, was in the welfare of the Expedition and not from any wish to remain behind on my part. I know you will see that I am righted on this point, should unfortunately any necessity arise. The world is uncharitable and one's motives are often misconstrued. I think I have told you my ideas frankly on the situation, not in any opposing spirit to the commander of the camp, but in a friendly chatty manner to you.

Ward's main worry at this time was that he would be left behind again. He wanted to know what would happen if, when he got back from the coast, the column had already marched. Barttelot assured him that he would make arrangements with Tippu-Tib to provide him with men to enable him to catch up with the column.

28 March was Barttelot's birthday; he was twenty-nine. It rained heavily all morning and Troup and Ward got off to a late start. Barttelot wrote, 'Ward left for Banana [on the coast] and Troup for Lomami to buy goats, but had I known when they started what was told me afterwards they should never have gone. They have both been false to me and to Stanley.' A day later he was writing, with more than a suggestion of cause and effect, 'I feel tons better. Bonny and I left alone.' And the day after that: 'More disclosures concerning Ward, which caused me to send a letter after him.' Bonny's tongue had not been idle. 'I told Barttelot today,' he wrote on 30 March, 'that Troup, unable to unlock his chop box, took out the screws at the back to open it to look for fat or lard, also that he wished to strike a piece of handkerchief off my mess account if I said nothing about him taking three pieces which he intended to replace by purchasing them from Ward with *mitakos* then in his possession and private . . .' Yet on 15 March, when Barttelot was still away, Bonny had written: 'We found that Barttelot and Jameson had hidden away for private consumption some of the European provisions. What a shame and what meanness. It is not the first time that both are guilty of this sort of thing.' Now he went on: 'I told Barttelot that Ward had received a present from Selim to bring up a present in return from the coast as a matter of business. Barttelot then wrote Ward a stringent letter . . .'

Ward got the letter while he was still as Raschid's camp on the Lomami. It was 2 April and he was leaving early the next morning. He and Troup were standing by the river, watching the men prepare the canoes for the journey down the Congo, when a messenger came up with the letter. This is what they read:

WARD, I am sending this to warn you to be very careful in the manner you behave below—I mean as regards pecuniary matters. I shall require at your hands a receipted bill for everything you spend, and should you be unable to purchase the champagne and the watch, you will not draw that £20. The slightest attempt at any nonsense I shall be down upon you for. I have given you a position of trust, so see that you do not abuse it. You will send me a receipt of this letter.

(Signed) EDMUND M. BARTTELOT, Major.

Ward replied: 'Consider letter gross insult, and will demand explanation and satisfaction on my return.'

But that was a long way off. Ward had a long and extremely hazardous canoe journey ahead of him. He and Troup stayed up half the night discussing the situation at the camp, Ward's journey and the reasons for it. They came to the conclusion that it was a waste of time and money and effort, for there was nothing the Committee could possibly say in reply to Barttelot's cable except: 'Carry out Stanley's instructions.'

17

IN THE absence of Ward and Jameson, who were both on friendly terms with Selim Mohammed, relations between the Arabs and the rear column went from bad to worse. Petty disputes over the purchase of a knife from a Manyema or the alleged theft of a paddle from a native canoe led to angry words between Barttelot and Selim. While Selim accused the Zanzibaris of making trouble, Barttelot blamed the Manyemas; he was convinced that Selim himself was 'egging on his men to have a row with mine, in order to have a shy at the stores'.

It had been reported to him that Selim had said, after the business with the Manyema women, 'This will be a second Stanley Falls palaver.' In fact, it was a quite different sort of affair, but Barttelot was prone to make comparisons between his situation at Yambuya and Deane's at Stanley Falls. He felt that he, like Deane, was the dupe of Arab Machiavellism.

'Things look black,' he wrote on 3 April. 'Selim Mohammed is drawing the string tighter.' He had heard that Selim was sending a man to the Falls to prevent him leaving his loads there. '*Perhaps my days are numbered,*' he went on. 'I had a palaver with Selim Mohammed this evening, and of course I had to eat dirt. We parted, he with many professions of friendship, but evil in his heart. I shall go to the Falls unless stopped, and try to get Nzige's aid.' (Nzige was in charge at the Falls during Tippu-Tib's absence.) He wanted to have Selim Mohammed removed from the immediate vicinity of the camp or, alternatively, to get the loads transported to the Falls, thereby obviating the danger of an attack.

The next day he consulted Bonny, who agreed that he should go to the Falls. (Bonny later told Troup that *he* had suggested Barttelot go to the Falls, because he felt things had reached such a pitch that not only were their lives and the camp in danger, but the Arabs might also attack Troup on his way back from the Lomami and make Jameson a prisoner at Kasongo. He would look after the camp while Barttelot was away—or out of the way, as the implication clearly was.)

The letter of instructions Barttelot gave Bonny when he left emphasised the need to keep peace with the Arabs. It urged him to prevent, as far as possible, all intercourse between the two lots of men. It also contained a sentence which represented a personal triumph for Bonny: 'You will retain command till my return, for though Mr Troup may return before I return, yet it will be such a short period before, that it will be best for you to retain the command.'

At Stanley Falls Nzige agreed to recall Selim Mohammed, so Barttelot returned to Yambuya. On the way back he bumped into Troup, who was also returning. Nowadays the very sight of Troup was enough to exasperate him. 'Troup, sick as per usual,' he wrote contemptuously 'and with no goats, arrived.' Troup had waited as long as he dared but he had not been able to get any goats. Raschid was engaged in retaliatory action against some natives who had had the gall to eat two of his men; he was not thinking about goats until that business was over. (In fact, though he refused all payment, he did send goats after Troup; they arrived at Yambuya towards the end of April.)

Troup was very surprised to come upon Barttelot so far from the camp and looking, as he put it, 'terribly ill and very disturbed . . . He was evidently much excited over the recent events in camp, and could not give me a clear statement of what had taken place.' But Barttelot was obviously most anxious about what might be happening there during his absence; as Bonny was the only white man present, he was afraid that Selim Mohammed might take the opportunity to launch an attack. Troup was amazed to hear that things had come to such a pass.

The following morning it rained heavily. Barttelot and Troup set off early and went at such a pace that most of the men were left far behind. 'On the march,' Barttelot wrote, 'Troup plausibly entered into certain matters. I gave him to understand that I considered he had acted with breach of faith towards me.' As if to emphasise his rejection of him, Barttelot left Troup and went on to the camp alone.

He got there in the afternoon of 15 April: 'On arrival in camp a tale of woe greeted me.' Bonny himself was alive and well, but what he reported was anything but reassuring. In the past the natives at least had been friendly, if at times a little suspicious. Now they too were making trouble. Ngungu had started to break up a canoe right in front of the sentry's eyes. When he was brought up before Bonny he said Selim Mohammed had told him to do it.

Barttelot wrote down the story just as Bonny had told it to him:

Selim Mohammed, being confronted with him, and asked if this was true, said: 'Cut the white men down when they go to the jungle.' Bonny turned to Selim and said: 'Look here, Selim Mohammed, there is only one white man here, and he is not afraid to lose his life; but rest assured if he loses his, yours goes before.' Selim Mohammed slunk off with the native. Next day the natives came and shouted out, 'The white men are bad.' Being asked who told them so, they said, 'Selim Mohammed.' That evening a crowd of natives and the chief met Bonny and made impertinent gestures at him. He sent for his revolver, and they dispersed.

The extraordinary thing is, Barttelot appears to have accepted this story at its face value. Leaving aside the fact that Bonny always features as the hero of his own stories, cool and decisive in the face of danger, he transforms Selim Mohammed into a quite preposterous figure. The officers had always thought of Selim as a gentleman, whatever else he might be, and he had shown himself a good deal more sophisticated than that remark about cutting the white men down in the jungle would suggest. Nor was he the sort of man to 'slink off' at the sound of Bonny's brave words. It is much more likely that Bonny lost his nerve, and was merely whistling in the dark when he wrote in his diary: 'I do not intend to die like a rat in a hole. If there is really no alternative I will at least try to see Selim Mohammed fall.'

Troup arrived the day after Barttelot. He still found it hard to believe that relations with the Arabs had deteriorated so far. When Bonny told him that it might be necessary to shoot both Selim and Ngungu, he commented drily, 'It seems possible that owing to the absence of the interpreters there was some misunderstanding between Bonny and Selim.' He had thought it odd when Barttelot had told him that Bonny had been left without a single interpreter. Bartholomew had been with him on the Lomami; Assad Farran had gone to Kasongo with Jameson; and John Henry had accompanied Barttelot to the Falls. And now rumour had it that John Henry, whom Barttelot had left along with the other men in his hurry to get back to camp, had 'bolted', taking with him the Major's revolver. So Barttelot sent out a party to look for him.

After lunch on the day of his arrival, Troup went to see Barttelot, who wrote of this interview: 'I had an explanation of his conduct while in command of the camp. I told him my opinion of him and have taken away charge of the stores from him.' Troup found he had already been turned out of his hut, which contained the stores. Barttelot himself was living there and he told Troup he could have Ward's hut.

That afternoon Troup was surprised, after all the talk about him, to see Selim Mohammed. He came in person to ask Troup if he or his men had brought the letter of recall which Barttelot had told him was on its way. (In fact, Selim was never recalled, though a couple of days later he went off of his own accord, taking a large body of men on a raid down river.)

Neither Troup nor Barttelot was fit, but they went through the procedure of handing over and receiving the stores. With Bonny's help, Troup made out his accounts and gave them to Barttelot, who checked all the stores with him. They also shifted the remaining stores from Jameson's hut, so that all the loads would be together in one place. The work was completed on Saturday 21 April, when Barttelot wrote, 'Had a row with Troup. He called himself a dog and thought I called him one, because I did not disagree with him. In the evening I caught him out in a lie which he had told Bonny. My temper with all these worries and vexations is none of the best.'

Bonny wrote on the same day: 'There was a big row between Barttelot and Troup, each accusing the other of certain things. Barttelot charged Troup with being a drunkard and having been in police courts, etc., Troup charging Barttelot with having been kicked out of the Egyptian army, etc. . . . Barttelot ordered Troup to leave the camp. Troup said, "You are not head of this expedition".'

As far as Troup was concerned, this was the last straw. Deprived of all responsibility, he took to his bed and remained there for six weeks. He had fallen over some slippery logs and injured himself on his way back to camp and the injury was getting no better. That Sunday he wrote in his diary, 'Still much troubled with the severe strain, resulting from my accident. Consulted Bonny about it; he ordered me complete rest, and said I had been very foolish to walk about while suffering so.'

With Troup sick and confined to his hut, Barttelot and Bonny were once again—to all intents and purposes—alone together. Barttelot would have nothing to do with Troup; he would not even visit him in his hut. So Troup's welfare was entirely in Bonny's hands. It suited Bonny very well to be the go-between; he could interpret the behaviour of each to the other, while at the same time making himself indispensable to both. Troup was duly grateful to him. He called him 'my kind nurse' and wrote, 'Bonny attended me, and did all in his power to alleviate my sufferings.' And Bonny could say what he liked to Barttelot without fear of contradiction.

Yet if Bonny could be said to have had a friend in the rear column, it was Troup. He turned to Troup for advice, and Troup provided him with companionship. But that did not stop him, of course, from telling tales to Barttelot.

The day Troup took to his bed, Barttelot sentenced the interpreter John Henry—who had been captured and brought back to the camp two days earlier—to be shot. The Zanzibaris threatened to desert in a body if the sentence was carried out; but Barttelot told them that if they did, they could give up any idea of ever seeing Zanzibar again. He said they would lose their money and their freedom; Tippu-Tib would make them all slaves again. He had made up his mind, he said, and he would not change it. But Bonny prevailed upon him to commute the sentence—if commute is the word—to 300 lashes.

'Flogged John Henry 300 lashes,' Barttelot noted the following day, 'his posterior a spectacle'.

Troup could hear what was going on from his hut. 'I was much disturbed by this,' he wrote, 'as I do not approve of such a severe punishment.'

Then Barttelot was away for two days visiting an Arab settlement. He left Bonny, not Troup, in charge of the camp, and when he returned he wrote, 'I heard on arrival that John Henry had died yesterday of mortification from his flogging; a terrible death but I am certain he must have been shot or hung, sooner or later, for he was a monstrous bad character.'

Barttelot's main hope now was that he would hear from Jameson before long. In the meantime, he and Bonny entertained themselves as best they could. Barttelot's diary tells its own story:

Monday, April 30. Light rain in the early morning. After breakfast we fought Sala's cock against Muni Katoto, but it was no good; Muni Katoto game, but out of condition. Bonny got a dinner out of me thereby. Bonny told me of Troup and Ward's suspicions against Jameson and me. They must have sunk very low in character to entertain such thoughts, but men who open other people's private boxes must have reached a lowish pitch.

Tuesday, May 1. Sala sent in last night two fowls and a lot of plantains, very fine ones. I sent his men and a present back this morning. Bonny told me, by way of a refresher, that Ward had told him that Stanley had told him (Ward) that he (Stanley) had left me behind because I was of no use to him. Certainly, I don't think I am much, but then, it is because Stanley does not attempt to utilize me, and hates me like poison.

Wednesday, May 2. Showery. Troup has something wrong with his testes, which Bonny says may be serious . . .

Friday, May 4. Rained last night. Bonny and I measured to-day. I am a smaller man altogether than he is; round the chest I measure 34 inches; I used to measure 36. I must have shrunk. Round the arm 9 inches—very small; round the forearm 10 inches, round the waist 31 inches, round the calf 12 inches.

In spite of their enforced intimacy, Barttelot's feelings towards Bonny remained equivocal. Later in the month he would sum up his feelings in a letter to his fiancée, Mabel Godman:

Bonny is a good honest man, but rough, and not a man I could make a close friend of were I shut up for years alone with him . . . [he] is the queerest specimen you ever saw. A mixture of conceit, bravery and ignorance, born a gentleman, but by circumstances a non-commissioned officer in the army, he purchased his discharge to come on this expedition. His continual cry is that he is every bit as good as we are, and must be treated the same. Stanley was very down on him, and he was very bitter about it. Since he has been with me I have done all I can for him. He is most useful with the natives and Arabs, of an unchanging slow temperament, he is just suited to them. He purchases all supplies for us and doctors the sick, for he was in the Army Medical Department. He is in charge also of the Zanzibaris.

On 5 May there were rumours that Selim Mohammed was on his way back—that he was just one day away by canoe—and once again, that Stanley was approaching. He was supposed to be four days away. 'If he comes,' Barttelot wrote, 'I shall catch it about the telegram.'

Whatever the truth about Stanley, it was certain that Selim Mohammed was returning. He arrived the next day with 'much beating of drums'. He too had heard about Stanley, so Barttelot decided to go up and take a look for himself.

Before he could leave, however, there was a welcome interruption to the monotony of camp life. At about midday on 8 May the officers heard the cheerful sound of a steam-whistle, and the steamer *AIA* hove into sight round a bend in the Aruwini. There was great excitement in the camp; even Troup felt it, though he was unable to move from his bed and relied on Bonny to tell him what was happening.

The officer in command of the steamer was a Belgian, Lieutenant Van Kerckhoven, by all accounts a rather flamboyant character, who sported shoulder-length hair, an enormous hat and pyjamas. The engineer on board was one J. R. Werner, who—nearly two years before—had made a similar journey to go to the relief of Captain Deane at Stanley Falls.

18

WERNER WAS the only Englishman still in the service of the Congo Free State. Exactly a month earlier, he had been sitting at dinner with his Belgian colleagues at Bangala when a Hausa sentry burst in on them and said that he had just heard Swahili being spoken by some people in canoes on the river. The Belgians were filled with alarm; they thought it must be the Arabs. Perhaps Tippu-Tib had sent to find out what had happened to the officers and men promised him by the State; he was not to know that of the two officers appointed to go to Stanley Falls, one had died at Leopoldville and the other had been so ill as to be forced to return to Europe, and that their replacements had only just arrived on the upper river. The whole station turned out in panic, only to find that the canoes contained not Tippu-Tib's Arabs, but Herbert Ward with 30 Zanzibaris and five Sudanese. Their relief was considerable.

So too was their curiosity. Werner and the Belgians had assumed that Ward, along with the rest of the expedition, had long since arrived at Wadelai, if they had not gone on from there down to the east coast. They were astonished to learn that Major Barttelot was still encamped on the Aruwini and there was no news of Stanley.

Ward had made excellent progress. He had travelled some 400 miles in only five days. He spent the night on the *AIA* and set off again early in the morning, this time with a skilled crew of Bangala natives. He was hoping to overtake the *Stanley*, which had started down river only hours before his arrival at Bangala.

Van Kerckhoven, who was in charge of the station, undertook to return the 35 Zanzibaris and Sudanese to Barttelot's camp. The journey reminded Werner of that earlier occasion when he and another Belgian, Captain Coquilhat, had gone to Deane's rescue: 'Once more was the little *AIA* on her way to relieve a distant outpost of white men, but this time under happier circumstances;

and the memory of those other days now seemed like a bad dream of long ago.' The steamer reached the mouth of the Aruwini on 6 May and Werner soon descried evidence of the Arab presence in the neighbourhood:

> Next day, approaching the bend of the river, where we expected to find the town of Yambumba—described by Stanley as truly metropolitan—I noticed that the bluff where he saw it in 1883 was completely bare of huts, only a few banana plants remaining. The Arabs had burned the whole place, and the natives had removed to the low bank opposite, where they were dragging out a wretched existence, having for houses only a sort of palm-leaf awning, supported on four sticks; while a detachment of Manyemas, left by the Arabs to keep them in subjection, kept them also in constant fear of their lives.

When the *AIA* arrived at Yambuya, Barttelot and Bonny came down to meet it. Werner thought they both looked well considering what they had had to live on for so many months. He wondered where Troup might be—Ward had told him he had been away. He found him in his hut, lying on a camp-bed, looking 'as if he had not a week to live'. Troup told him what had happened, how he had strained his leg and a large tumour had formed, which had not only lamed him but affected his health in general. After dinner, Van Kerckhoven, Werner and Bonny all went and sat with Troup in an attempt to cheer him up.

Barttelot had gone off in the afternoon to check the rumour of Stanley's approach. He found, as he had expected, there was nothing in it; and he returned to camp the following evening. Van Kerckhoven made him a present of tea, biscuits, jam and a tin of sardines. Barttelot noted grimly in his diary, 'Heard about Ward and his untrustworthy carryings on.' Not a word about the danger of his mission or the notable speed with which he had accomplished the first, and most hazardous, leg of the journey with only a small force and a totally inexperienced crew of Zanzibaris.

In spite of the arrival of the steamer and Van Kerckhoven's attempt to establish cordial relations with Selim Mohammed, the bad feeling between Barttelot and Selim persisted. Barttelot (wrongly) accused Selim of withholding a letter from Jameson and, though Selim denied it, Barttelot made no attempt to conceal the fact that he thought he was lying. As a precaution he got Van Kerckhoven to provide him with petrol so that he could blow up the stores, 'if necessary'.

Van Kerckhoven meanwhile was offering to transport the ivory that the Arabs had amassed at Yambuya to Stanley Falls. He felt obliged to do this, as Tippu-Tib was now an official of the State. Selim, for his part, readily accepted the offer. So the spoils of many months of indiscriminate raiding were loaded on to the steamer belonging to the Free State for delivery at the home of its appointed representative.

The ivory, some 1,500 pounds of it, was in poor condition, mostly cracked and blistered, because it had been looted from villages which the Arabs had burned first. 'These tusks,' Werner wrote in disgust, 'contrast very unfavourably with the fine ivory bought peaceably and cheaply by European traders on the Congo, which is worth about four times as much; and afford a striking proof of the low value set on human life by the Arabs, who for the sake of a few such, will murder scores of men and women.'

The *AIA* left Yambuya at 5 a.m. on 11 May. Troup wrote in his diary:

> They are coming back here again. Bonny tells me that Barttelot is very anxious that I should go home. Bonny informs me that Barttelot wishes him to give me a certificate that I am unfit for further service, adding that if he does so I shall be forced to go whether I like it or not. Barttelot said that in the service when a medical officer in charge gave such a certificate it was compulsory for the patient to go. Bonny tells me that if I don't get better before the steamer goes down he will send me back in it. At present he finds there is not much improvement in my condition.

With the departure of the steamer, normal hostilities were resumed. Barttelot wrote:

> In the evening the natives were insolent to me, and one man tried to knock me off the path as I was walking up and down our promenade. I knocked him flat with my stick—wrong on my part, perhaps, but almost unavoidable. This man went straight

to Selim Mohammed, and came back escorted by about 20 Manyemas armed with sticks, spears, and guns. They met me on the road. I stood still in the centre of the road; I had only my stick; but for some reason they sheered off on one side and left me clear. They made a great noise, and no doubt cursed me. Close to the fort-gate, but of course outside it, stood Selim Mohammed with a man whom I swear had a gun under his clothes. They were talking to Bonny, who happened to come out just at that moment. This evening we heard that Tippu-Tib had come to the Falls; also that the natives had been told to take my life. I expect Jameson back about the 14th.

In fact, Jameson and Tippu-Tib were still ten days away from the Falls. But the rumour of Tippu's return was enough to decide Barttelot to go and see for himself. Once again leaving Bonny in charge of the camp, he set out on 14 May, hoping to cut across to the Congo in time to intercept the *AIA* on its way up to the Falls. He managed this and so was able to complete the journey in comfort—which was just as well as he was in some pain: his hands were a mass of small suppurating ulcers which stiffened the joints and made it almost impossible to move his fingers.

It was during this part of the journey that Werner tackled Barttelot on the subject of Troup, who had complained that Barttelot did not consult him as Stanley had instructed him to do; and if he did consult him, took no notice of his advice. Later, Werner recalled what Barttelot had said. 'Troup thinks he ought to be in command of the camp,' he had said, 'because he has been on the Congo before; and he won't back me up in anything I do. As for the rows with the Arabs, for which he blames me, they began when Troup was in command of the camp, while I was away at Stanley Falls.'

Werner was inclined to believe Barttelot. He found it hard to reconcile the fact that he was supposed to be the cause of quarrels between the whites and the Arabs with the obviously friendly welcome he received at all the Arab stations on the Congo and at the Falls as well: 'He was even better received than Mr Van Kerckhoven [Werner did not like Van Kerckhoven]—Selim Mohammed and Raschid being the only ones who appeared to dislike him, except old Nzige, who appeared to be greatly frightened when the Major arrived at the Falls on a steamer in company with Mr Van Kerckhoven.'

Of course, Werner may not have been a good judge of the situation. He was not very experienced in the ways of the Arabs, and what he took to be friendliness on their part may have been nothing more than their normal courtesy—it was perfectly natural that they should give Barttelot a bigger welcome than Van Kerckhoven; they had known him longer. And it must be said that Barttelot himself had no very high opinion of the engineer of the *AIA*. On 19 May, the day after they had arrived at the Falls, he wrote in his diary, 'In the evening Werner and I went for a walk. He is mad, I fancy.'

Barttelot, restless as ever, had not long to wait for Jameson and Tippu-Tib. They arrived at 4 p.m. on 22 May. Barttelot paid his respects to the Arab leader and then drank the health of his 'dear old Jameson' in champagne provided by Van Kerckhoven. It was the first they had tasted in fourteen months.

19

JAMESON HAD been away two months. His canoe journey up to Kasongo (like Ward's down to Bangala) had not been free of danger. At the beginning of April, he and his companions had come upon a wild lot of natives who wore their hair in knots on the top of their heads, but spoke Swahili and dressed in white garments like the Arabs. Jameson observed that 'the Arabs appear to be very much afraid of them, which seems a curious reversion of their relations, compared with the state of affairs on the Aruwini, where the natives only ask to be let alone'. In spite of this, these natives received the same treatment as those on the Aruwini: the Arabs set fire to their villages. But this bunch did seem to have more fight in them; and Jameson was warned, quite superfluously, that they were in 'a very dangerous mood'. Drums sounded all around and they came threateningly close in their canoes. Unlike the Aruwini natives, who aroused his pity, these warlike fellows challenged the sportsman in Jameson. He even offered to take a few pot-shots at them with his Remington, which had a longer range than the Arab guns. The Arabs readily accepted his offer.

> I got the rifle and sat down. I fired several shots at the most conspicuous canoe, some 300 or 400 yards away, and so far as I could see hit two or three of the men in it. There was a tremendous getting away in every direction, and after putting some bullets right beside two or three more, there was not a man to be seen. I think it gave them a lesson, which will be useful for us tomorrow, for we have to go up the rapids right through the middle of them.

After that there was no more trouble and Jameson reached the Arab stronghold of Nyangwe on 9 April. Two days later he was at Kasongo. Tippu-Tib was glad to see him, but reluctant to discuss the question of the men. He refused even to consider a separate contract with Barttelot; his contract was with Stanley and he had no intention of making another. He urged Jameson to be patient; if he would wait another ten days the two of them could travel back to Stanley Falls together with the remainder of the men. When Jameson raised the question of who should command the Manyema, Tippu told him he was going to approach Selim Mohammed. Jameson, who of course had no idea what was happening at Yambuya, was delighted:

I told him he was the very man Major Barttelot wanted; that of course, as he would command and give all orders with regard to marching and fighting, it would be a splendid thing to have a man whom we all knew and liked. He said that if Selim would not go, he would give us the very best man he could. I next asked him for a definite date, at which all the men would be delivered, and we could leave Yambuya Camp. He said he thought 1 June would be the very latest, and he certainly thought it would be before then, for he would only wait one day at Singatini [Stanley Falls], and come on straight to the camp himself. He is evidently now in a desperate hurry to get us off. There are two causes for this—1st, he has been hurried up from Zanzibar; 2ndly, he has other big games on hand, which he cannot attend to until we go.

The pressure from Zanzibar came in the form of letters from the British consul, Holmwood. And the conviction, that Tippu-Tib was just as anxious to see the rear column leave as they were to go, was one that Jameson reiterated several times over the next few weeks.

The country around Kasongo was open, hilly and pleasant, and the soil was fertile. There were acres of cultivated land; rice and Indian corn, manioc, ground-nuts and sweet potatoes, all grew in abundance. The town itself was large, built on two sides of a valley, and the house Jameson was given was the best Arab house he had ever stayed in. He was amazed how cheap everything was: 'A man can live here for two days on one "cloth" or less than half a *mitako*.' 'Notwithstanding the slavery,' he wrote in a letter home, 'I don't think I have ever seen a country where there is so much general happiness, and so little misery; one sees far more of the latter at home. There is no starvation here, and no one without work.'

Jameson took advantage of his stay there to discover all he could about Tippu-Tib's position in his own country. He found that there were several independent Arab chiefs, but only three 'great chiefs'. These were Tippu-Tib (of course), Said bin Habib and Said bin Abede. The other two owed no allegiance to Tippu-Tib, but would act with him in a common cause. Tippu's two chief towns were Kasongo and Singatini; the headquarters of the other Arab chiefs were at Nyangwe. 'At first,' Jameson learned,'there was much quarrelling and fighting amongst them, but now they are settled, and each chief owns large districts in which they hunt for ivory and slaves.'

Yet it was not entirely plain sailing. Disputes still did take place, as Jameson soon found out:

At Nyassa the English and the Arabs have had a fight, in which the Arabs have been driven out. They have come to Tippu-Tib to ask for men and powder, which he refused them, telling them that he wanted all his powder and men in case of having to fight Said bin Abede, whose father had some dispute with Tippu-Tib about some villages which they both claimed. The matter was settled by the Sultan in Zanzibar, but on Tippu-Tib's arrival here Said bin Abede came and stayed for two or three days, and at once reopened the quarrel (his father had died on his way to Muscat); but Tippu-Tib told him that it had all been settled in Zanzibar, and that he would not talk to him on the subject, as he was only a boy, but that his son Sefu, who was young, might do so. Said bin Abede then said he had strength enough now to settle the matter. Tippu-Tib told him to use it, but warned him that if there was a row he would not leave him a station, and would drive him clean out of the country. Tippu-Tib then went and burned the three villages in dispute, and took from them a number of men, 100 of whom he sent to us . . .

At Kasongo Jameson met Tippu's son, Sefu, and many other chiefs. He found they were all 'very much puzzled at the non-arrival of any steamer at Stanley Falls up to the time I left, and I do not wonder at it'. He also met the notorious Said bin Habib— 'a venerable white-bearded old Arab, with whom Tippu-Tib was having a conference. He was on his way to Zanzibar; he is very rich, and is one of the Arabs who questioned Tippu-Tib's authority as an officer of the Free State, as he had no visible signs of authority.'

Jameson and Tippu-Tib prepared to depart on 27 April, but they did not get under way until 5 May, as there were people Tippu still had to see (Said bin Habib for one) and he was having difficulty in mustering enough canoes to transport all his men, their women and belongings. The Manyema would not move without their women; it was the women who carried things and did all the work. When Jameson made some reference to the delay, Tippu-Tib lost his temper; so Jameson refrained from mentioning it again. His own temper was sorely tried by his interpreter, Assad Farran, whose idleness and generally gross behaviour were a constant affront. In exasperation he wrote, 'A dirtier, more helpless and useless specimen than Assad Farran I have never met in my life.'

He elaborated on this in a letter he was writing to his wife:

My interpreter is a Syrian from Jerusalem, and about as good-for-nothing a specimen of a Jerusalemite as I ever saw. He has succeeded in making himself properly ill here, through over-eating and taking no exercise. He would come to me at least four times a day, and say he was going out to 'try his chance,' which is a great expression of his. He would then go to the Arabs and eat with them, and return very much swollen out, and tell me of all the things he had eaten. It has, however, done for him, as I warned him, and to-day he has done nothing but lie on his back and groan horribly. I had no medicine for him, having scarcely an atom for myself, but I procured a large half breakfast-cup of native castor-oil from an Arab; it is fearfully strong, and I made him swallow the whole. It has done him a world of good, and I tell him he will be a new man tomorrow.

Jameson was missing the other officers, in particular his friend Barttelot, whom he described to his wife as 'a real honest gentle-man, and I cannot say more'. But most of all he missed his wife and children—'little Gladys and the small baby that I have never seen'. He was tired of the expedition and longed for a rest. 'I shall surely have wrought out my mission in the way of travel after this long journey is over,' he wrote. 'My ambition to do something good in this world before I died was right, but there were a thousand other things which I might have done which would never have called me away so far . . .'

By 10 May Jameson and Tippu-Tib had reached Riba-Riba, an Arab settlement nearly halfway down to Stanley Falls; and the next day Jameson watched an unusual native dance. The Arabs explained to him that these were the Wacusu people, that they had suffered a number of deaths recently and had gone into a kind of collective retreat to make medicine. They had disappeared into the bush, and nobody had seen them until their return that day. While the dance was going on, Tippu-Tib came in and sat down by Jameson. He told him the dance would degenerate into an orgy of killing and feasting on human flesh—the Wacusu were terrible cannibals, he said. He went on to tell a story about a fight which had taken place some years earlier. His men had killed a number of the enemy, but not a single body could be found the next morning. During the night Tippu had sent for water to drink and wash his hands in, and when the water was brought to him he had not been able to understand why it was so oily and nasty to taste. In the morning he went to inspect the well and was horrified to discover that there was a thick yellow scum on the surface of the water. Apparently the natives who had fought for him had taken the flesh of their enemies to the well to wash it before eating. Jameson did not believe a word of it. He told Tippu that such stories were known in his country as 'travellers' tales' or, more simply, lies:

He then said something to an Arab called Ali, seated next to him, who turned round to me and said, 'Give me a bit of cloth, and see.' I sent my boy for six handkerchiefs, thinking it was all a joke, and that they were not in earnest, but presently a man appeared, leading a young girl of about ten years old by the hand, and then I witnessed the most horribly sickening sight I am ever likely to see in my life. He plunged a knife quickly into her breast twice, and she fell on her face, turning over on her side. Three men then ran forward, and began to cut up the body of the girl; finally her head was cut off, and not a particle remained, each man taking his piece away down to the river to wash it. The most extraordinary thing was that the girl never uttered a sound, nor struggled, until she fell. Until the last moment, I could not believe that they were in earnest. I have heard many stories of this kind since I have been in this country, but never could believe them, and I would never have been such a beast as to witness this, but I could not bring myself to believe that it was anything save a ruse to get money out of me, until the last moment.

The girl was a slave captured from a village close to this town, and the cannibals were Wacusu slaves, and natives of this place, called Mculusi. When I went home I tried to make some small sketches of the scene while still fresh in my memory, not that it is ever likely to fade from it. No one here seemed to be in the least astonished at it.

Jameson did not have long to reflect on the implications of his action, and perhaps that was just as well. Tippu-Tib had heard from the Falls that Barttelot had had a row with Selim Mohammed. Nzige, he told Jameson, had written to Selim, 'telling him on no account to have any row with the Major'. (This must have been the letter which Barttelot imagined contained Selim's recall.) Jameson tried to defend his friend: he told Tippu that Barttelot was a quick-tempered, but not a bad-tempered man; that they had all had rows with one another in camp and he was sure this one would be settled by the time they got back.

A couple of days later Tippu-Tib informed Jameson that whether or not Selim Mohammed went up with the rear column, the man who would command the Manyema was Muni Somai, one of two chiefs at Riba-Riba. When Jameson passed this on to Assad Farran, Assad coolly told him he knew it already: the other chief at Riba-Riba had said that Muni Somai was paying Tippu-Tib £300 to give him the job. Jameson was furious with Assad for not volunteering this information earlier; he realised that Assad would have said nothing at all if he had not brought up the matter himself. As far as his relationship with Assad Farran was concerned, this was positively the last straw.

20

ON THE way down to the Falls, Tippu-Tib was in an expansive mood, and he confided in Jameson:

You see all this river from Nyangwe to the Falls; it is all quiet now, but when we first came the natives were very warlike, and we had to fight every village in turn. The Belgians have made me chief of Stanley Falls station down to Bangala, and I want to see all that part of the river like this. What I propose doing is to fight each lot of natives on both sides of the river all the way from Basoko to Bangala, and leave men in charge of each large place; but the Belgians have never communicated with me since I came up to Stanley Falls last year.

Jameson agreed that this was appalling negligence on their part. He said the officers had often discussed it in camp, and that Ward might well say something about it on his way down to the coast. Tippu went on:

We were at the Falls long before the Belgians. I had been wandering about and fighting in Central Africa for fourteen years, when I met a Belgian officer near Tanganyika, who asked me whether I agreed to the Falls belonging to Belgium. I asked him whether he had consulted the Sultan of Zanzibar. He said, 'No.' So I replied, 'Unless the Sultan gives the Falls to you, I will not.'

At that time the Sultan was not prepared to give up the Falls. But after the fight with Deane, when Tippu again went to the Sultan, he found—as he put it—'his power all gone'. Referring to the present state of affairs Tippu, laughing, told Jameson: 'If I find all the power gone from the Belgians as it is from the Sultan, then I will take it all myself.' Jameson recalled:

He told me that if no steamer arrived before we left Yambuya, he would go himself to Bangala and ask for an explanation. I told him I thought he was perfectly right, as they had no business to keep him in suspense all this time, and that, when Mr Stanley left, I did not think he ever expected they would have behaved as they had done . . .

The way the Belgians have treated Tippu-Tib seems very strange. He is extremely anxious to have a definite settlement made about the matter, and they have kept him for a whole year without any communication whatever. Tippu-Tib naturally cannot understand this way of doing things, and looks upon it as a decided slight upon himself.

That Tippu-Tib himself might go to Bangala and demand an explanation was precisely what the Belgians had feared most— hence the panic at Bangala when Herbert Ward had turned up unannounced and after dark in a canoe.

At about the time that Jameson was hearing Tippu-Tib's point of view, Ward was getting the other side of the argument:

During a conversation with a Belgian officer, Monsieur Baert [who was shortly to become Tippu-Tib's secretary], upon the Arab situation in the country round about the Falls, he said: 'Among us it was pronounced very short-sighted policy on Stanley's part, appointing Tippu-Tib to be Chief of the Falls.' 'But stay,' said I; 'Stanley only suggested such an action, for before finally settling anything at Zanzibar, the agreement, etc., was sent home to His Majesty the King of the Belgians to be ratified and sanctioned; therefore Stanley cannot be in any way blamed.' 'No, but if he is not legally accountable, he is at least morally responsible. It was Stanley who brought the Arabs to the Falls eleven years ago, and he is really the cause of their being where they are to-day!' I stated that I thought if the State officers who are going up to the Falls only temporise and are politic, there will be no trouble. I know the Arabs are very eager to get traders up from the West, and they would very soon conform to the State regulations, as far as confining their raiding within certain limits is concerned . . . Monsieur Baert replied that what I had said might be true; but that during the next few years, after the Khartoum Arabs had met and comingled with Tippu-Tib, as they assuredly would after Stanley opening up this Aruwini route, there would be trouble. He said that if Tippu-Tib had been appointed Chief of the Falls in the first instance, all would have been well; but now, after the loss of the station, the appointment was very serious. Better it would have been if the station had been forcibly retaken, and then for Tippu-Tib to have received his post. 'And,' inquired I, 'what are your propositions now for confining the Arabs to the South of the Falls?' 'Well,' he continued, 'we Belgian officers out here think that a station or line of stations should be made across the country at Basoko, fully fortified and armed; that all the natives should be armed with cap-guns to the extent of several thousand, and that they should be led on to fight for themselves against the Arabs.' 'That's very good,' said I; 'but, supposing you wanted to disarm the natives afterwards, their strength would be very great, and they would probably turn out to be as bad as the Arabs.' 'Oh, that is a very simple matter,' was the quick retort. '1st, stop giving them caps; or, 2nd, give them dynamite in place of powder, and then they would all blow themselves to bits.' I am quite confident that the Belgians will have much trouble before settling the slave-raiding business. They do not know the country, and they are not strong enough, and never will be in my opinion, to cope with the Arabs.

The meeting of Tippu-Tib and the Belgian, Van Kerckhoven, at Stanley Falls on 22 May must be seen against this background of mutual mistrust and suspicion. The Belgians had always feared that Tippu-Tib would try and extend his territory down the Congo at their expense, and though he was now their appointed representative, they still saw him as a rival rather than an ally. Van Kerckhoven, as chief of the station at Bangala, would be the first to know if the Arabs came down river in force; so he was most concerned that Tippu's attention should be occupied elsewhere. While Barttelot was engaged in discussion with Jameson (who was able to tell him that Tippu had now promised them 800 men), he nipped in to see Tippu and put forward a scheme carefully designed to whet the Arab's appetite. He proposed that Tippu should take possession, in the name of the State, of the area to the north-east of the Aruwini as far as the Welle or Mobangi River. This would serve the dual purpose of keeping the Arabs out of Bangala and of deterring potential intruders in a large area of Free State territory which the State itself was not yet strong enough to occupy.

Barttelot described the effects of Van Kerckhoven's tactics in a letter to Consul Holmwood:

This officer being afraid of Tippu advancing on Bangala, his station, to divert him told him of the Mobangi River (Junker's Welle) and advised him and begged him to send men there at once, as it abounds in ivory, etc. I had not had my palaver with Tippu when this was put in his head, but that evening I did, when he (Tippu) told me he could only let me have 400 men and not 800, and pretended all ignorance of ever having promised 800 . . .

The reasons for his not giving the men are in my opinion as follows:

(i) The Lomami River [where Raschid was always in need of reinforcements in his constant pursuit of slaves and ivory]

(ii) The Mobangi River

(iii) His personal dislike to Stanley, because he had not fulfilled his promise made to Tippu when crossing Africa [in 1877—Stanley had promised Tippu all kinds of presents if ever he succeeded in reaching the west coast. Jameson wrote in his diary on 19 May: 'From that day to this he never sent him a thing, and Tippu-Tib told him so on board the *Madura*.* Mr Stanley replied, "Did you not get the beautiful cloth and gun I sent you?" Tippu said, "No. You sent the gun, a Winchester, to the Sultan, and the cloth to Tarya Topan (Tippu's agent in Zanzibar)".']

(iv) The intense dislike of all the other Arabs to Tippu giving any aid to Stanley's Expedition.

The reasons why he eventually gave us men:

(1) Because of your letters to him when he was at Kasongo.

(2) Because he learnt I had sent a telegram home.

(3) His fear of having a bad name in England.

* The ship which transported the expedition from Zanzibar to the Congo.

To his brother-in-law, Major Sclater, Barttelot wrote, 'I don't think Van Kerckhoven meant us harm, but he has certainly done it.' During the next week or so of negotiations with Tippu-Tib, though, Van Kerckhoven had almost as difficult a time as Barttelot himself. Tippu was far too astute not to see through the Belgian's plan to distract him from what he felt was his proper course of action: namely, the pacification of the Congo River as far down as Bangala itself. On 7 June Jameson heard that relations between Tippu-Tib and Van Kerckhoven were 'decidedly strained'. And Barttelot wrote, 'Van Kerckhoven and Tippu have just had a tremendous row. Tippu says he will send men to Bangala. Van Kerckhoven says he will shoot every man of Tippu's who goes near the place. Tippu-Tib means to have Bangala.'

Barttelot and Jameson might be forgiven if they had got a certain satisfaction out of Van Kerckhoven's discomfiture. But by that time they were far too busy preparing for their own departure to spare much thought for the Belgian.

21

TIPPU-TIB HAD never been to visit the rear column until he went there with Van Kerckhoven on the *AIA*. While they were still on the Congo they met the *Stanley* coming up with the latest Belgian officers to be appointed to serve with Tippu-Tib on board. As a result of this meeting, the *Stanley* turned round and followed the *AIA* up the Aruwini. They arrived at Yambuya on 4 June.

Barttelot and Jameson had got back a few days before; they had marched across country with the 400 Manyema and their head-man, Muni Somai, whom they had contracted for the enormous sum of £1,000 (which they guaranteed personally, in case the Committee should jib at having to pay so much). During the journey Barttelot took time off to continue the letter to his brother-in-law which he had begun at the Falls:

> No doubt you will see many reports against me, no doubt some of a very infamous nature, such as I am to blame for [the] delay, that I have been hard on the men, etc. But don't believe them; wait till I can come home and clear everything up, and in company with Jameson disprove all false reports.

Was Barttelot thinking only of himself when he wrote this passage, or was he more worried on his friend's behalf? Jameson would certainly have told him about the incident at Riba-Riba and shown him the sketches he had made—of which he was rather proud. Barttelot went on:

> I am writing a long letter to you, but dear old Harry it does me good to write to you and more or less unburthen myself especially as I know I can rely upon you, for beyond Jameson I have not a single friend in this accursed country. Him I love, but my other three officers don't care much for me; two of them positively hate me and the third has not a great affection for me,

because I am constantly what he calls 'on to him'. He is trustworthy but too fond of his own way . . .

Barttelot urged his brother-in-law to call on Mackinnon at the Burlington Hotel in London:

He will tell you all news, and what he thinks of my conduct. I have no doubt he will get some damaging accounts of me from de Winton, who receives reports from an officer in my camp. Such are the people I am surrounded by. Jameson is my only stand-by.

At the camp nothing had changed. There had been further incidents involving the Zanzibaris and Selim's Manyema, but Selim had acted swiftly on Bonny's complaints; there were now over 80 graves outside the camp and many more of the men were little better than dead; and Troup was still very sick indeed. Yet Jameson found himself 'quite glad to get back to the old place again, for it has been a kind of home to me for a long time'.

Ten days earlier Troup had had a consultation with Bonny to decide his future. He wrote:

Bonny has been talking over with me my present critical state of health, and my inability to move; we also discussed whether I could be of any further service to the Expedition by staying here. We weighed the matter calmly over, and he came to the conclusion that it would be best for me to return home, and much as I regret to leave the Expedition, it is clear to my mind that I would only be an incumbrance instead of an assistance in my present condition, so it was agreed that it was best for me to go. Bonny wrote to Barttelot, saying he had advised me to take this step, and enclosed a certificate. I wrote also, saying I agreed under the circumstances.

What Troup could not quite bring himself to admit was that he was sending in a *request* to be invalided home—at least, that was how Barttelot took it. He acknowledged Troup's request with a note and readily gave his consent to his departure. In his diary he wrote, 'On arrival here I found Troup in a dying state, and he will have to go home.' But it gave him some satisfaction that it should be at Troup's own request.

His own health was none too good, as he told Major Sclater with a characteristic flourish: 'Am now laid up with swollen fetlocks, caused by abscesses, the same as on my hands.' Bonny, too, was suffering with a badly swollen hand, which made it impossible for him to do any work. This was a nuisance as there was plenty to be done: all the loads had to be repacked as a result of Tippu-Tib's insistence that no load his men were to carry should weigh more than 40 pounds. With Barttelot fully occupied writing official letters and reports, the bulk of the work fell on Jameson, who undertook it with his customary cheerfulness and application.

The *Stanley* brought up the officers' letters, and among them were two addressed—in English—to Tippu-Tib. Tippu sent for Barttelot, who read them to him. Barttelot told his fiancée:

One was about centrifugal pumps, and the other about reclaiming slaves, from some religious society in America! Tippu and I both roared over it. The simple idea of the biggest slave-dealer in Central Africa having anything to do with reclamation is too absurd.

Tippu said to me to-night, 'You look happy, Major!' I said, 'Yes; I have heard from home.' He asked me all about it, and took a keen interest in all I told him.

Tippu also professed himself full of admiration for the lay-out and defences of the camp. But such moments of harmony were rare.

Barttelot had decided that he would send all surplus loads down river to Bangala rather than leave them at the Falls. Van Kerckhoven and Werner—not to mention Troup, who no longer had any say in the matter—opposed this scheme on the grounds that, once they were sent to Bangala, the loads would be a write-off as far as the expedition was concerned; whereas if they were at the Falls and Stanley returned, as he had promised he would, they were at least retrievable. Barttelot refused to consider this argument. At the time Werner put it down to obstinacy on his part, but later he was inclined to think Barttelot was justified in mistrusting the Arabs.

The arrival of the steamers was a godsend to Jameson, as Werner volunteered to help him repack the loads and brought three carpenters with him. It was no chore for him. 'I was in that camp three days and two nights,' Werner remembered (wrongly, as it happens—he was there five days and nights in all), 'and I do not ever remember to have enjoyed a piece of work more than I did the altering of those loads at Yambuya, for Jameson kept up a continuous string of yarns, songs, and jokes, which, in spite of the labour, made me sorry that the day was over when the watchman came to *piga ngoma* (beat the drum) at 6 p.m.'

While Werner helped Jameson with the loads, Barttelot was busy drawing up final agreements with Tippu-Tib and Muni Somai (he spared no pains in trying to squeeze out of Tippu-Tib a few extra men, and succeeded in getting another 30) and writing his reports. In his letter to William Mackinnon, he wrote: 'Mr Troup, who is in a terrible condition of debility and internal disarrangement, is proceeding home at his own request. Mr Bonny's certificate of his unfitness is attached . . . The interpreter Assad Farran I am also sending home. He has been and is utterly useless to me and is in failing health.'

Barttelot made Assad Farran sign an agreement (modelled on Stanley's contracts with his officers) in which he swore on oath not to divulge, 'or cause to be divulged any information concerning the Expedition, its movements, the movements of any individual of the Expedition, during my period of service with it, till six months after the official report has been published in England, on pain of forfeiting all claims to pay and character.'

Even so, the dismissal of Assad Farran strikes one as an extraordinary decision; it shows a quite astonishing naïveté on Barttelot's part. Assad Farran was noted neither for his reticence nor for too exacting a regard for truth; in fact, he was just the man to start a malicious rumour of the sort the Anglophobe Belgians on the Congo would particularly relish. Yet, instead of keeping Assad closely under his observation, Barttelot sent him away, apparently oblivious to the damage he might do to his own and Jameson's reputations. Did he imagine he had frightened him into silence? Or was it that he thought his insignificance and the stigma attached to his dismissal would ensure that no one believed him if he did talk? Whatever the reason—and since Barttelot was so impetuous, it may have been that he (and Jameson, too) simply could not stand the sight of him any longer and took no thought to the consequences—he did neither himself nor Jameson any good by sending Assad Farran down river along with Troup.

By 7 June (the day that Tippu-Tib had a row with Van Kerckhoven), all the loads 'had been reduced and Barttelot believed they were ready at last to march. He hastened to finish his letter to his brother-in-law.

Stanley is in a fix I am sure, but I don't think he is dead. I pray God we may succeed. In Jameson I have one of the finest men I have ever met, but I must say I am disappointed in Bonny, for for the last five days the pressure of work has been enormous and he has done literally nil. He has a bad hand and so have I, and feet also and yesterday and the day before I had bilious fever from eating too much tinned bacon. Giving orders, palavers with the Belgians, with Tippu-Tib, writing letters has occupied my whole day and far into the night for the last five days, but we are pretty nearly squared up now . . .

22

BARTTELOT SPOKE too soon. The next morning Tippu-Tib came to inspect the loads and Werner, who was in Troup's hut, suddenly heard an extraordinary noise which he described as 'something between a yell and the howling of hyenas'. He hurried out to see what had happened.

Troup, of course, was unable to follow. So he sent his boy to find out what was going on. 'He returned after a time, and from what I could gather there had been a big row, which he described in broken English, helped out with Swahili and most graphic gestures. He said, "Major, he make big palaver with Tippu-Tib. Manyemas say loads too big, not fit to carry." He added that Tippu-Tib was very angry, and he heard Tippu-Tib had said, "If Major *piga* (strike) Manyema, Manyema he *piga bunduki* (strike gun—that is, shoot him)." '

Tippu-Tib refused to accept the loads because he said they were overweight. It is true that some of the loads of ammunition were a pound or two over 40 pounds, but to reduce them would have meant opening sealed cases and removing just two small packets of cartridges and then resealing them. Barttelot was livid, but he had to give way; the loads were once again reduced. Barttelot believed that the reason Tippu-Tib refused the loads was because of the poor quality of the cloth he had given him the day before as part of his advance payment for the men. Barttelot admitted, 'The cloth he bought of me was not up to much.'

In negotiating with Tippu, he was handicapped by the fact that he still could not carry out to the letter Stanley's side of the contract over the carriers. He was able to hand over the gun-powder which Stanley had promised to supply, but not the ammunition caps. When he looked into the loads, he found 'all satisfactory till the issue of caps, when 80 per cent of them were found to be bad, and I had to purchase fresh ones from Tippu-Tib'. Now if the caps had simply deteriorated due to the climate

Stanley could hardly be blamed. But this was not the case, according to Jameson, who wrote: 'Nearly all the caps turn out to be bad. When passing them on board the S.S. *Madura*, I tried some of them, and told Mr Stanley that they were bad, but he would not listen to me; the consequence is we have had to buy from Tippu-Tib.'

In the afternoon of 8 June Troup was carried down to the *Stanley* in a hammock; it was the first time he had seen daylight in six weeks. Bonny had looked after everything, and Troup felt he owed his life to him. 'At the landing-place I parted with Bonny, who had down to the very last moment attended me like a brother. I cannot dwell further on this scene, my wretched state and the forebodings of disaster completely unmanned me. Some of my old Zanzibaris came down and kissed my hands, and so did some of the Sudanese.'

Both steamers went the next morning, leaving Tippu-Tib, who was anxious to see off the rear column, to find his own way back to the Falls. The *Stanley*, with Troup and Assad Farran on board, was the first to go. Werner, on the *AIA*, was determined to say a final farewell to the officers before he too was called away.

So I dashed up the bluff, through the water-gate into the camp, and into Major Barttelot's hut. The Major was sitting on some boxes, his face buried in his hands, and his elbows on his knees; he seemed more depressed than I had ever seen him before. 'Good-bye, Major!' I shouted; 'I have only two minutes to spare.' On hearing my voice he jumped up like a shot, and seized my outstretched hand, exclaiming, 'Don't be in a hurry, old fellow. We may all be dead in another week, you know.' Just then, the notes of a bugle sounding the recall, and a long whistle from the *AIA*, came floating up on the still morning air, and one of my men rushed into tell me she was going to start. I turned to the Major, who continued, 'I should like to get home to the old place again. If you get home before news of me arrives, tell my father I was all right when you saw me.' 'All right,' said I, as I rushed out. Jameson and Bonny were in the mess-room, the former in high spirits at the prospect of starting at last. A few hurried words of farewell, and I ran down to the landing-place.

Werner was horrified when Van Kerckhoven told him casually that Tippu-Tib had said the Manyema were to shoot the Major if he did not treat them right. Yet it was common knowledge; everyone on board confirmed it. Werner wanted to turn back and warn Barttelot, but Van Kerckhoven would not hear of it. The two steamers reached Stanley Falls on 15 June. After two days Tippu-Tib still had not arrived; so the commander of the *Stanley*, Captain Vangele, prepared to depart. He left two of his officers with Van Kerckhoven on the *AIA*, and went on down the river. He had not got far when he met Tippu-Tib on his way up. Tippu came on board and demanded to speak to Troup. There followed what Troup described as a 'most painful interview'. Tippu was clearly very agitated—'the man fairly shook with rage', Troup wrote:

He said that the contract made at Stanley Falls was to the effect that the loads should not exceed 40 pounds, but this agreement had not been kept, he asserted. When he objected, Major Barttelot accused him of breaking faith with the Expedition. He was surprised at this as he (Tippu-Tib) was only asking that the contract should be kept. He added excitedly, 'You are going home to the big white men, ask them if I have ever broken faith; ask Bula Matadi (Stanley); ask Cameron, ask Wissmann; and hear what they will say.' He went on to inform me that had he known at the Falls, when he arrived with the men from Kasongo, the facts that he had since heard from Selim Mohammed, when he met him at Yambuya, he would not have given us the men, and he now regretted very much that he had done so. He says he had great difficulty in getting the men to go at all, as the Manyemas who had been round our camp for months had spread evil reports all over the country.

By this time Herbert Ward, who had been down to the coast and sent the cable, had received a reply, which ran: 'Committee refer you to Stanley's orders of 24 June 1887. If you cannot march in accordance with these orders then stay where you are, awaiting his arrival or until you receive fresh instructions from Stanley. Committee do not authorise engagement of fighting men . . .' And Ward was now well on his way back to rejoin the rear column.

On 3 July, near the Equator station, he met the *Stanley* coming down and was very surprised to find Troup on board. This was his first opportunity to hear news of the camp since his departure in March. Not that Troup could tell him much; his illness had kept him apart and even now he was in no state to talk for long. But Ward did learn that there had been 'the devil's own row' between Barttelot and Tippu-Tib, and that it 'at one time threatened to result in Tippu's people attacking Major Barttelot for a supposed insult to their chief'. He also learnt that Jameson had brought back from Kasongo some very good sketches, 'some of which had been prepared after a cannibal feast at which he had been present'.

At the same time he received a letter from Barttelot:

SIR, On arrival at Bangala you will report yourself to the chief of the station, and take over the stores from him belonging to the Expedition. You will remain at Bangala till you receive orders from the Committee concerning yourself and the loads ... On no account will you leave Bangala while you remain in the service of the Expedition, till you receive orders from home. Should you do so, you will do it at your own expense.

Your orders from home must be submitted to the chief at Bangala. On receiving your orders you will inform the Committee of your proceedings ...

Should you bring a telegram of recall for me, you will make arrangements with the chief of Bangala to forward it to the Falls, where a messenger awaits it. You will not, however, send any other message after me, nor will you on any account leave Bangala station unless you receive orders to that effect from the Committee.

EDMUND M. BARTTELOT.

Ward could hardly find words to express his anger and dismay. 'This letter,' he wrote in his diary, 'is the unkindest act which has been done to me since I have been with the Expedition. On the impulse of the moment I feel inclined to throw everything up and go back home. I have travelled night and day for twenty-eight days, and have walked upwards of 235 miles, in ten days and a half, in my anxiety to obey orders and get back quickly—and this is my reward!'

Barttelot had confided in a letter to his brother-in-law his intention of dismissing Troup and Ward as soon as he could, but he had done better than that. He had got rid of them without the trouble of dismissing them. Troup, through illness, had voluntarily withdrawn; and Ward he had managed to employ at such a distance from the theatre of action as to rule out the possibility of his taking any further part in it.

[23]

ON MONDAY 11 June, Barttelot, Jameson and Bonny marched out of Yambuya with 430 Manyema, their women and slaves (amounting to a further 150 camp followers), in addition to the remaining 22 Sudanese and 115 Zanzibaris—seven of whom were boys. Those who were too sick to march were left behind in Tippu-Tib's care. The others followed the example of the Manyema and fired off their guns to express their feelings. It took some time to check this waste of ammunition, but on the first day out the men marched well.

Jameson feared there would be trouble between their own men and the Manyema. 'Our men are afraid of them,' he wrote, 'but taunt them for not carrying heavier loads, and for being cannibals, as, for a fact, the majority of them are.' He only hoped Muni Somai would have sufficient authority over the Manyema. He did not doubt his good intentions—'Muni Somai seems very anxious to get on well with us and to make the whole thing a success, but he evidently has a good deal of trouble with the Manyemas.'

From the start the Manyema found the work uncongenial and made life hell for their headman, refusing to move on for days at a time when they stopped to rest and gather food. The officers could do little about it as they had no direct control over them. That was part of the agreement; the Manyema would only come on their own terms. They had seen for themselves, or heard from others, how the Zanzibaris and Sudanese were treated by the white men and they would not go with them unless they were more or less free to do as they wished. However he treated them himself, Tippu-Tib had taken care to point out to the officers that the Manyema were free men, not his slaves, and he could not force them to do anything against their will.

Free men or not, Muni Somai had a pretty low opinion of them. They had not gone far before he was telling Jameson that they were not men at all, but 'meat-like beasts'.

'How can they be men,' he argued, 'and yet love to eat men as they do? If there were two goats and one man offered them to choose from for food, they would take the man; all they think of now is what a lot of natives they will eat further on. The first lot of natives that they fight,' he went on, 'they will eat as many as they can, and when their stomachs are full they will then catch others to carry their loads.'

It was not the Manyema, however, who caused trouble at the beginning; it was the Zanzibaris. On the fourth day of the march, 14 of them deserted, taking twelve loads. These were precious loads, containing the best quality cloth, provisions and vital medicines; they had to be recovered. So Jameson went back to Yambuya, where he found Selim Mohammed preparing to leave. Selim promised to block all roads to the Falls and guaranteed to get the loads back within a week. 'I left Yambuya full of bright hopes,' Jameson wrote, 'but I must say they have received rather a damper at the start.'

While Jameson tried to recover the missing loads and hold the Manyema rearguard together, Barttelot and Bonny struggled on with the Sudanese and Zanzibaris and tried to prevent further desertions among them. Only a fortnight before, in a letter to his fiancée, Barttelot had written:

My little boy, Sudi bin Bohati, is a slave, but I shall purchase his discharge, for, though a wooden-headed little beggar, he is honest and willing and will do anything for me. He is the queerest little mite you ever saw, and, when he has his long clothes on, looks like a baby in its nightdress. He cannot be more than ten years old, yet he can walk 25 miles in the day, carrying an axe, my food and tea, and will sit up half the night drying my clothes, and be fit to start again next morning.

Now, on the morning of 23 June, Sudi deserted after Barttelot had seen fit to thrash him—'for idiocy'. Barttelot wrote in his diary, more in sorrow than in anger:

My revolver and 75 rounds of ammunition were gone, also my table-knife. The poor little beggar only took what he considered absolutely necessary, and was advised to it by the men. On being informed that they all knew where he was, I offered a reward for him, but no one responded. I was told that many others intended to desert. I fell them all in, and took away all the arms from the Zanzibaris, and their ammunition. The Sudanese are faithful. I told Bonny I should go to the Falls the next day and get some chains, and that I would not return the rifles to the Zanzibaris for some lengthened period. He thought it good.

The situation was critical. Out of more than 550 men, Barttelot had only 20 he could rely on. He had been obliged to deprive the majority of his own men of arms, thus creating more loads to be carried, and at the same time rendering himself more vulnerable to attack from outside; he had to return yet again to Stanley Falls to get chains from Tippu-Tib so as to make his own men prisoners and drive them forward as the Arabs drove their slaves; and the whole column must come to a halt once more while he tried to obtain from Tippu-Tib that authority which, in all probability, only his actual presence could have commanded, in order to continue at all.

Bonny was left in charge of the camp in the forest until Jameson should arrive. Barttelot's orders to Jameson were to take over command from Bonny and proceed with the whole force to Abdullah's camp at Banalya (also called Unaria). This was Tippu-Tib's most advanced post on the Aruwini (there were other Arabs further along but they owed no allegiance to Tippu). Abdullah was the same Abdullah who had conducted Jameson and Ward to Stanley Falls on the first journey the officers had made out of Yambuya, and had incurred their enmity on account of his cruel treatment of Ngungu and his people. Once at Banalya, Jameson was to halt the column and wait for Barttelot's return.

The boy, Sudi, was captured and brought to Barttelot after only two days on the run; he still had Barttelot's revolver. 'He said he was with the other deserters, but that they had left him as he slept. I don't think this is true, otherwise they would have taken the revolver also. I did not punish him, as it was partly my fault that he ran away, and the boy is not a bad one'—a judgment that showed unusual clemency on Barttelot's part.

By 27 June Barttelot was back at Yambuya, where he found one or two of the sick men he had been forced to leave behind; evidently Selim Mohammed had left them too. As he followed the old route to the Falls, he came upon more of those he had left behind: on 28 June, 'I passed five dead men on the road, two of whom were soldiers . . . This day last year Stanley left Yambuya, and still no news'; on 29 June, 'All along the road single and small parties of Zanzibaris were found, who had been handed over sick to Tippu-Tib. They were without food or water. My carriers had gone on, so I could give them nothing. They amounted to ten, also one dead.'

He reached the Falls on 1 July. Tippu-Tib was surprised to see him, but gave him what he wanted in the way of chains—though, according to Barttelot, 'Selim Mohammed begged him not to.'

Barttelot stayed with the Belgian officers who had taken up residence at the old Falls station. While he was there—on the day before he left, in fact—he made his last entry in his diary. It recorded the fact that he had written letters to his fiancée, Mabel, to his father, his brother-in-law, and to William Mackinnon. After that the diary ceases; he wrote no more. It is as if he had a premonition of his end, quite deliberately put his affairs in order and determined that the rest be silence.

If this interpretation should seem a little fanciful, there is corroboration in something Tippu-Tib's Belgian Secretary, Lieutenant Baert, said later—in an interview he gave the *New York Herald* (30 October 1890). Baert maintained that Barttelot 'constantly spoiled' his negotiations with Tippu-Tib 'by his intractable character', and thereby brought about his own disasters. He went on:

As a matter of fact, Barttelot knew his unpopularity and foresaw his fate. He spoke of it with magnificent courage and coolness. Dining with me at Stanley Falls just before starting to join Stanley, he said: 'These are the last pancakes I shall ever eat. I am doomed to be killed.'

I asked, 'Why don't you carry a revolver instead of a simple stick?'

'Because I shall surely be shot or stabbed from behind.'

The Belgians showed Barttelot a letter of testimony against Jameson which Assad Farran had written and—in spite of the agreement he had signed not to divulge the affairs of the expedition for the duration—handed over to the State. Barttelot wrote at once to Jameson's brother. And in his own last letters home, he took up the matter with his brother-in-law, Harry: 'The interpreter, Assad Farran, whom I sent home, has been making the best of his time traducing all of us, and spreading the most abominable stories about us. He has written an official letter to the State about Jameson; and Troup, who was on board the *Stanley* with him, never attempted to stop it.'

The next day (6 July) Barttelot left the Falls to go up country, knowing that the damage was done and that his name and Jameson's were already the subject of rumour and malicious gossip the length of the upper Congo.

Jameson, meanwhile, was still trudging through the forest with Muni Somai and the unruly Manyema. Barttelot had once described him, in a letter, as 'sweet-tempered as a woman'; but with several loads missing, others broken into and their contents stolen or scattered, even his patience was tried to the limit. 'I am more sick of the whole business tonight,' he had written on 25 June, 'than I have been since we started.'

It was becoming increasingly obvious that Muni Somai had no authority over the Manyema. By 30 June, Jameson had caught up with Bonny. He tried to get Muni Somai to provide men to escort Bonny's party to the next camp, but Muni Somai had to admit that all his men had gone back to the village where they had camped the night before to get food. 'I asked him when he would ever be able to obey my orders,' Jameson wrote in exasperation, 'to which he replied that the Wacusu and Manyema were very hard to deal with, and would not leave the village until it pleased them . . . I can now see that Muni Somai is utterly useless as a commander, although himself willing.'

Over the next few days Jameson and Bonny struggled on, often losing their way. An outbreak of smallpox among the Manyema added to their worries and, to give their own men some protection, Jameson sent Bonny on to Banalya with the Zanzibaris and Sudanese. Once he got there, Bonny was to send back some men to carry extra loads.

On 9 July, which he called 'a day of disaster', Jameson wrote in the Log (which the officers kept assiduously during the march):

Last night, as if at a given signal, nearly every man in camp began to fire off his gun; several of the shots were fired beside my tent. I jumped out of bed, sent for Muni Somai, got my rifle, and told him before everyone that I would shoot the next man that fired close to my tent. There were no more shots. Had I men to carry the rifles I would take every one from his men.

Muni Somai was so ineffective that Jameson decided to send him on to Banalya; he himself would wait for the men Bonny was to send back for the remaining loads. These men eventually turned up on 18 July, bringing a letter from Bonny which told of his troubles on the march—who had deserted or escaped, where there was a road and where there was not, where there was food and where there was none. The day before, Jameson had heard that Barttelot had taken a short cut to Banalya and would be there before him. Now that he had carriers Jameson hastened to join him.

He had been on the march two days when he received by messenger another letter from Bonny. While he was opening it he overheard some of the men saying that Barttelot was dead. The letter was dated 19 July 1888:

My dear Jameson, Major was shot dead early this morning. Manyemas, Somai, and Abdullah all gone. Have written to Tip through Baert. Push on. Yours, BONNY.

Leaving a headman to bring up the men and loads, Jameson went on alone to Banalya. He thought Bonny's note was 'shorter than a telegram ought to have been', and he was impatient for details. He wrote in his diary:

It is a fearfully sad piece of news to me, for ever since we were left alone together at Yambuya camp, more than a year ago, there has been the closest friendship between us, never so much as a single quarrel. In all difficulties we went to one another for advice, and many a happy picture did we draw of times at home together after all this unlucky Expedition was over. He was a straightforward, honest English gentleman; his only fault, being a little too quick-tempered. He loved plain, straightforward dealing far too much ever to get on well with the Arabs. He hated their crafty roundabout way of doing everything, and showed it to them, and, of course, was disliked in turn. He was far too good a man to lose his life in a miserable way like this, and God knows what I shall do without him.

[24]

As BARTTELOT had ceased to keep a diary, his last days can only be seen through the eyes of William Bonny. Bonny was the only European to see him between the time he left the Falls and his death. But Bonny, of course, was a profoundly unsympathetic witness. Writing his diary, even filling out the semi-formal Log, he took no pains to conceal his animosity.

Barttelot arrived at Banalya on 17 July, two days after Bonny and only hours after Muni Somai and his force. He brought with him two letters from Tippu-Tib, one admonishing Muni Somai for his lack of control over the Manyema and the other instructing Abdullah to provide him with 60 slaves as well as such provisions as plantains and palm-oil.

Abdullah had neither men nor food to spare. He explained that the arrival of so large a force had frightened the natives away. Barttelot told him—according to Bonny—'If you do not get me the men I will go again to Stanley Falls and I will order my men to eat up everything they find in your village.' Bonny felt that he might have had more success in getting slaves out of Abdullah 'if he had gone a different way about it'.

Barttelot showed Bonny a copy of the statement which Assad Farran had made 'in reference to Jameson giving handkerchiefs to have a girl killed and eaten in his presence'. Bonny noted in his diary that Assad had also said 'that at one place Jameson saw a canoe containing five men and wishing to show the people how well he could shoot, shot the five men in the canoe before they had time to get away'. Barttelot was plainly very upset about the whole business.

That evening the Manyema indulged in their practice of firing their rifles indiscriminately, a hundred of them going off in five minutes. Barttelot and Bonny did their best to prevent it while Muni Somai bemoaned the fact that the men would not obey him. Barttelot threatened to stop him and his entire force a month's pay. Then, when everything had quietened down, a gun went off just outside Barttelot and Bonny's house. The culprit was caught by the Sudanese and brought to the Major, who flogged him so severely that Bonny commented: 'If he is not dead he ought to be, for it would have killed ten white men.' There were no more disturbances that night, but Bonny wrote in his diary, 'They threaten to shoot the Major.'

The next day the camp was quiet. Bonny put in the Log that Barttelot ordered Abdullah to accompany him to the Falls on 20 July and said, 'I shall be back on 9 August.' He represented himself as opposing the Major's decision and suggesting he would do better to hand out rifles to the Zanzibaris—and thus do away with 14 loads—than to try and get slaves to carry more loads. He claimed that when *he* tried to purchase slaves, he 'was at once shown seven women and told that the people would do business with me, but not with the Major. I told him this.'

In his diary, Bonny now wrote of Barttelot, 'I begin to think he is half-mad . . . [He] threw his knife at the poor boy Sudi who never escapes one hour without a thrashing. He bit a woman on the cheek and he is generally bashing the men about, and without reason.'

At daybreak on 19 July, some of the Manyema started drumming and singing. Barttelot sent Sudi to stop them. When this had no effect, he got up himself and went out. As Bonny understood it—he was still in bed at the time—'The Manyemas at once rushed off to their places of shelter. The Major, revolver in hand, followed but when about to pass between two houses was shot dead, the shot passing through him just below the centre of the chest bone. I went out on hearing the shot . . .'

At this moment of crisis the Sudanese refused to follow Bonny; the Zanzibaris were nowhere to be seen—they had all gone into hiding. Bonny found himself alone in the midst of a Manyema stampede. 'The screaming, shouting, firing and yelling was something fearful,' he wrote later. At first, he thought a massacre was about to take place; but then all the Manyema fled into the bush, Muni Somai and all the other headmen among them. After a while some of them returned, and a headman called Sadi told Bonny he was sorry the Major had been shot.

The panic over, Bonny tried to piece together what had happened:

From the time the shot was fired until I got to where the Major fell was about two minutes. I was not dressed. He had tried to force his way into a house with his revolver in his hand and [was] there shot dead. The muzzle of the gun must have been close to his chest because his shirt was burnt by powder. The hole was large where the charge entered and it passed out at the back of the heart—my belief is that the charge passed through the heart.

Death was instantaneous; not a muscle of his face had moved. Bonny removed his body and buried it at the edge of the forest. He then wrote a letter to Lieutenant Baert (as well as his cursory note to Jameson) and sent messengers to the Falls. He urged Baert to press on Tippu-Tib the need for more men and a chief with authority to replace the useless Muni Somai.*

Next he set about recovering the loads; some had been flung away and many more had been looted in the general scramble that followed the Major's death. Bonny told those of the Manyema who had returned that the trouble was not his, but Tippu-Tib's: 'All loads lost he would have to pay for; they were Tip's loads, not mine; I was only showing the Manyema where Tip wanted them taken. Tip had got a list of loads carried by each headman . . .' etc. This tactic worked, and gradually the loads started to come in to him.

When he came to write up the day's events in the Log, Bonny's conclusion was little short of triumphant:

I had now housed 300 loads, buried the Major, quieted the people, opened communication with Stanley Falls, written to Sir Walter Barttelot and Mr Jameson, which brought this trying day to a close.

WILLIAM BONNY, Commanding.

* This letter, if indeed it was sent, never reached its destination. Baert first heard about Barttelot's death from the Manyema, some of whom got to the Falls on 26 July. The only letter he had was from Jameson.

142

Nowhere—not even in his diary—did Bonny express the slightest regret at the Major's death. *

But this was Bonny's supreme moment, when he transcended his position of hired medical assistant and became, if only for a day or two, 'WILLIAM BONNY, Commanding'.

The following morning Bonny learned that the man who had shot Barttelot was called Sanga; he was one of the Manyema headmen, and he had run away with the others. Needless to say, *he* had not returned.

It rained throughout the next day; and the rain, the filth and squalor of the camp, and the dangers attendant on armed bands of Manyema roaming the bush, all contributed to a sudden depression of Bonny's spirits. He confided in his diary: 'I would thank God and pray that Stanley may return here soon or that I may hear he has arrived at Zanzibar, the Expedition being at an end and we ordered to return.'

---

* Unless his stiffly formal letter to Sir Walter Barttelot comes into the category of condolence:

Sir, I regret to inform you of the death of your son, E. M. Barttelot, Major, who was shot through the chest early this morning by a Manyema. The gun used was [an] old Tower 62 and of large bore. He was shot dead. I buried him just within the forest, sewing him up in his blanket, and placing green leaves at the bottom of the grave and covering the body with the same. I read the Church service over the body, and have ordered a wooden cross over his grave.

I am, Sir, your most obedient servant, WILLIAM BONNY.

JAMESON ARRIVED at Banalya an hour before sunset on 22 July. He wrote, 'Bonny has done all that a man could do under very trying circumstances.' He listened to Bonny's recital of events connected with Barttelot's death. As he understood it, one of the Manyema had started drumming and singing at daybreak and Barttelot, who had been annoyed by the same noise earlier in the night, had sent his boy to stop it. In protest, a couple of guns were fired off—at which point Barttelot jumped up, grabbed his revolver and went out. Bonny said he had tried to dissuade him. 'Immediately afterwards,' Jameson wrote, 'a shot was fired, and shouts were heard that the Major was killed.'

The following morning Jameson made an inventory of Barttelot's personal effects and began a long letter to Sir Walter Barttelot. He also offered a reward for the capture of Sanga, the Manyema chief who had fired the shot that killed the Major.

It was a busy time for Jameson. On 24 July, he made a list of all the loads which had been recovered, instituted a search among the Sudanese for missing cloth and told the remaining Manyema headmen that he was going to Stanley Falls to see Tippu-Tib. They told him that Muni Somai and six other headmen—including Sanga—had gone there already.

With the memory of Barttelot's death so fresh, Jameson found the atmosphere at Banalya unbearably oppressive: 'There is a sadness hanging over everything, which no amount of work will shake off.' He was also weighed down by his new responsibilities as commander of the rear column. As he hurried off to Stanley Falls on 25 July, the oppression lifted a little. 'I am glad to get on the march again, for one has not so much time to think. I have not slept more than six hours altogether in the last three nights.'

On the road he caught up with Muni Somai, who—as he wrote to Bonny—was 'in an awful fright' about everything. His excuse for leaving Banalya was that once the Major had been shot, his own life was in danger. Jameson was scornful: he accused him of simply running away, and warned him that he would have to answer to Tippu-Tib for 47 missing loads.

Tippu-Tib had already sent out his interpreter, Salem Masoudi, to find out what he could. He had found Sanga and sent him to the Falls in custody; and now he came upon Jameson, who wrote: 'I hear Tippu-Tib is in a terrible state about the whole matter, and Muni Somai received such a letter from him that it made him quite sick, and he asked my leave to go ahead, as he felt bad!'

There was a steamer at the Falls when Jameson got there. The *En Avant* had arrived the day before with the new Belgian chief, a M. Haneuse, on board. But as his business was with Tippu-Tib, Jameson decided he would stay with the Arabs rather than go over to the island where the Belgians were.

He had an interview with Tippu in which he explained that he had come to ask for such assistance as would enable him to get the expedition under way again as soon as possible, and to demand that justice be done on the murderer of Major Barttelot. Tippu, for his part, was most anxious to know whether Jameson thought he would be held responsible for the Major's death and the subsequent loss of loads. Jameson wrote:

> I told him the truth, that according to his contract he was not, but that Muni Somai was, according to *his* contract, certainly answerable for all: that this was my opinion, but that the real people to judge the matter would be the Committee, when they knew all the facts of the case.

Jameson never doubted that Tippu was innocent of Barttelot's murder. In this letter to Sir Walter Barttelot, he wrote: 'Tippu-Tib cannot I think be blamed in any way for this, and I assure you he has taken it very deeply to heart, being, as one of the Belgian officers told me, quite a changed man since this happened.'*

* When he edited his brother's diaries and letters for publication, Walter Barttelot suppressed this passage (though he included the rest of Jameson's letter to his father). The reason for this omission is not hard to fathom: it did not suit the Barttelots' purpose to allow Tippu-Tib any humanity when so much of their case against Stanley was built on the Arab's alleged treachery. Walter Barttelot made much of the fact (which he learned from one of the Committee) that, in order to protect Stanley, Sir Francis de Winton had wanted to delete 'all remarks as to Tippu-Tib's treachery' from the version of Major Barttelot's last report which was to be released to the press. Yet he himself used the same tactic in order to discredit Stanley.

(When the officer in question, Lieutenant Baert, was privately approached by the Barttelot family two years later, he remembered that when news of the assassination came, 'Tippu-Tib rushed into my house like a madman, and appeared dismayed at the news. He immediately despatched Salem Masoudi the interpreter to get Information.' Tippu himself, in a letter to his brother and son in Zanzibar—and why should he lie to them?—wrote, 'At that time i was stupefied and knew not what to do.')

Jameson now requested that Tippu-Tib and his fellow chiefs should try the case of Muni Somai; he did not wish to appear harsh or unjust in his treatment of this man. So they all assembled and listened to his description of Muni Somai's abject behaviour from the moment he had signed the lucrative contract up to the time of the Major's death and his own desertion. When Jameson had finished, they asked Muni Somai if he had anything to say. He started to 'mutter something' but Tippu-Tib interrupted him.

'Stop,' he said, 'you have not one word to say in defence; I know all this to be true.'

He then turned to Jameson and asked him what he wanted done. Jameson said he would like to see the contracts torn up, all the ammunition, rifles, the tent and revolver issued to Muni Somai—as well as the sums of money paid out to him and his men in advance—returned. Tippu promised to settle the matter as Jameson wished.

It certainly helped that Jameson and Tippu-Tib got on so well together. Troup said of Jameson that 'he never seemed to fully believe that Tippu-Tib was treacherous', and Tippu often referred to Jameson as his friend. Indeed, on at least one occasion, Jameson acted as intermediary between him and the Belgians. Tippu was puzzled by the arrival of a Belgian chief of the station; he believed himself to have been appointed chief by the King of the Belgians. Jameson passed this on to Baert, who explained that Haneuse was not chief but Resident—a distinction he promised to elucidate to Tippu himself.

Tippu, in turn, would do what he could for Jameson. He needed to clarify his position vis-à-vis the expedition with the Belgians. He told them there were only three men in the country with sufficient authority to lead the Manyema: his son Sefu, who was too far away to be called upon, his nephew Raschid and himself. The Belgians flatly refused to consent to his going; but they urged him to use his influence to persuade Raschid to go with Jameson. So Tippu sent to the Lomami for Raschid. He told Jameson that Raschid was 'a perfectly free agent', and he should treat with him accordingly.

While he was waiting for Raschid, Jameson occupied himself writing letters. He scribbled a note to Ward at Bangala, telling him of Barttelot's death and his own hopes of getting away in two or three days' time. He added, 'Do not on any account leave your post at Bangala until hearing from home, as I might have to employ you at any moment relative to either telegrams or loads.' He sent this letter off by the steamer *En Avant*, which was about to leave the Falls. Then he settled down to write to his brother Andrew, to his wife and to William Mackinnon. He was chiefly concerned to clear his name of the charges Assad Farran had brought against him.

To his wife he wrote:

The reports that Assad Farran, the dismissed interpreter, wrote down on paper for some of the Belgian officers are one tissue of falsehoods. They are about my shooting natives on the way to Kasongo, and buying a girl to be eaten by cannibals at Riba-Riba on my way back. I am almost sure that in my letter to you from Kasongo I mentioned the fact of having shot at some natives for the protection of the caravan of canoes I was going with. I have sent a true account of both affairs to Mr Mackinnon, and I am having the necessary witnesses examined here before one of the Belgian officers, and papers signed to send home. It is a blessing that I am enabled to do so. It is an awful thing to think that a low scoundrel like Assad Farran should be allowed to traduce one behind one's back, when one has not a chance of defending oneself! I am so anxious about everything that I lie awake for hours at night thinking, but when once on the march again, all that will pass. I only do pray that I may get the Expedition started again, but the Arabs are very hard customers to deal with. Whatever happens, you, at any rate, will know that I have done my best.

In his letter to Mackinnon, Jameson did not attempt to deny that he had shot at the natives in the canoe—'I believe I hit three men, but whether they [were killed or] jumped into the water, which is more probable, as it was so dark that I could not see the sights of the rifle, will remain a mystery'—or that he had caused a girl to be killed and eaten before him; he only denied that he had done these things in the cold-blooded and calculating manner imputed to him by Assad Farran.

Raschid arrived at the Falls on 6 August. Jameson knew that among the Arab leaders Raschid was the least favourably disposed towards the white man (it was he, more than anyone else, who had been responsible for the attack on Deane); but he hoped to play on his susceptibility to money, fame and flattery. Raschid was not to be lured into an adventure, though—even for £1,500. He had his own interests to look after, and just then he was expecting 500 tusks of ivory.

Tippu told Jameson that the *real* reason for his refusal was that 'he feared death'. He now suggested Selim Mohammed, but that was out of the question after all the unpleasantness that had developed between him and Barttelot and, to a lesser extent, Bonny at Yambuya. Jameson was near to despair when Tippu jumped out of his chair and said, 'Give me £20,000 and I and my people will go with you, find Mr Stanley, and relieve Emin Bey.'

This put Jameson in something of a quandary. £20,000 was an awful lot of money. But Tippu-Tib would not consider it for less and no one else with authority, it seemed, was prepared to consider it at all.

A decision had to be made and this called for another conference with the Belgians. 'You and I, M. Haneuse,' said Tippu-Tib, 'are both officers of the State; will you tell me if I am right in going?' But Haneuse would only concede that if he were bent on going, there was precious little he could do to stop him. And a decision was postponed until Sanga had been tried for the murder of Major Barttelot.

Sanga's trial took place on the morning of 7 August, in front of Tippu-Tib and the Belgians. He pleaded not guilty, said he did not have a gun, that someone beside him had fired the shot and he only ran away because all the others had; but Jameson's evidence, based on what Bonny and all the other Manyema had told him, led to his unanimous conviction. When Haneuse told him he was going to be shot, Sanga replied with a laugh, 'Well, do it quick.'

Jameson remained to see justice done.

He was chained to a large log, and when carried outside said again with a laugh, 'It is all right; the white man is dead, I am going to die too.' He was carried down to the rocks on the shore, where a firing-party of six Hausas, at six paces, fired at him; then one of the Belgian officers ran up with a revolver, and fired two shots into his head. Only four bullets had hit him, two in the right breast, one in the knee, and one in the throat, besides the two from the revolver. After the first discharge, when he was hit by some of the bullets, the look he gave us was the most horrible I think I ever saw on a man's face.

That afternoon Tippu-Tib outlined his conditions for entering into a contract to go with the rear column. He would accept nothing less than £20,000 no matter how quickly the march was accomplished; and if, beyond the limits of his domain, he came upon a man with a stronger force than his own, he would not stay to fight it out but would return home and still expect £20,000. He also wanted to take the familiar southern route to Unyoro via Kasongo and Tanganyika.

Jameson could not agree to this; he had to carry out Stanley's instructions and follow his route. So in the end he said to Tippu:

You cannot get me a headman to put over the Manyemas; you yourself say you will turn back (should you go with me) if any serious loss is threatened to your men; the only thing left for me to do now is to get a canoe at once and go to Bangala. If I find the reply from the Committee [to Barttelot's cable] to be 'go on at all hazards', I will return at once and start with your men myself. If I find that it does not tell me to go on at all hazards, I will send Mr Ward with a telegram to Banana stating my present position, your proposals, and asking for orders.

When it was settled that he should go, Jameson wrote to Bonny to recall him to the Falls, where Tippu-Tib would look after him and his men and loads. He also took the opportunity to send Bonny a couple of sacks of rice and 20 fowls.

Jameson left the Falls by canoe on 9 August. The next day he wrote in his diary, 'I was frightfully seedy, having caught cold inside after a big dose of medicine'. But he kept going and two days later recorded that he and his men had 'got through the worst of the natives during the night'. He went on:

One very curious scene; shot out of an open reach—fine clear night—into a dark narrow channel, not more than 40 yards wide. All at once it became lit up with dozens of fires on both sides, throwing a bright light back into the forest and across the water. We glided on without a sound from us but the zip-zip of the paddles, drums beating, horns blowing, shouts and cries on every side, the white loin-cloths of our men showing plainly who they were. Down this lane of fires and noise we went for nearly half a mile, when suddenly it opened out into a grand open reach of the river on our right, the fires, drums, etc., going on for more than a mile away down on our left. I don't think I ever heard such a noise before. We shot out away to our right, and soon left all the tumult behind.

Those were the last words he ever wrote.

[26]

AFTER JAMESON had come and gone, Bonny had no one to talk
to; so he occupied himself at Banalya writing a long and rambling
letter to William Mackinnon. With his customary venom he
reported to that worthy:

At one time it was thought by Messrs Barttelot and Jameson of
going a different route than that taken by Mr Stanley. They
were going via Ujiji. I cannot tell you why it was given up but
now they only desire to explore the lake Muta Nzige [the Albert
Nyanza] and to relieve Emin Bey.* Of course they conclude
that Mr Stanley is dead. They have taken the precaution of
spending a lot of money by sending you a cablegram etc., asking
you for instructions, but telling you what they were going to
do and that they would not be there to receive your instructions.
The man who brought the cablegram and who brings back an
answer has been stopped at Bangala by order of the Major and
on no account is he to be allowed to proceed to Stanley Falls by
way of the Congo steamers. Mr Jameson tells me that the
Major left instructions with M. Van Kerckhoven to detain
the despatch unless it contained an order of recall, but Mr
Jameson is very cross at the delay for fear the despatch will

* Evidently Bonny began this letter before the Major's death—presumably
when Barttelot was at the Falls. The plan to explore Muta Nzige is not an
invention of Bonny's. On 1 June, Barttelot had written to his brother-in-law:
'. . . I shall now tell you something very private . . . viz, my intentions. I shall
make the best of my way to Kavalli on the south-west corner of the Albert
Nyanza where Stanley intended making a camp . . . If I find Stanley is gone out
to Uganda, and is away with Emin, or that Emin is gone and that Stanley's
force has been annihilated . . . I shall come back to Ujiji by way of Muta Nzige,
which lake I shall explore, and thence to Zanzibar, so that our trip will not have
been entirely fruitless.' It seems that Barttelot's geography was a little confused,
that the Arab name for the Albert Nyanza misled him into thinking it was
another lake.

arrive and order a recall. This gentleman would rather that this part of the Expedition was out of reach of a despatch of that kind . . .

The next sentence is scratched out; perhaps even Bonny thought he might go too far—especially as Jameson, so far as he knew, was liable to return.

The account Bonny gave Mackinnon of Barttelot's death was much as he wrote it elsewhere, though he did not hesitate to provide his own commentary:

The Major was simply Hated, not feared, by every Arab and the whole of the people belonging to them, and this feeling of Hatred was brought about by himself through his mannerisms and want of tact; he had not sufficient powers to discover when he was insulting or pleasing. He did not understand the Arabs who could buy and sell him at their pleasure, and the wonder is that the Major was not shot or knifed months ago before we left Yambuya . . . After sitting quietly and reviewing the Major's conduct of late I am compelled to come to the conclusion that his mind had become affected. His strange way of staring at people, calling them names and showing his teeth at them without any cause and a lot of other items go to show that there was something wrong with him.

On 11 August, Bonny copied—both into the Log and into his letter to Mackinnon—instructions which he said Barttelot had given him on 22 April (when there had been no other white man in camp but Troup, who had just been relieved of his duties; Jameson, of course, was at Kasongo). These instructions put Bonny in charge of all the men and stores at Yambuya in the event of Barttelot's 'death, detention by Arabs, absence from any cause from Yambuya'.* They had naturally long since ceased to apply, but Bonny made out they were somehow timeless. He wrote triumphantly to Mackinnon:

* There is no record of Bonny having received any instructions on 22 April. He *was* given two letters of instruction: one on 5 April; the other on 24 April. Though these put him in command of the camp, neither mentioned any such eventuality as Barttelot's death or detention by Arabs. Bonny must have added this clause himself.

I therefore take command of this the Second Column of the Emin Pasha Relief Expedition until I see Mr Stanley or return to the coast. It shall be my constant care under God's help to make it more successful than heretofore. I have been alone with the vanguard as far as Unaria [Banalya] and I can lead it through the other portion of our journey. Mr Jameson will occupy the same position as shown in Mr Stanley's instructions to Major Barttelot. He has gone to Stanley Falls to settle with Tippu-Tib for another leader for the Manyemas. He has free hands believing himself to be in command. I did not undeceive him . . .

Bonny wrote to Baert as well, asking him, among other things, to write to the chief administrator of the Congo Free State on his behalf to get him to forward his mail. He went on, 'Also kindly state that I am now in command of this portion of the Expedition by written order left by Major Barttelot. Mr Jameson is only in temporary command for the despatch of business while at the Falls.' But Bonny did not actually send this letter; perhaps he feared that Jameson might still be at the Falls when it arrived.

Of course, he fully intended to put Jameson in the picture; on his return he would show him Barttelot's letter of instructions. But it may have occurred to him, in the midst of his dream of glory—of becoming in fact, as well as in his imagination, 'WILLIAM BONNY, Commanding'—that it might be just a little tactless to break the news by letter—and a letter addressed to somebody else at that! He was also very sensitive to ridicule.

27

AT ABOUT 8 o'clock in the morning of 16 August, Herbert Ward was lying in bed, feeling a little feverish and out of sorts, when a boy rushed into his room and told him a white man in a canoe had just arrived at Bangala from the Falls. Ward immediately threw off his lassitude and leapt up: 'I hurried to the beach, and there saw a figure lying back in the men's arms, insensible. I jumped into the canoe, and, great heavens! it was Jameson!' It was only four days since Ward had got Jameson's letter telling him of Barttelot's death and now Jameson himself had arrived and looked to be dying. In his diary, Ward kept a detailed record of what followed:

I soon got an umbrella over him, and we carried him up into Van Kerckhoven's room. He did not recognise me. I took his hand and knelt in front of him. His eyes were half closed and his skin was ghastly yellow. No recognition, until after having arranged him upon his bed, he gained consciousness and said, 'Oh, Ward, is that you?' and again relapsed.

I got a warm bath ready, and my boy Msa and I bathed him carefully. Poor, poor fellow! Nine days in a canoe without any help and without nourishment! After his bath he brightened up a bit—took some Madeira and chicken soup. He said he had had an awful journey down, exposed to the tornadoes, wind, and rain, lying helpless in a canoe. It is really remarkable that he lived through it. Another day would certainly have finished him. He was not able to converse, only to make an occasional remark, such as, 'You know, Ward, if I could only get a square show at this sickness, I should soon be all right.'

When the Belgians came in from time to time to see him and inquire if he was better, he would reply, 'Oh yes,' (pause) 'much better!' but so faintly as to be scarcely audible.

August 17, '88. * *Friday.* Poor Jameson does not seem any better, I think not so well. His pulse is feeble, he cannot retain his senses for more than a minute or two, and can only take a spoonful of soup at long intervals. I am still by his bedside; every quarter of an hour or so he 'comes to', and with a gaunt smile of recognition, he stretches out his poor thin hand and clasps mine, as if by so doing he steadied his nerves. He said just now, 'You're so well and clean-looking that it does me good to look at you.'

His reply to almost every question is a feeble 'Splendid', and to every inquiry about his condition, 'Oh, in-fi-nitely better,' but so feeble, and with such an effort to utter it, that he relapses after every such answer into unconsciousness.

1 p.m. I asked him just now if he was in any pain. 'No, old chap; no pain, only tired—oh, so tired! I think it's time to turn in, it's so dark—so tired!' and again he became unconscious.

2.10 p.m. I watch poor Jameson's face as he lies with his eyes half closed, breathing fitfully. How I wish I could get him home to his wife and child, and brothers! For me to go it would be nothing as, except for my dear mother, I care little, and am cared for little, by my kindred; but he is so popular, and his future so bright.

It is sad to look upon his pallid face and attenuated limbs, his finely chiselled features, high broad forehead, and long wavy hair, which has not been cut for months. He is a fine, intelligent, brave fellow. Even exhausted and weak as he is, he still retains his old courageous spirit, and bears up most pluckily. Never a word of complaint, and always so abundantly thankful for even the slightest service.

He has spoken very little to-day and seems completely prostrated, notwithstanding the nourishment and brandy and quinine.

3 p.m. I put mustard leaves on his calves, but I fear the mustard has become useless from the climate. Although I have given him nourishment regularly, he does not rally and only gets feebler.

6 p.m. Daenen [a Belgian officer] and I put hot bricks

* Jameson's birthday—he was 32 years old.

around him, as his extremities have grown cold. He grows weaker and weaker.

The drums have just beat to knock off work in the station. He opened his eyes and stared at me, clutching my hands and saying with a husky voice, 'Ward, Ward! they are coming! Listen!'

The drums continued to rumble in the distance. 'Yes, they're coming! Let's stand together!'

7 p.m. He moans and breathes heavily. Msa and I replace the hot bricks every few minutes. He is quite prostrated and unconscious.

7.20 p.m. His pulse grows weaker ar. 1 weaker.

7.32 p.m. As I supported him to administer brandy with a spoon, he drew a long breath, and his pulse stopped—

The Belgians were at dinner. I sent Msa to bring them. They came a minute or two after all was over—

12 a.m. I have arranged him as well as I could, sealed up his box, and had a Hausa guard stationed by the house. I have got the Belgian carpenter to make a coffin, although the poor chap had been ill in bed with fever all day. I promised him a couple of pounds for his work. Daenen has gone across the river with men to dig the grave. It rains heavily. I cannot rest. Never in my life have I experienced such a deep regret as I have now for this poor chap's death. How vividly I picture him up at Yambuya, and how well I call to mind his future plans! We used to talk over our future together with sketching and collecting.

Ward walked all night—'quite beside myself with sadness'. The next day he supervised the burial of Jameson. The coffin was covered with black velvet and the initials 'J.S.J.' were engraved on a piece of copper plate which was then nailed on the top. The cause of Jameson's death was haematuric fever, which had developed from the chill he had caught the first night out in the canoe. Now Ward, too, caught a chill as a result of walking about all night, became feverish and lost his voice. But he soon recovered. He wrote to Bonny on 19 August, announcing Jameson's death and outlining his plans:

From his papers I have gathered that no headman can manage the Manyemas but Raschid, who refuses to go; Sefu (Tippu-

Tib's son), who cannot leave his post at Kasongo; and Tippu-Tib himself, who requires £20,000 irrespective of men's pay, and who will give no guarantee, but states that if he meets with any strong opposition en route he will turn back and still require his £20,000.

Therefore there can be no doubt that my duty is to proceed at once to the coast and telegraph the state of affairs ... (I personally expect that we shall be recalled, for further action on our part seems impossible.)

28

ON 17 AUGUST, as Jameson lay dying at Bangala, a fleet of thirty canoes carrying 200 men arrived at Banalya—700 miles away. Stanley was back. He had returned, as he promised he would, to fetch the rear column. But he was too late. He had been away fourteen months—nine months longer than he had allowed for. It was too late now to save more than a remnant of the force he had left behind.

Stanley's account of his arrival is as highly coloured as most of what he wrote for publication:

About 200 yards from the village we stopped paddling, and as I saw a great number of strangers on the shore, I asked 'Whose men are you?' 'We are Stanley's men,' was the answer delivered in mainland Swahili. But assured by this and still more so as we recognised a European near the gate, we paddled ashore. The European on a nearer view turned out to be Mr William Bonny, who had been engaged as doctor's assistant to the Expedition.

Pressing his hand, I said, 'Well, Bonny, how are you? Where is the Major? Sick, I suppose?'

'The Major is dead, sir.'

'Dead? Good God! How dead? Fever?'

'No, sir, he was shot.'

'By whom?'

'By the Manyema—Tippu-Tib's people.'

'Good heavens! Well, where is Jameson?'

'At Stanley Falls.'

'What is he doing there, in the name of goodness?'

'He went to obtain more carriers.'

'Well then, where is Mr Ward, or Mr Troup?'

'Mr Ward is at Bangala.'

'Bangala! Bangala! what can he be doing there?'

'Yes, sir, he is at Bangala, and Mr Troup has been invalided home some months ago.'

These queries, rapidly put and answered as we stood by the gate at the water side, prepared me to hear as deplorable a story as could be rendered of one of the most remarkable series of derangements that an organised body of men could possibly be plunged into . . .

It goes on like this for pages in *In Darkest Africa*—impossible to stem the flow of Stanley's titillating journalese with its pseudo-archaic cadences and clusters of adjectives. What it reveals, of course, is not so much what Stanley saw and felt as how he wished others—namely, the great Victorian public—to see and feel:

The life of misery which was related was increased by the misery which we saw. Pen cannot picture nor tongue relate the full horrors witnessed within that dreadful pest-hold. The nameless scourge of barbarians was visible in the faces and bodies of many a hideous-looking human being, who, dis-figured, bloated, marred and scarred, came, impelled by curiosity, to hear and see us who had come from the forest land east, and who were reckless of the terror they inspired by the death embodied in them. There were six dead bodies lying unburied, and the smitten living with their festers lounged in front of us by the dozen. Others worn to thin skin and staring bone from dysentery and fell anaemia, and ulcers large as saucers, crawled about and hollowly sounded their dismal welcome—a welcome to this charnel yard! . . . I sat stupefied under a suffocating sense of despondency, yet the harrowing story moved on in a dismal cadence that had naught else in it but death and disaster, disaster and death. A hundred graves at Yambuya—thirty-three men perishing abandoned in the camp, ten dead on the road, about forty in the village about to yield their feeble hold on life, desertions over twenty, rescued a passable sixty! And of the gallant band of Englishmen? 'Barttelot's grave is but a few yards off, Troup went home a skeleton, Ward is somewhere a wanderer, Jameson has gone to the Falls, I don't know why.' 'And you—you are the only one left?' 'The only one, sir.'

An affecting scene it is too; it seems to call for one of those massive Victorian set-pieces with a title like 'The Rescue of the Last Survivor', or 'The Wreck of the Rear Column'. No doubt Stanley hoped that this heavy swell of emotion would deflect the awkward question of responsibility.

He was not, of course, so shocked as he would later have others believe. He had been anxious about the rear column for months, at least intermittently, and he had written two long letters to Barttelot—one in September 1887, and the other in February 1888. Neither letter got through, but he certainly wrote them and did what he could to ensure they reached their destination—short of sending a European officer.

The first he wrote from a camp on the south bank of the Aruwini opposite an Arab settlement; he called it 'Ugarrowwa's'. It had taken him longer than he had anticipated to hack his way through the dense forest, but he had now reached an area which freebooting Arabs and their Manyema followers had penetrated from the south. He formed a camp there and, on 18 September, wrote to Barttelot urging him on:

> If Tippu-Tib's people have not yet joined you I do not expect you will be very far from Yambuya. You can make two journeys by river for one that you can do on land. Slow as we have been in coming up and cutting our way through, I shall come down river like lightning. The river will then be a friend indeed for the current alone will take us twenty miles a day—and I will pick up as many canoes as possible to help us up-river for our second journey up-river. Follow the river closely and do not lose sight of our track. When the caravan which takes this passes you look out for your men, or they will run in a body taking valuable goods with them.

Even Stanley, it seems, had a difficult time with the Arabs and Manyema. His next letter, dated 'Fort Bodo, Ibwiri District, February 14, 1888' tells a grim story. The advance column had to travel through country which had been depopulated and devastated by these Manyema. There was no food to be had, and the men inevitably sickened. Stanley was forced to leave one of his officers, Captain Nelson, who had such bad ulcers he could scarcely walk, with 52 of the sick, while he went on to look for food. When he returned ten days later, only five of the men remained. Many had deserted, many had died, some were out foraging for food. All the men who remained with Stanley were reduced to skeletons, living (if that is the word) on wild fruit and fungi. In four months, Stanley lost over a third of his men one way or another.

When they got clear of that part of the forest which the Manyema controlled, it was like entering another land. There were people, and there was food. Their troubles were over for the time being. Stanley wrote in his letter:

We first met the Manyema on the last day of August and parted from them January 6. In this interval we have lost 118 through death and desertion. In their camps it was as bad as in the wilderness, for they ground us down by extortion so extreme that we were naked in a short time. They tempted the Zanzibaris to sell them rifles and ammunition, ramrods, officers' blankets etc etc, and then gave them food so sparingly that their crimes were of no avail. Finally besides starving them, tempting them to ruin the Expedition, they speared them, scourged them and tied them up until in one case death ended his miseries.

Never were such abject slaves as our people had become under the Manyema, yet withal they preferred death by scourging, spearing, starvation, ill treatment, to the duty of load bearing and marching on to happier regions. Out of 38 men left at the Manyema camp 11 have died, 11 others may turn up but it is doubtful—however we have only received 16. Sixteen out of 38 !! Comment is unnecessary.

Stanley had been right up to Lake Albert, but still he had not succeeded in contacting Emin Pasha. He had been obliged to leave the expedition's whaleboat behind at the Manyema settlement because he no longer had the men to carry it. He had hoped to be able to buy, seize or—as a last resort—make out of trees a sizeable canoe to go on the lake, but when he got there he found neither trees nor ready-made canoes. He was forced to return for the boat, and for a number of other loads he had had to leave behind. At this point he had to make up his mind what to do next: whether to go forwards or backwards. In his letter to Barttelot, he stated his dilemma:

You will understand then that Emin Pasha not being found, or relieved by us, makes it as much necessary that we should devote ourselves to this work as it was imperative when we set out June 28, 1887 from Yambuya. And you will also understand how anxious we all are about you. We dread your inexperience, and your want of influence with your people. If with me people preferred the society of Manyema blackguards to us, who are known to them for twenty years, how much more so with you, a stranger to them and their language. Therefore the cords of anxiety are strained to exceeding tension. I am pulled East to Emin Pasha and drawn West to you, your comrades, people and goods.

But Stanley would not seriously consider turning back at this juncture; the pull to the east was stronger. So he called for volunteers at £10 a head to take his letter back, even as far as Yambuya—'as it might chance, for all we know to the contrary, you have not started'—then to return with news of the rear column. An officer, Lieutenant Stairs, was detailed to escort the volunteers as far back as Ugarrowwa's, where he would pick up the remnant of Stanley's advance column—those who had been too sick to move—and bring them up. (When Stairs got to Ugarrowwa's, he found Stanley's letter of the previous September and sent that on too.)

Stanley believed that he would meet Emin and settle everything with him before the end of April and be back at Ugarrowwa's himself—should it be necessary to go that far back to come upon the rear column—by 29 May. He urged Barttelot to send his messengers back at once—'because the sooner we hear from you, the sooner we will join hands, and after settling the Emin Pasha question we shall have only one anxiety which will be to get you safely up here.'

He ended his letter with an 'earnest prayer' that it reach Barttelot 'in time to save you from that forest misery and from the fangs of the ruthless Manyema blackguards'.

It is pointless to speculate what difference it might have made, had the letter ever reached its destination. It didn't. What is significant is Stanley's own state of mind, his anxiety about the rear column. He knew just how difficult Barttelot's situation was;

he did not trust Tippu-Tib to keep his side of the contract and thought it probable that he had 'been faithless' and sent no men— the one eventuality for which he had made no provision in his original letter of instructions to Barttelot. At the same time he plainly did not think the rear column had much chance of getting far without Arab aid; if he, with his twenty years' experience of African exploration, had almost met with disaster, how could the Major and his party hope to come through unscathed?

In the end it was not enough that he should write a letter, however concerned, however full of useful advice. The only hope for the rear column would have been if on that day in February Stanley had sat down and, instead of writing a letter, decided to come in person to re-unite the expedition before going forward once more in search of Emin. In Stanley's view that would have taken too long and put the whole purpose of the expedition at risk. He chose to go after Emin and left the rear column to its fate.

Twice he failed to meet his own deadlines. He had failed to return in November and he failed to return in May; so that when he did return, in August, he can hardly have been surprised at what he found.*

* In view of the fact that he was later to accuse the officers of the rear column of 'total disregard of his written instructions', there is a revealing note in a discarded draft of In Darkest Africa in which he specifically exonerates Barttelot from that charge: 'Major Barttelot has not been guilty of disobedience. There is no breach of orders in his act, but he has been heedless of advice and singularly unwise in choosing to waste his time, his energies, his patience, and the lives of his own men, rather than move on.'

AFTER JAMESON's death, Ward took over his canoes and for a second time set off down the Congo to cable the Committee for instructions. Still suffering from fever and deeply grieved at Jameson's death, he kept no record of this journey; but he travelled as fast as before, hardly pausing even for rest until he reached the coast.

The Committee replied to his cable on 25 September, declining Tippu-Tib's terms outright and promising further instructions. A series of cables followed until, on 4 October, Ward received his final orders:

> Return Stanley Falls; leave powder, Remington cartridges and portion of goods in charge officers there in case communication with Emin opened. Sell remainder goods to State. See Governor about this. Bring Bonny, all men Expedition, all Barttelot's and Jameson's effects and collections Banana; ship them England, care Gray, Dawes & Co. If help wanted engage and take back Casement. Wire if these instructions understood.

In the event Ward did not call on the services of his friend Roger Casement. He reached Leopoldville at the beginning of December, and only then did he hear of Stanley's return. He determined to follow him. He would pick up the loads—particularly the ammunition—left at Bangala and then, perhaps, he could still make a useful contribution to the expedition. On 1 December he wrote to the novelist, Joseph Hatton, the father of his friend who had died in Borneo and now something of a father-figure to him, too:

> I expect to start from here by the middle of this month for Stanley Falls, hoping to overtake Stanley. My success entirely

depends upon the Arabs, and I may find it utterly impossible to proceed. You may be sure that I shall lose no opportunity, and if I once get started I shall stick to it as long as I last . . .

I am bitterly disappointed at being left behind, more so than I care to write. I will say nothing of the dead, but perhaps some day in the privacy of your little room, to you alone, I will explain how I have been wronged.

Ward had every reason to be concerned. The news of Stanley's return had reached Leopoldville by means of the *Stanley*. On board was Baert, who—for reasons of health—had left the Falls and was on his way home. He handed Ward a letter from Bonny, addressed to Jameson. It was an altogether truculent letter, in which Bonny told Jameson it had been his intention to take over command of the rear column from him if Stanley had not turned up at that moment. On no account would he have obeyed Jameson's orders to move back to the Congo.

It was clear from this letter that since Stanley's arrival Bonny's tongue had not been idle. 'I told him everything I knew in detail,' he wrote, 'hiding nothing from him, telling him all about the Major, Troup, Ward and yourself.' The only question was, would Stanley give credence to Bonny's stories and insinuations as readily as Barttelot had?

Baert also had in his possession a letter from Stanley to Tippu-Tib, which he allowed Ward to copy. Stanley had written in a friendly spirit, making no reference to Tippu's delay in providing men. He minimised his own difficulties on the march through the forest and spoke of his meeting with Emin Pasha, who—he said—had 'ivory in abundance, cattle by thousands, sheep, goats, fowls, and food of every kind. We found him to be a very good and kind man. He gave a number of things to our white and black men. His liberality could not be exceeded . . .' Evidently, Stanley hoped to tempt Tippu-Tib to follow him—though, at the same time, he was careful to seem indifferent: 'We have gone the road twice over. We know where it is bad and where it is good. We know where there is plenty of food and where there is none—where all the camps are, and where we shall sleep and rest. I am waiting to hear your words. If you go with me it is well. If you do not go with me it is well also. I leave it to you. I stay here ten days, and then I go on slowly . . .' *

This letter was dated 17 August, the day of Ṣtanley's arrival at Banalya. It made Ward all the more impatient to get up to the Falls, but steamers were few and far between. He did not get away from Stanley Pool until 7 January; he went on the *Stanley*, which reached Bangala on 22 January. There he had to face another delay as Van Kerckhoven wanted the steamer to settle some scores with the local natives. Ward was also frustrated in his efforts to get hold of another of Stanley's letters—this one addressed to Jameson. Baert had told him about it, but did not know what it contained. Van Kerchkoven had it, but he insisted that if it were opened, two copies would have to be made and one of them sent to the Governor of the Free State at Boma. Ward did not feel justified in giving Stanley's letter such publicity; so he would not take it. He made his own arrangements to continue his journey to the Falls.

Tippu-Tib welcomed him with his usual courtesy but would not hear of his attempting to follow Stanley. He said that Stanley would already be on his way down to the east coast with Emin Pasha. Ward wrote despondently:

> What is there now for me to do? I have only six half-hearted Zanzibaris, and no goods to buy our way to Tabora, and even if by a remote chance we did succeed in overtaking Stanley, I would probably be asked what the devil I had come for. Much as I have longed to make that journey through East Central Africa, I have no reasonable excuse for going there except for my personal satisfaction—and as it is obvious as things have

---

* Needless to say, Tippu-Tib was not tempted. When he heard that Stanley had returned he sent Selim Mohammed to see him, and Stanley told Selim— according to Tippu-Tib's autobiography—'I am going off, not by any recognised route. I have seen Emin Pasha; I went to him. Now we're going to the coast. Furthermore I'm going to say that Hamed bin Mohammed [Tippu-Tib] was responsible for killing the Major.' Tippu had Selim reply: 'That is up to you, say what you like. But your men here are those for whom you contracted with Hamed, and he sent me here to deliver them to you. He's under no obligation, is Hamed, except to provide you with men.' In the end, though, only 65 of Tippu's men and three chiefs went with Stanley. And Selim tried to prevent even those few going, according to Stanley.

166

turned out that I cannot now be of any service to Stanley, I feel I should make up my mind to carry out the Committee's instructions, collect the sick men abandoned by Barttelot and take them down country . . .

When eventually he got down to the coast again, Ward was shown an old newspaper which contained a letter from Stanley to Mackinnon, dated 28 August 1888, in which Stanley averred that after rumours of his death had reached Yambuya, Ward—at an officers' meeting—had proposed that his instructions to Barttelot be cancelled; and as a result Stanley's personal kit and baggage had been shipped down the Congo. Ward was astonished. 'I could not realise at first that I had read correctly,' he wrote. 'What ingenious misrepresentations must have been made to Stanley.'

The shock of this discovery, on top of the exhaustion he suffered as a result of what one newspaper was to describe as a year of 'rushing up and down the Congo like a shuttle in a loom', finally affected his health. He wrote in his diary:

> I never remember spending such a wretched time. My spirits have been very low. I have neither eaten nor slept. My mind has been so shocked since reading Stanley's letters that even the banging of a door startles me. Were the allegations founded upon truth I should feel justly punished, but being the least concerned in the whole affair, and being blamed for it, is to me, with my disappointment in being left behind in the Expedition, the bitterest experience of my life. I have suffered intensely during the past week, both in mind and body. Last night I walked up and down the beach from 11 p.m. until dawn almost beside myself with pain.'

It may have been then, or it may have been later, that he first saw in print the letter from Stanley to Jameson which he had wanted so much to get hold of. Either way, it must have been an additional shock; it was a most intemperate letter. After the briefest of preliminaries, Stanley had written:

> I cannot make out why the Major, you, Troup, and Ward have been so *demented*—demented is the word! You understand English—an English letter of instructions was given you. You said it was intelligible, yet for some reason or another you have

not followed one paragraph. You paid £1,000 to go on this Expedition, you have voluntarily thrown your money away by leaving the Expedition. Ward is not a whit better; he has acted all through, as I hear, more like an idiot than a sane being. You have left me naked—I have no clothes, no medicine; I will say nothing of my soap and candles, a photograph apparatus and chemicals, two silver watches, a cap, and a score of other trifles. You believed I was dead, yet you brought along my boots, and two hats, and a flannel jacket . . . Though, as reported to me, you, and all of you, seem to have acted like madmen, your version may modify my opinion . . .

At last a cable arrived, recalling Ward to England. Though his five years in the Congo were to form the basis of his life's work as a sculptor, he never went back. He left Banana at 7 a.m. on 25 May 1889, and wrote in his diary: 'I took a singular satisfaction in watching the mouth of the Congo grow dim in the distance as we steamed away.'

IN HIS book, *In Darkest Africa*, Stanley wrote:

> By his written report, and his oral accounts, by the brave
> deliberation of his conduct during the terrible hours of the 19th
> of July, and by the touching fidelity to his duties, as though
> every circumstance of his life was precisely what it ought to be,
> Mr Bonny had leaped at a bound, in my estimation, to a most
> admiring height. I was sure, also, that Major Barttelot must have
> discovered remarkable elements of power in him, which,
> unfortunately for my credit, had been unseen by me. But no
> sooner had permission been given to the men to speak, than I
> was amazed at finding himself [*sic*] listening to a confession that
> the first day's march to the eastward under Mr Bonny was to
> be the signal for his total abandonment by the Zanzibaris.

Another thing that Stanley was amazed to discover at this time,
but did *not* reveal in the pages of his book, was Bonny's addiction to
opium—to which (as officer in charge of the medical stores) he
had easy access. Ten years later, replying to an enquiry from the
Charity Organisation Society, Stanley wrote from an hotel in
Monte Carlo giving a summary of Bonny's history. 'I might add,
however,' he remarked, 'that had I known he was addicted to
opium he should not have accompanied us to Africa. I only
discovered the habit when I relieved the rear column in 1888 after
he had been with us about twenty months. Something strange in
his manner then induced me to put the question to him and he
confessed it at once.'

After this discovery Stanley kept a sharp eye on Bonny.
Initially, Stanley had seemed favourably disposed towards Bonny.
Bonny remembered him saying, 'You will act as my lieutenant,
attend to the sick and take charge of the land force [Stanley
himself would travel by water], but you must not flog the
people.'

But soon after this he took away all responsibility from Bonny. When Bonny complained that a guide had misled his men in one part of the forest, Stanley said to him, 'I do not want you to interfere with the men or the guide. They are doing very well. They are satisfying me. If you do not interfere, then you will not fall foul of me. Leave well alone.' And Bonny was effectively reduced to the status of William Hoffman, Stanley's servant and the only other European with him at this time—a shadowy figure who never even gets a mention in Stanley's books.

To begin with, though, Stanley was so anxious to know all that had happened to the rear column that he had no option but to talk to Bonny and find out what he could. On 23 August, Bonny wrote peevishly, 'I am very ill. Mr Stanley asked me a few questions about Ward and Troup, if or why they did not oppose the Major. I said Troup did sometimes oppose him, but Ward said that he considered Mr Stanley's instructions to the Major cancelled and that the Major was justified in taking what course he thought best . . .' Even as he rejected his services as an officer, Stanley recognised Bonny's serviceability as a witness.

Bonny, for his part, was not very pleased at the turn of events. He had a fever and was full of self-pity. In his diary he accused Stanley of not giving him proper food; he went so far as to suggest he was being starved. He even toyed with the idea of going home 'through illness'. When he put this to Stanley, he got little sympathy. Stanley merely replied, 'If you want to go home I will make you the bearer of my despatches, but you will have to make up your mind quickly. We shall get no food from here for two months.' In the end, Bonny decided against returning. He probably felt it was safer to remain with Stanley.

Stanley patronised Bonny just as his officers had done, and Bonny did not even have the satisfaction of despising him as he had despised—or affected to despise—the others. He had to admit that Stanley was 'a good worker' and, in spite of himself, he was impressed. 'He has shown an amount of patience with his men that is very creditable,' Bonny wrote. 'He is just the man for the work he has undertaken, but he should be alone or without white men for as a rule they do not care to be made a laughing-stock for the coloured races. It will not always succeed with Mr Stanley.'

And when Stanley told some of the officers at Fort Bodo—in his presence—that Bonny had behaved like a man and marched well, Bonny groaned inwardly: 'Is it praise to be a man and able to walk? Oh lord, what a recommendation!'

In February 1889, the entire expedition—or what remained of it—was reunited for the first time since June 1887. Mounteney Jephson wrote:

The officers are not very pleased with Bonny's story of events which happened in the rear guard and do not give credence to a good deal of what he relates; it is certainly peculiar that when he tells his story one is struck by the fact that any grain of sense which is shown in the many senseless councils they held should have invariably come from Bonny—according to his own account—he was never very remarkable for common sense, so one is rather inclined to distrust this evidence. He has stocked his outfit with numbers of things belonging to the other officers such as European provisions, boots, clothes, books, boxes and even Jameson's ammunition and collecting gun, and seems to have been the residuary legatee of all the officers. It is all very strange and one looks at such things askance, for Bonny is in a different position to the rest of us, first of all he is paid for his services, he is only a hospital sergeant and came merely as Parke's assistant, and we do not therefore think it likely that the officers would have given him their things in the way he said they did. Even the Zanzibaris speak about it and say he came with only two small loads and now he has eight. Stanley and the officers are terribly down on him and speak out plainly about him, I myself hardly know what to think; it seems impossible that any man could dare to do the things they accuse him of doing, however we can only know what is true when we again see Jameson.* The thing which is so bad is that Bonny seems to take such a pleasure in telling all the most dark and disreputable stories of the officers, and he has certainly done his best to blacken their character as much as possible, for even were all the stories true—which we all of us doubt—still there is no necessity to repeat them with such pleasure. He says he thinks Barttelot became insane, and he tells a story of his running after a woman and seizing her by the cheek with his teeth, and

* No one with the expedition yet knew of Jameson's death six months before.

relates a story of Jameson having bought a slave woman and handed her over to the Manyema on condition that they would kill and eat her before him. Stories like these are incredible . . .

Jephson tried very hard to be fair in his assessment of Bonny. He recognised that Bonny *was* in a different position to the rest of them and that he had good reason to resent their superciliousness towards him. He saw the way the others treated him and there is a generous element of doubt in his appraisal—'I myself hardly know what to think.'

Jephson had had an eventful time during the year that had passed since the first, historic meeting between Stanley and Emin Pasha. This meeting has been described almost as often as the Stanley–Livingstone meeting, on which Stanley himself probably modelled it. Only on this occasion the roles were somehow reversed. There was Emin, smartly dressed in a white drill suit, his steamer, the *Khedive*, anchored nearby; and there were Stanley, his officers and men, starving, dressed in rags, having survived their first terrible journey through the Ituri forest. The only thing Stanley had to offer that Emin lacked was ammunition; while Emin could provide Stanley and his officers with essentials such as food and clothing.

But ironically, the arrival of the force sent to his rescue pre-cipitated Emin's downfall. For some time past Emin had only maintained his position in Equatoria by telling his people of the powerful force that was coming to his support. When they saw the rabble that actually emerged from the forest, these people (some of whom secretly supported the Mahdists) knew they had nothing to fear.

On the assumption that Emin was a strong leader with a devoted following, Stanley had been empowered by both Leopold II and William Mackinnon to make him offers of future employ-ment. Leopold's proposal was that Emin should remain Governor of Equatoria, only not under the government of Egypt (Sir Evelyn Baring favoured evacuation of the Equatorial province) but as part of an enlarged Congo Free State; Mackinnon wanted to take advantage of Emin's expressed desire to serve the British and was prepared to shift him and his people on to the territory Stanley was to acquire for his Imperial British East Africa

Company. Emin noted that when Stanley put these alternatives to him, he urged him to reject Leopold's proposition (which was, in fact, impracticable given the nature of the terrain between the Congo and Equatoria) and accept Mackinnon's plan. (When the expedition was over, Stanley received two new honours from the King of the Belgians; but he was probably telling the truth when he claimed that as far as he was concerned there was never a conflict of loyalties—'I considered myself only your agent', as he wrote to Mackinnon.)

Stanley found Emin a slippery customer, and maddeningly evasive when it came to discussing his future. Emin wanted to stay put; he would leave only if it were impossible to remain in Equatoria. He told Stanley that he was the servant of his people and must respect their wishes. The only certainty was that his Egyptian officers did not want to return to Egypt. They led very comfortable lives and, as they had been more or less banished from Egypt in the first place, they could scarcely expect to be welcomed home.

Stanley's officers knew nothing of the deeper political game he was playing; as far as they were concerned their mission was a simple one: to relieve Emin Pasha as the earlier military expedition up the Nile had failed to relieve Gordon. So when Mounteney Jephson was sent off with Emin on a tour of his Nile stations to read out Stanley's proclamation urging a return to Egypt, he could not know that this would simply fan the flames of incipient rebellion. He had plenty of time to think about it when he and Emin were grabbed and locked up by the rebels in August 1888 (about the time Stanley was busy 'relieving' the rear column). After two months in prison they escaped. But by then the province was reduced to anarchy. Emin's five-year rule was over, his power—which for a long time had been pretty fragile—gone and he himself a fugitive.

The second meeting between Emin and Stanley was a very different affair to the first. By the beginning of 1889 it was Emin who was the suppliant. There was no longer any question of annexing Equatoria to the Congo, or of establishing Emin and his people on the shores of Lake Victoria for the IBEA Company. *They* were now no more than a rabble. And Stanley, dominant by virtue of his position as well as his character, was not prepared to put up with further hesitation on Emin's part. He issued him with an ultimatum: either he could join his column, along with those of his followers who wanted out, and march to Zanzibar—they would leave in a month's time—or he could stay where he was. But in that case he would get no help from Stanley. The first lot of ammunition he had handed over was in rebel hands; the rest—in guarding which so many of the rear column had lost their lives— was now quietly buried, there being no further use for it.

When the march finally got under way, in April 1889, Emin had no choice but to accompany Stanley. By now there was no love lost between them; and tempers generally, during this last leg of the journey, were not of the best. Even Jephson was running out of patience—particularly with regard to Bonny. Seeing him every day, his attitude had hardened. On 16 June, he witnessed an ugly scene between Captain Nelson and Bonny. Bonny had been ordered by Stanley to look after the expedition's cattle and goats, 'but like everything else he has to do, he simply neglects his duty to such an extent that he might just as well not be there at all'. Nelson was so exasperated by Bonny's unco-operative behaviour that he reported him to Stanley, at which Bonny went berserk and 'said all sorts of evil things about Nelson in a sort of shrill scream—whether true or not I can't say—and finally called Nelson a liar, upon which Nelson struck him and a rather disgraceful struggle took place in Stanley's hut in front of him; the combatants were finally separated, and Stanley read them both a lecture on the disgrace of two Europeans fighting.'

Jephson's sympathy was entirely with Nelson. He wrote in his diary:

Bonny is a most exasperating, low sort of fellow; he is just a sergeant with all the feelings, ideas, and loafing propensities of a typical 'Tommy Atkins'. Added to this he has an overweening conceit which is quite wonderful, seeing that he has absolutely nothing to be conceited about; he has done nothing for the Expedition and is despised by the men. We have treated him much as an equal, being all Europeans together in Africa, and he has come to think that he actually is our equal in every way and so has become spoilt. He is a man none of us ever liked or trusted, for he is simply dishonest.

Yet Jephson, for all his anger and disdain, would in the end do more for Bonny than anyone else connected with the expedition.

For Bonny, the expedition ended much as it had begun. After the farcical muddle at Fenchurch Street station, only Stanley's intervention had saved him. But there was no Stanley around to intervene when he got involved in a brawl on board ship, returning from Zanzibar. He had taken a violent dislike to a certain Dr Charlesworth and, as a consequence, he had to be locked up for much of the journey.

As Stanley explained in the letter he wrote to the Charity Organisation Society; while he was with the expedition, Bonny could not be discharged—'therefore we had to endure him right across Africa. You will have to ask the other survivors what the word "endure" means in Bonny's case . . .'

PART TWO

The Scandal

FROM EVERY practical point of view the Emin Pasha Relief Expedition was a failure, if not an unmitigated disaster. The time taken, the lives lost, the abysmal personal relations between Stanley and Emin—the ruthlessness of the one and the vacillations of the other—make a dismal story. And it had a fitting climax. At a party given by the German East African authorities on the coast at Bagamoyo to celebrate the arrival of what remained of Stanley's expedition, Emin (who was extremely short-sighted and had been a long time away from civilisation) stepped out of a first-floor window under the illusion that it was a ground-floor door and fractured his skull and several ribs. This was the final accident in an expedition which might be characterised as one long chapter of accidents.

Yet for Stanley, who looked after his own publicity, it was a personal triumph. And of course it was an astonishing feat of endurance. The expedition was more than two and a half years in Africa. Stanley himself crossed the great Ituri forest (previously unexplored) no less than three times, exposing himself and his men to every sort of danger from having nothing to eat to being themselves eaten. By the end of the third journey through the forest, his men dying all round him, Stanley came nearer to taking his own life than he had ever done before on an expedition. But he survived—and triumphed.

He did not return to Europe at once, but settled in Cairo to write—in less than four months—his two-volume epic account of the expedition, *In Darkest Africa*. The publishing process, too, was swifter in those days and the book came out in another two months. It was an instant bestseller. Stanley and his officers (Parke, Nelson, Stairs and Mounteney Jephson; not Troup, Ward or Bonny) were wined and dined wherever they went and, to crown it all, Stanley got married—to Dorothy Tennant, a fashionable painter of portraits and studies of slum children—in Westminster

Abbey. He was so ill at the time he could hardly walk, but when he and his bride emerged from the Abbey they were mobbed by a delirious crowd and had to be escorted by mounted police the short distance to their home in Richmond Terrace.

For Stanley, the triumph was all the sweeter in view of the rejections he had suffered earlier in his career. The 'American' upstart who had had the gall to find Livingstone and then return to the coast before the Royal Geographical Society's sponsored expedition had even left Zanzibar—and worse, had done it as a newspaper stunt—had at last gained acceptance from those he had upstaged all those years before.

For six months he enjoyed his celebrity. Then came Nemesis, demanding an explanation of his virtual abandonment of the rear column, and Stanley was once more fighting for his reputation.

In his book, Stanley wrote that the rear column 'was wrecked by the irresolution of the officers, by the neglect of their promises, and their indifference to written orders'. This harsh judgment stung the influential Barttelot family into retaliating with a polemical account of the expedition from the point of view of the late lamented Major.

The publication in 1890 of *Major Barttelot's Diaries and Letters*, edited by Edmund's brother, Walter, sparked off a fierce controversy in the newspapers. *The Times* led the field in the sheer volume of its published statements and counter-statements, accusations and affidavits, letters to the editor and editorial comment as 'neutral', solemn and portentous as the Chorus of a Greek tragedy; but no newspaper could afford to ignore what was *the* scandal of the hour.

Stanley himself was in New York on a lecture tour when Barttelot's *Diaries and Letters* was published, but he made a statement which *The Times* printed in full on 8 November. In it he argued, in so far as he argued at all, *ad hominem*. Discredit the witness and who will believe his testimony? Do it in the words of others and who can say you lie? So he prefaced his specific allegations against Barttelot with the remark: 'Much of the following information I obtained from Mr Bonny, the Zanzibaris, the Arabs, and the Manyema.'

The first things that had caught Stanley's attention were two cryptic entries in Barttelot's diary (24 November and 6 December 1887) in which he recorded his determination 'never to partake of Stanley's hospitality while out here'. What did this mean? Stanley had asked Bonny, who told him: 'Well, Sir, Major Barttelot said, "Don't you think Stanley is a Pritchard?"—a poisoner, and that one of your ways was to leave Africa alone, so that no one would know what had transpired; and he, Barttelot, said that he had heard the story of your leaving an officer in some part of Africa and never going back for him.' Stanley dismissed this by saying that Barttelot and Jameson had 'picked up a skit from some irresponsible newspaper to the effect that "it was odd Stanley had never returned from Africa except alone".'

Warming to this theme, Stanley went on:

I was told that Major Barttelot had expressed great curiosity to learn the probable effect of a dose of cyanide of potassium, and at one time was caught tasting it on his tongue in order to ascertain whether its taste would be likely to be detected in a cup of coffee. I was at the same time told that the person for whom this dose was intended was Selim Mohammed, the nephew of Tippu-Tib. I was also told that Major Barttelot's life was saved twice by Mr Bonny, once when Major Barttelot had suddenly seized a woman and fastened his teeth in her shoulder. I was told that frequently Major Barttelot would cause his black followers to shrink from before him by standing in their path in front of the advancing natives and grinning like a fiend—that is the expression that was used. I was told that with a steel-pointed cypress staff he had run about the camp prodding his people with it, and then flourishing the stick and hitting about him indiscriminately. And all this without apparent cause. A Manyema chief, a comrade of the man Sanga, reported to me that he had been prodded 17 times in one day only a day or two before he [Barttelot] was killed by Sanga.

The little boy Sudi, whose death I have recorded in *Darkest Africa*, was a little fellow ten years old ... Major Barttelot, irritated with little Sudi one morning, gave him a kick with his heavy boot, and from the effects of that kick the boy died.

John Henry, a mission lad, was flogged with 300 lashes, and died soon after.

Stanley gave a dramatic account of Barttelot's own death. He pictured the Major striding through the camp with his loaded revolver and that steel-pointed cypress staff:

With these weapons in his hands, he walked to the scene of the singing and the drumming, and there he saw a woman beating a drum, accompanying the music with her voice, in the usual habit of the Manyema, who thus start the day at dawn with wild music. * Major Barttelot, seeing the woman, ordered her to desist two or three times, accompanying each order with a prod with his steel-pointed staff or a blow with it. He then began to kick her, upon which her husband, Sanga, hearing the screams and seeing Barttelot armed with the revolver, thrust his gun through a loophole in a hut opposite the officer and shot him dead.

Mr Jameson went to Stanley Falls and, having proved that Sanga had shot Major Barttelot, the chief was sentenced to death. If Sanga had been brought before me, and if the story as reported to me in writing and orally had been confirmed, I would have acquitted him.

Jameson himself did not escape censure. If Barttelot's behaviour was generally scandalous, the single most shocking revelation was associated with Jameson's name. Stanley told the story as he had heard it from an eye-witness:

'Mr Jameson, returning from Kasongo, got into a conversation with Tippu-Tib and another Arab about cannibalism. He informed them that he did not believe there was such a thing as cannibalism, because, although he had heard much, he had never seen it, and no white man had ever seen it done. Tippu-Tib replied that it would be easy to prove it if he liked. Jameson asked how that was possible, and it was answered, "If

* Stanley gave a different explanation of this local custom in his book. There he wrote that 'among the Manyema were two insane women, or rather, to be quite correct, two women subject to spasms of hysterical exaltation, possessed by "devils", according to their chiefs, who prevented sleep by their perpetual singing during the night. Probably some such mania for singing at untimely hours was the cause of the Major's death. If the poor Major had any ear for harmony, their inharmonious and excited madhouse uproar might well have exasperated him.'

you will pay for a slave, and give it to those men there, they will show you." Twelve cotton handkerchiefs were then given in exchange for a little girl aged ten or twelve years. She was given to the cannibals, and Jameson is said to have then exclaimed, "Now let us see what you can do!" The girl was tied up, and Jameson took his sketchbook in his hand. The witness to this stood a few feet behind him. When all was ready a knife was plunged into the girl's heart, and Jameson stood still sketching while her life-blood spurted over her body. He made six sketches during the different stages of the affair, from the murder to the eating of the body.'

Stanley's accusations were not confined to the dead. Troup had also published a book about his experiences with the rear column, and Stanley now asked why he and Ward had not risen up and challenged Barttelot, since they plainly did not approve of his actions. Recalling his arrival at Banalya and meeting with Bonny, Stanley said:

I expected every minute to hear at least of one effort made to break the shackles, one effort made to resist this imperious despot. I thought that Lieutenant Troup, who was a strong, substantial man, weighing one third more than Major Barttelot, and that Mr Ward, with his physique—I thought that these spirited young men should have faced this despot and asked him to halt there and then. But it appears that they were all as submissive as Madras coolies.

It appeared that they also had the morals of Madras coolies, if Stanley was to believe what he had been told:

Major Barttelot alleged that Mr Ward was in the habit of abstracting brass rods from the camp stores, and he had actually sent a courier, it was said, with a letter to Mr Ward directing him to render a strict account . . .
    A good deal of ill-feeling, it is said, was excited in the camp, especially in the mind of Mr Jameson, by Mr Ward and Lieutenant Troup having unscrewed Mr Jameson's box with a view to find out whether or not there were concealed there some provisions that were missing from the camp. A bill also was sent from Banya [Bangala] station to Major Barttelot for 3,000

brass rods, which, it was stated, Mr Ward had received. I am told that Mr Troup applied to Major Barttelot for medicine while he was ill, and that Major Barttelot refused it. There were also frequent quarrels in the camp on account of expostulations from Mr Bonny, and Major Barttelot even went so far as to order the Sudani guard to arrest him.

Since he was cited as a source of the accusations against the others, it is hardly surprising that Bonny himself escaped censure and even got a crumb or two of praise from Stanley. In general, Stanley had him aligned with Troup and Ward—'I was told that there were two parties in the camp of the rear column: Major Barttelot and Mr Jameson comprising one party; and Mr Ward, Mr Bonny, and Lieutenant Troup comprising the other'—but he exempted him from the criticism he levelled at the other two. If challenged, he could have argued that Bonny's lowly position excluded him from responsibility: the others had been specifically mentioned in Stanley's letter of instructions to Barttelot; not Bonny. Of course Bonny was Stanley's principal witness; without his support Stanley's allegations might not be believed. Even so, prudence dictated that Stanley should add a disclaimer:

I have told these facts as they were told me. Whether every one of them is true or not, I have no means of knowing from personal knowledge. Some are attested by affidavits, others are stated in official reports which I, being bent upon saving the Expedition from scandal, tried to suppress. Under the circumstances I should have been only too glad to have gone into Court, where the facts could be fully ventilated.

In spite of Stanley's use of the past tense, this last statement was taken to imply that he was threatening an action. Walter Barttelot, when he was interviewed by a representative of the Press Association, declared his readiness to enter the legal arena: 'If he intends going to a Court of law we are prepared—amply prepared—to meet him, and let everything be known.' Troup, who—like Stanley—was in New York at this time, cut short his visit to America and hastened home. In a statement he made on 11 November he said, 'I am returning to England tomorrow. If Mr Stanley is going to bring an action against Major Barttelot's brother and against the surviving officers of the expedition I suppose I will be included. That will suit me immensely, for then I shall have a chance of cross-examining Mr Stanley.'

Ward too was drawn into the controversy, but unwillingly. In a letter to the Editor of *The Times*, he defended Barttelot's memory and claimed that his own position 'as regards the alleged atrocities' was similar to Stanley's—he too was hundreds of miles away at the time:

> But, unlike Mr Stanley, I should prefer not to attempt to injure the reputation of the dead by the use, or misuse, of allegations based on report only. For it should never be forgotten that Mr Stanley can at any time cast the whole responsibility of this degrading controversy, as it affects the dead, upon his informants.
>
> When Mr Stanley comes to dealing with the living it is not difficult to answer him. The statement that I abstracted brass rods (the currency of the country) is a lie.
>
> The bill for 3,000 brass rods referred to the rods paid by the Congo State to the Bangala natives who assisted me in my canoe journey down the Congo with despatches.

In a statement a day or two later he replied to the other accusation Stanley had made:

> The story that Mr Troup and myself miscarried and opened a box of Mr Jameson's is a proof of the ease with which a most innocent transaction can be so distorted as to appear dishonourable. The box mentioned was an ordinary provision case, and we opened it in order to find lard for cooking purposes. I now learn for the first time that on account of the brass rods and Jameson's box incidents I am said to have been suspended by Major Barttelot during my absence . . .

Protests against Stanley's statement came not only from Ward and Troup and the families and friends of Barttelot and Jameson, but from neutrals as well, and casual acquaintances such as the novelist, H. Rider Haggard, who wrote:

> Sir, I have read with much pain the horrible charge of aggravated child murder which Mr Stanley brings against the late Mr

Jameson. Necessarily I am unacquainted with the evidence on which he bases this accusation, but I hope I may not be thought presumptuous if, at this juncture, I venture to offer my testimony to character. It chanced that I travelled to Egypt with Mr Jameson when he was on his way to join Mr Stanley, and in the course of many friendly conversations I became well acquainted with him. So far as my judgment goes, a more gentle, kindly, good-hearted gentleman I never met, and all I can say is that if any one were to tell me the story which has been told to Mr Stanley, that with his own eyes he saw the horrors Mr Jameson is reported to have perpetrated, I should answer that he lied . . .

Meanwhile, on Monday, 10 November, Bonny's statement was published. Predictably, it corroborated Stanley's allegations in all but the smallest details and added a few more for good measure. Bonny concentrated his attack for the most part on Barttelot, whose diary had obviously been a subject of discussion between him and Stanley. He quoted the two entries for 24 November and 6 December 1887, which referred to conversations between Barttelot and him about Stanley, and wrote; 'Mr Stanley's statement reads as though it was in Africa where he first saw the foregoing entries. As a matter of fact it was on Sunday, October 26 of this year, after the publication of Major Barttelot's diaries, that Mr Stanley, reading these entries and wondering what they meant, asked me to tell him.'

'The poisoning story', as Bonny chose to call it, was quite true; the only thing Stanley had got wrong was the name Barttelot had used in that conversation—he had asked Bonny if he thought Stanley was 'a Palmer' (not Pritchard). Otherwise the details were correct. It was also true that Barttelot had wanted to poison Selim Mohammed, and only Bonny's timely action in removing all dangerous drugs from his reach had prevented him. Barttelot did indeed seize a woman and sink his teeth into her flesh—only it was her cheek he bit and not, as Stanley had said, her shoulder. And Stanley had made a slight factual error in his account of the shooting of Major Barttelot by saying that Barttelot had had his steel-pointed cypress stick with him when he went out to stop the woman singing: 'Major Barttelot did not have this staff on that morning and did not, therefore, stab the woman with it, but he did beat her with his fist and he did kick her, and he had his loaded revolver in his hand, as stated by Mr Stanley.' Bonny knew because he was there: 'I was myself at the moment going about the village attempting to quell the disturbance, and was not ten yards from the Major when he fell; and though I did not myself actually see Major Barttelot fall there is no question as to how he died and why.' * Stanley had also got the Jameson story right in all particulars but one: Bonny found, on examining his notes, that the price Jameson had paid for the girl the cannibals were to eat was six cotton handkerchiefs, not twelve.

There was one incident, however, that Bonny thought worthy of mention though Stanley had omitted it altogether. That was what he called 'the stabbing of Chief Ngungu by Major Barttelot'. He wrote:

This was on the occasion referred to by Walter G. Barttelot in his book, where it is stated that I captured eight women and a child in order to open up trade with the native tribes. This is correct. I had captured the women and the child, and I had succeeded in changing four of these women for 32 fowls, some fish, and palm oil, when Major Barttelot interrupted my trading. The Chief Ngungu was sitting down with me, and we were all laughing at the bargaining, I trying to get as much as possible for each woman, and the utmost good nature prevailed. Suddenly Major Barttelot came up, and without a word he drew a pocket-knife and stabbed Ngungu in the shoulder. Confusion followed, and I at once released the other four women and gave them back. Lieutenant Troup can testify to the truth of this statement. Two days after Ngungu came to me in secret to have his wounds dressed, and this I did.†

* In his original account of Major Barttelot's death (page 141) Bonny was still in bed when Barttelot was killed and only got up when he heard the shot.
† On 29 November, Walter Barttelot met Troup at the Westminster Palace Hotel and in the course of conversation asked him about this incident. He recorded Troup's response in a diary he kept of events connected with the rear column: 'Troup . . . laughed and said, "Why, your brother was always ready for a joke. He would laugh sometimes as if to split his sides and the truth is he came up in one of these laughing moods and gave Ngungu a prick with his pen-knife. It was nothing more than a joke and was never considered anything else."'

Bonny's description of trading with Ngungu provoked 'A Puzzled Reader' to write to *The Times* and enquire 'if this capturing of women and children was the ordinary and authorised method in which the expedition was in the habit of "opening up trade with the native tribes". Mr Bonny himself evidently sees nothing out of the way in it. I had an idea that any bartering in human beings by an Englishman was punishable by law; but it seems that "in Darkest Africa" Englishmen are a law unto themselves—unfortunately for the wretched natives.'

In his statement Bonny gave a detailed description of the part he himself had played during the last few days of Barttelot's life, when he was the only other white man present:

> It was on the 18th [July '88] that Sudi received the fatal kick and that I saved the Major's life when he bit the Manyema woman, and it was on the night of that same day that he killed [killed?] the Manyema, the comrade of Sanga. This man Major Barttelot prodded quite thirty times with his steel-pointed cypress staff, and finished up by beating the man's brains out before the eyes of all in the village. The scene which followed was like that which occurred when he bit the woman; and again I had to fight to save Major Barttelot's life. It was only by knocking him down myself that the natives held back, for then they thought I meant punishing him.

It clearly rankled with Bonny that Stanley's considered judgment of him, expressed in his book, was that he 'lacked initiative'. What Stanley had meant by this, Bonny explained, was that 'I should have taken Major Barttelot and bound him and sent him away.' He then argued that, had he done so, Barttelot's blood would have been on his hands as all the black men who so hated him would have torn him limb from limb once he was at their mercy. Bonny preferred it that Stanley should accuse him of lacking initiative than that he should be held responsible for the Major's death. He went on:

> Mr Stanley suggests that we might have done much by combined action, and I am willing to admit that by combined action we might, perhaps, have prevented the extremes to which Major Barttelot went. But there were many reasons why

combined action was impossible. I wish to be perfectly frank, and say that the strained relations existing between some of the officers had much to do with this state of affairs. There is no use going into details in this respect, but I cannot agree with Mr Stanley that the written protest of any single officer would have had the desired effect upon Major Barttelot. It is as certain as the fact that I am writing this, that the officer who would have dared to write to Major Barttelot as Mr Stanley suggests would have been a marked man, and it was no slight matter to incur the dislike of Major Barttelot.

At the end of his statement Bonny made public his contention that Barttelot went mad: 'I believe now, and I believed then, that he was insane, and it would have been better if his friends, who knew the circumstances, had placed this charitable construction upon them.'

At the same time he proudly asserted his own disinterestedness: 'I do not wish to defend Mr Stanley. I am not beholden to him nor to anybody else in this matter.' He was motivated purely by a desire to satisfy the public's legitimate demand to know the truth. He was simply doing his duty.

Bonny's statement provoked a number of letters, one of which raised a pertinent question. It was signed 'Veritas' and dated 'Edinburgh, November 12', and the point was this:

> Mr Bonny has given us in detail the revolting story of Major Barttelot's alleged atrocities, but why does he stop there? Why only inform against the dead, who cannot defend themselves? I know, on good authority, that Mr Bonny can say much more that would throw light on the dismal story of the rear guard, and it is to be hoped that he will not submit to be tongue-tied in exposing the culpability of the living when he has so freely exposed the actions of the dead.

This correspondent perhaps was personally acquainted with Bonny. His point was a fair one. Bonny's only mention of Ward and Troup had been in connection with one of 'the projects of Major Barttelot to start an expedition of his own'. Bonny claimed that he had attempted to get their co-operation in demanding an explanation from Barttelot:

I stated to them that if anything of the kind came to a head I would oppose it if I had to get the help of the Arabs, and that I would not allow a box of ammunition to go in any direction except in that decided upon by Mr Stanley. Neither Lieutenant Troup nor Mr Ward made any response to this, and in fact Lieutenant Troup had already volunteered to care for the goods which Major Barttelot proposed to leave behind him.

If that was all Bonny was prepared to say in public about his fellow survivors, they were scarcely less reticent about him. Ward chose to ignore him altogether, while Troup seemed anxious to appease him. In general, Troup said, he had no doubt that Bonny was correct, and he admitted Barttelot's cruelty, but:

Mr Bonny has made one error regarding myself, when he says . . . that I consented to take care of the goods which Major Barttelot proposed to leave behind him when he intended starting off on an expedition of his own. Mr Bonny has got these facts slightly mixed. Major Barttelot spoke to Mr Bonny about starting off on an expedition, and Mr Bonny came to me for consultation. I told him decidedly that I would not be a party to any such scheme. He asked me to talk to Major Barttelot, and, if possible, dissuade him from carrying out his project. I replied to this that as Major Barttelot had confided only in him, I was not supposed to know anything about the scheme, and that I should not mention it until Major Barttelot asked my advice. That was the last I heard of it.

In his own defence Troup was able to use the same plea as Ward had used, that he had not been there at the end, and even when he *was* there during those last months, he had been too ill to have any part in what was going on outside his hut. He said of Bonny's statement:

I have no reason to doubt the truth of most that he says, but only a few of those acts of cruelty were witnessed by me. Major Barttelot was cruel, terribly cruel—there is no doubt of that; and it is only reasonable to believe that another man might have brought the rear guard back to the coast with little loss of life and with few of the privations which we suffered.

But Mr Stanley, knowing what a temper Major Barttelot had, and knowing the Major's hatred of the blacks, appointed him absolute master.

This argument had already occurred to more than one reader of *The Times*. Stanley's opening statement had elicited a pithy letter from a Mr R. W. Essington, who wrote, 'If Major Barttelot was such a man as Mr Stanley now asserts him to have been, why did he not take him on under his own eye instead of leaving him in command of the rear guard?' And R. Bosworth Smith (a master at Harrow and author of a two-volume *Life of Lord Lawrence*) made the same point, adding:

> But I would go a step further back and ask why Mr Stanley, knowing Major Barttelot to be what he was before the expedition started, ever took him with him to Africa at all. When I was in Egypt in the winter of 1888 I met many personal acquaintances of Major Barttelot, who, from their knowledge of his character and of his acts in that part of Africa, did not hesitate to express their belief that he had been justly slain; and, more than this, it is within my knowledge that the traveller of all others most entitled to give advice to Mr Stanley when starting on his expedition, and a member of the Emin Relief Committee [Colonel Grant, presumably], implored him not to take Major Barttelot with him, on the grounds of his ungovernable temper and of his notorious hatred of the natives.
>
> If I take a man, of whom the best defence that can now be urged for his acts of fiendish ferocity and cruelty is that he is insane, with me upon an expedition undertaken in the interests of humanity and civilisation; if I put arms into his hands and place him in a position of vast responsibility among a people towards whom he is known to cherish a savage hatred, am I not responsible, at least in a secondary degree, for the natural result?

Other correspondents questioned the fitness of this portrait of Major Barttelot as a dangerous lunatic, citing 'his proverbial kindness to and love for children'—as if they were a safeguard against any form of hatred and cruelty. Stanley had his defenders, too. A clergyman, who had been reading the Life of a prominent

African missionary who had died during the Emin Pasha Expedition, wrote:

> In Mackay's Life just published ... I find the following testimony: 'Wherever I find myself in Stanley's track, in Uganda, Ugogo, or even Ukerewe itself, I find his treatment of the natives has invariably been such as to win from them the highest respect for the face of a white man.'

Interest in the controversy had reached a peak. Even the French, with not too distant memories of the rivalry between Stanley and their man, de Brazza, in the Congo, were eager to get in on the act. The *Débats*—'from which,' *The Times* commented acidly, 'greater fairness might have been expected'—saw the dispute as a prime example of English hypocrisy: 'Let us compare our countrymen with the English. We have fewer evangelical pretensions; but on which side is the true spirit of humanity?' In the French view a lawsuit was not only inevitable but also mandatory, as the matter now concerned 'not merely certain Englishmen, but the very honour of the civilised world'.

It was at this moment, with the English and French press alike clamouring for a lawsuit, that Stanley, in New York, calmly announced that he had no intention of taking legal action in the matter. In this decision he was supported by at least one correspondent, who sought to widen the scope of the debate. This correspondent signed himself 'Anglo-Australian' and gave as his address the Oriental Club in London. He wrote:

> Sir, The thing that is most astonishing about the disclosures of cruelty made by Stanley and Mr Bonny is the incredulous astonishment with which they appear to have been received. Those, however, who hold up their hands in horror and complain of the stain on human nature must be singularly ignorant of what has taken place without exception, as far as our records go, when a superior race is placed in contact with one much inferior.
>
> No nation and no age has a monopoly of this monstrous cruelty. The Romans in Gaul, the Spaniards in South America, the Yankees in North America, the English in our own day in Australia and the islands of the South Pacific, all have per-

formed horrible deeds on the lower races with whom they have been brought into contact. It is not many years since it was the custom in Northern Queensland when the blacks were troublesome, and many cattle were found speared, for the overseer to get up a party armed with rifles to go out potting blacks. The unfortunate victims were left to live or die as they liked. It is a great mistake to suppose these young Englishmen were worse than most of us. Low-class natives are most irritating people, and one hardly recognises in them the rights of humanity. Besides which, everyone degenerates truly awfully in the absence of civilised restraints unless he happens to be a man of exceptional moral fibre such as was Livingstone.

Let me add one other word. It is a great folly to demand a legal inquisition into this matter which occurred in the centre of Africa. The actors are dead and the rules and canons of legal evidence will exclude much that is properly to be believed.

If all history was to be credited only on such evidence as a Judge receives at *Nisi Prius*, history would be nearly a blank page. I certainly believed the story from the first and think it is far more in accordance with human nature than would have been a story of kindness and consideration. The latter would have been unique and, though not impossible, highly improbable. *

* In the 1890s there was much discussion of what constituted the proper relationship between the 'superior' and 'inferior' races. It was the age of Jingo-ism. The poet and politician, Wilfrid Scawen Blunt, who deplored the growth of Imperialism, recorded in his diary a conversation with Gerald Balfour (brother of Arthur) in 1892:

'7 August (Sunday). Drove with the Balfours and Conny Lytton to Blickling, where we lunched. On the way we had a grand discussion about patriotism, Gerald maintaining that patriotism was the imperial instinct in Englishmen, who should support their country's quarrels even when in the wrong. This of course is not my view. Gerald has all his brother's scientific inhumanity in politics, and it is a school of thought distinctly on the increase, for it flatters the selfish instincts of the strong by proving to them that their selfishness is right . . .

'Gerald's argument, I recollect, was based on an application to inter-racial politics of Darwin's law of the selection of the fittest, or rather of what is an exaggerated interpretation of that law. Those who put forward this view forget that Man by the abnormal development of his reasoning powers and his invention of lethal weapons, has put himself outside the unconscious working of

[*continued overleaf*

the natural law. Darwin is in no way responsible for this application of his doctrine, as is clearly seen in the sympathy he shows with the backward races of mankind, especially in his *Voyage of the Beagle*. Though individual strives with individual in the natural world, there is never a combination of a whole species or race to make war with and destroy a feebler race. This was my argument with Gerald. Three years later he was appointed by Lord Salisbury and his brother Arthur, Chief Secretary for Ireland, and proved a kindly ruler while in office there, being by nature an altogether amiable, kind-hearted man, but infected, as so many of our Imperialists were beginning to be at that date, by the politico-scientific doctrines so crudely preached in Germany.'

Later that summer, Blunt was writing:

'27 Sept. On a visit to Frampton ... There is a Miss Fetherstonhaugh staying in the house who showed me letters she had received from young de Winton from Uganda, written in the mixed missionary and fighting language one is familiar with in Gordon's letters to his sister. These people believe they have a mission from God to establish the British flag, "the dear old Union Jack," throughout the world and to maintain it there with fire and sword. Pizarro, no doubt, wrote in the same strain from Peru, when he destroyed the beautiful old world of the Incas. Truly "civilisation is poison." '

JUST WHEN the controversy seemed to be losing some of its impetus, Stanley placed at the disposal of *The Times* various documents, including an affidavit written by the interpreter, Assad Farran. The publication of this sensational account of events gave the dispute its second wind.

Stanley claimed that while he was in Cairo in March 1890, writing *In Darkest Africa*, Assad Farran 'delivered a written document to me, on reading which I saw that the details were so circumstantial, and related with such wonderful clearness, that I asked him if the facts were true which the document contained. I asked him if he had written them himself, and he answered in the affirmative. Two witnesses were called . . .' One of these witnesses was Stanley's private secretary, whose name was Leonard Wilson. He remembered Stanley bursting into the room where he was 'engaged upon the manuscript of *In Darkest Africa*', followed by a Syrian whom he had seen a couple of times before. Stanley also called in his courier, a Mr Zerilli, and after catechising Assad Farran in their presence, demanded that they witness his signature —which they did. Wilson wrote:

> I most heartily concur in Mr Stanley's statement that, if the document affecting the character of the late Mr Jameson is not absolutely true, then the man Assad Farran is the most consummate and accomplished liar in existence, for, to my mind, the man's face at the moment of signing the document bore the stamp of utter truthfulness.

Assad Farran began by describing the capture of native women and children and explaining how they were bartered for food by the officers:

> Another time Mr Bonny, after his arrival in the steamer with the men and the loads, also captured seven women and brought

them to the camp. This time they were tied by a rope round their necks and in the night they were taken to the officers' quarters. These were also kept weeks in the camp till they got a chance to run away. Not one day passed without a dozen or two of the men were flogged with either 100 or 50 or 25 lashes each; even to the very sick persons no mercy was shown.

And he related in sickening detail—down to the very worms that crawled out of the sores on his back—the story of the Sudanese soldier, Burgari Mohammed, who stole the leg of goat from Ward's hut, was flogged with 150 lashes and then shot, after he had deserted and been recaptured.

But it was when he came to the cannibal incident that Assad Farran's evidence was most damaging. His story was indeed circumstantial:

After talking on different matters through Salem Masoudi, Tippu-Tib's interpreter, Mr Jameson said he was very anxious to see a man killed and eaten by cannibals, because, he said, 'In England we hear much about cannibals who eat people, but, being myself in the place, I should like to see it done.' This was interpreted by Salem Masoudi to Tippu-Tib and the other chiefs, whereupon, after consulting each other, told Mr Jameson that if he wants to see a thing like this, he should buy a slave, and which he can present to the cannibals and they will eat him before him. Mr Jameson then asked how much is the price of a slave there. They told him half a pice of handkerchiefs (six single pieces). He then told them that he will pay that price and went to his house where he lodged and brought half a pice and came back; this was handed to a man who went away and in a few minutes came back leading a girl of about ten years old.

This girl was led by the orders of Tippu-Tib and the other chiefs, at the request of Mr Jameson, to the native huts to be eaten. Mr Jameson and myself, Salem Masoudi and Farhani, Jameson's servant, presented to him by Tippu-Tib, and many others, followed. On reaching the native huts, the girl, which was led by the man who brought her, was presented to the cannibals, and a man told them that 'This is a present from the white man, he wants to see how you do with her when you eat her.' The girl was taken and tied by a hand to a tree; about five of the natives were sharpening their knives; then a man came and stabbed her with a knife twice in the belly, the girl did not scream, but knew what was going on; she was looking right and left as if looking for help, and when she was stabbed she fell down dead. The natives then came and began cutting her in pieces, one was cutting the leg, another the arm, another the head and breast, and another took the inner parts of the belly. After the meat was divided some took it to the river to wash it, others went straight to their huts. During this time Mr Jameson had his book and pencil in hand, and was making rough sketches of the scene. After this was over we also went back; I went to the chief's house, and Mr Jameson went in his house. On my return to Mr Jameson, he had his sketches already finished, painted with water colours. They are six small sketches neatly done, the first when the girl was led by the man, the second when she was tied to the tree and stabbed in the belly, the blood gushing out, another when she was cut in pieces, the fourth a man carrying the leg in one hand and the knife in the other, the fifth a man with a native axe and the head and the breast, and the last a man with the inward parts of the belly. Mr Jameson, when he finished these sketches, took them to the chief's house and showed them to all the people there, with many other sketches that he did.

Another person to whom Jameson had shown these sketches was Troup. In an earlier statement Troup had admitted as much— 'but I did not say that Mr Jameson had been guilty of buying a girl and giving her to the cannibals'. He had pointed out then that that charge rested only on the word of Assad Farran, whom he described as 'an inveterate liar, who afterwards retracted the charges under oath'. Yet at the same time he had to admit that when they were travelling together down the Congo, Assad Farran had equally solemnly sworn that his original story of events was true. Troup said, 'I was too ill to take down his statement in writing, but the recital distressed me like a nightmare.' And then there was the evidence of the sketches themselves which Jameson had brought in to show him when Troup lay on his sickbed at Yambuya. Jameson had been in the habit of showing Troup his sketches and jokingly called him his 'art critic'. In his statement, Troup explained what had happened on this occasion:

> When Mr Jameson came to me after luncheon, he asked me if I thought he had improved, and I replied, 'What an awful subject you have here!' He replied to the effect that he had not been present at the actual killing of the girl, and that part of the sketches had been drawn from description, but that he came in afterwards, just when they were feasting.

Troup added, 'I thought nothing more of it then.'

Assad Farran, on his return from Africa two years earlier, had been virtually forced to sign a retraction of the statements he had made to the Belgian authorities in the Congo. Jameson's widow now sent *The Times* a copy of his retraction along with Jameson's own last letter to William Mackinnon, the Chairman of the Emin Pasha Relief Committee—now Sir William. But the juxtaposition of these two documents was an unfortunate one. As *The Times* editorial rather ponderously put it, '[Jameson's] letter of exculpation strikes a heavier blow at his reputation than any of the statements it has been our duty to publish during the past week.' It showed up the accompanying retraction for what it was, a misguided and bungled piece of expediency on the part of the Emin Pasha Relief Committee.

Jameson had not attempted to deny the substance of Assad Farran's story, only to claim extenuating circumstances. He had handed over the cloth, he wrote, because he had thought it was just another Arab ruse for getting a present out of him:

> Then followed the most horrible scene I ever witnessed in my life, and Assad Farran even here cannot help lying. The whole thing happened so quickly that, had I wished, I could not have sketched it, and I had nothing with me to sketch with, they all being in my house. The small sketches I made were done in the evening afterwards in my own house.

Jameson's intention, in his letter, was to discredit Assad Farran. He had written:

> Assad Farran openly boasted that he had swindled the British government out of £300 in the hiring of camel drivers at

Suakin, and told me on the road to Kasongo that he had had a good chance there. When I asked him what it was, he told me that whoever was then in command had stopped all gambling, but he knew of places where it still went on. If he found out any soldier inclined to gamble with plenty of money, he used to take him to one of these places and watch who won most, then he would slip out, get a policeman, and point out to him the man, upon which there would be a general rush, the policeman catching the man with the money, and Assad and he dividing the spoils . . . It is a low brute like this whose word the Belgian officers take, and who is allowed to try and destroy my character.

But it was quite beside the point that Assad Farran was a low brute or scoundrel when, in this instance, and on Jameson's own admission, he was telling what was substantially the truth—even if it was with malice aforethought.

On the same day that Assad Farran's affidavit was published, there was in *The Times* a further statement from William Bonny, who now set out to establish that the act of cannibalism and the disaster to the rear column were more closely related than most people would probably have suspected. Bonny was certainly doing Stanley's work for him. Stanley had made his several but disparate allegations against the officers of the rear column in the hope that some, if not all, of the mud would stick. He had not—as Troup had complained—attempted a coherent argument; it was up to the reader to make any connections that might suggest themselves. But Bonny, as the one European who had been with the rear column throughout, had greater freedom to speculate: he had 'very strong reasons for believing,' as he put it, 'that, had Mr Jameson's name never been connected with this unfortunate incident, both Major Barttelot and himself would be alive to-day.'

He argued that the knowledge that Assad Farran's story was being so eagerly taken down by the Belgians, and would therefore be reported in Europe, had excited Barttelot to such a degree of apprehension that when he returned to Banalya after his last trip to Stanley Falls he was even more violent than usual. According to Bonny, Barttelot had shown him the pages of his diary which contained the cannibal story and said to him, 'Look at that, Bonny! Read that! I shall lose my commission!' Bonny went on:

> I have never doubted that Major Barttelot was becoming insane through privations, anxieties and other causes; but the cannibal incident was unquestionably the 'last straw', and from that time he can hardly be held responsible for what he did.

As for Jameson, he too had become very anxious once he realised what a stir Assad Farran's story was causing among the Europeans in the Congo, and he had been trying to get to the coast to stop the story getting any further—or at least to send home his own explanation of it—when he had contracted the fever from which he died. Bonny maintained that he would not have suffered an attack of fever in the first place had he not been so anxious and worried. So both men could be said to have died as a result—an indirect result, to be sure—of the cannibal incident. Such was Bonny's considered opinion.

Bonny had still more to say about the incident itself. He reminded his readers that Jameson was an ardent naturalist who had gone on the expedition 'in search of novelty and adventure and for scientific research'. The best excuse that could be made for him—for the story could not be denied—was that he had been carried away by scientific enthusiasm and simply had not paused to think how his actions would be regarded at home. It was no use pretending that he had merely happened upon a cannibal feast commonly held by Central African tribes:

> Cannibalism with them is not an habitual practice. When they fight they eat their dead enemies, but it not their custom to kill little girls and eat them. Therefore it could have been only by some special inducement, or for some particular reason, that this act of cannibalism which Mr Jameson witnessed was perpetrated.

Nor could it be denied, Bonny argued, that Jameson had carried his enthusiasm to extremes; there had been another little matter of a native head—not a skull, but 'a preserved head, with skin and hair upon it'—which Jameson had sent home, and which now occupied a glass case in Mrs Jameson's house in London. Bonny remembered how it had been acquired:

A native with whom we were well acquainted was shot and killed by an Arab.* Mr Jameson sent some soldiers to get the body and bring it into camp. This was done, and Mr Jameson then had the head cut off, packed in salt, boxed, and shipped to London. When it arrived here it was handed over to Messrs Rowland Ward and Co., of Piccadilly, who dressed the head for Mr Jameson's representatives. While at the house of Mrs Jameson upon one occasion she showed me the curiosity, asking me as she did so, 'Do you know this gentleman?' I replied, 'Yes, I know him well. I have shaken hands with him many times.' Mrs Jameson informed me that at times the odour from the head was extremely disagreeable, and asked me the reason why. 'You have a human barometer in the house,' and I explained that the salt in which the head had been packed not having been entirely removed, the skin was liable to become moist in certain conditions of the atmosphere, and this would account for the disagreeable odour.

When approached by *The Times*, Mr Rowland Ward, head of the firm of naturalists which carried his name, declined to comment on a matter which, he said, concerned only himself and his clients.

* See page 83.

[3]

WITH THE support of such documents as Assad Farran's affidavit and Bonny's official report, Stanley had done all the damage he needed to do; and if he had rested his case there, his point of view would probably have prevailed. But, perhaps because he was in New York and therefore in no position to gauge public opinion in Britain, he now made a tactical error and overplayed his hand. He gave to the representative of *The Times* in New York a signed statement by his Zanzibari servant, Saleh Ben Osman, who had not even been with the rear column and whose account of events was so manifestly incorrect, biassed and malicious as to undermine the very case it was designed to support —as readers of *The Times* were quick to point out. Saleh Ben Osman had Jameson himself taking the slave-girl by the wrist and personally handing her over to her 'savage executioners'. As one correspondent wrote, 'The absolute inaccuracy of the first part of Saleh Ben Osman's statement throws the greatest discredit on the remaining portions; and in what way Mr Stanley is trying to strengthen his case by publications of his description will, I think, remain a mystery to the majority of the thinking public.'

At the same time, Herbert Ward spoke out for the first time on the general issue rather than purely personal ones. Stanley had finally goaded him into it by causing to be published a statement by Ward's friend, E. J. Glave, who had translated Saleh Ben Osman's statement and who admired Stanley to the point of idolatry—as Ward himself once had. Glave said that Ward, in private conversations with him, always spoke of Barttelot's mismanagement of the affairs of the rear column, his cruelty to the men, his tactless and high-handed dealings with Tippu-Tib, and his tyrannical behaviour towards the other white officers. Ward was also in the habit of complaining that Barttelot and Jameson 'always held counsel together, but kept everything secret from the other officers'. He and Barttelot had never got on together, but he could not account for the great change that came over Barttelot during their long stay at Yambuya; he could only think that the life and conditions there had thoroughly brutalised him.

Asked by *The Times* to comment, Ward did not deny that he had spoken thus in private conversation, but maintained that he had a duty to defend Barttelot in public in his character as a British officer, the more so since Barttelot was dead and could not speak for himself. Ward stressed once more his reluctance to enter into the controversy at all. But in spite of this he wrote a long letter to the Editor of *The Times* in which he showed not only his contempt for Stanley's press campaign but his own very considerable powers of argument as well.

Sir, I have always been loyal to Mr Stanley. By loyal, I mean that where praise was possible it was ungrudgingly given, and where censure might have been indulged in it was withheld. I had hoped to maintain this attitude towards the leader of the Emin Pasha Expedition, but recent events have made it necessary that I should depart from this position and deal with matters frankly and fully. It will be obvious that in anything I say there can be no malice, no sudden expression of ill-feeling.

The controversy regarding the rear guard has drifted altogether away from the main point at issue. This was, the question as to responsibility for the disasters of the rear guard. Personal matters have been thrust into prominence, side issues have been raised, and the vital question altogether obscured.

This particular matter is what I wish to deal with now. The dispute as to whether or not Mr Jameson bought a slave girl and the hundred and one other matters which have been introduced may be very useful in assisting Mr Stanley to form a public opinion in his favour; but the matter with regard to which the whole controversy has arisen is quite distinct from these and must not be ignored.

Mr Stanley's contention is that 'the rear guard was wrecked by the irresolution of the officers and their total disregard of his written instructions.' I quote his own words. This was the charge.

Mr Stanley may or may not be a scrupulous man. He is

undoubtedly a bold and farseeing one. It is impossible for anybody calmly regarding the matter to avoid coming to the conclusion that a man of Mr Stanley's character must have had a purpose in making such a charge as this. It would appear as if he feared that one day he might have to answer the charge that has since been made, that he himself was responsible for the disaster.

Except Mr Stanley's personal apprehensions, there was no reason whatever why the details of the Yambuya camp should not have been left untold. The story of Barttelot's death was known to his relatives, his comrades, and his employers, and until Mr Stanley chose to thrust it before the public, there was a generous conspiracy of silence. But Mr Stanley's vanity was alarmed, and lest it should happen that some one should say, 'No doubt he did a fine thing, but how about his loss of his rear guard?'—he collected all the tittle-tattle of tale-bearers, all the passing trifles of petty individual impatience, and, thus equipped, attacked the characters of his subordinates; yet all this time he knew that he himself was in part responsible for the catastrophe of Yambuya. Mr Stanley would fain have us believe that his treatment of the natives was above criticism in every respect.

The keynote of the expedition was struck by Mr Stanley himself when, after disembarking, he started through the cataract region of the Lower Congo, and left it to his officers, then inexperienced in African travel, to drive the load-bearers along as best they could, when his peremptory orders could only be carried out by the exercise of great severity. Mr Stanley now talks in a very high and exalted way of the indifference of the officers of the rear guard; but, as a matter of fact, he himself left sick and dead behind him from his first day's march. I, who came up a few days afterwards, had to bury some of the dead whom he left in his track.

Mr Stanley says Major Barttelot and the rest of us were responsible for the disasters; but who appointed Major Barttelot to the command of the camp? It was Mr Stanley himself. It is now stated on all sides that Mr Stanley was informed beforehand that Major Barttelot was a thoroughly unsuitable man for the work before him, yet he not only took him out with him, but actually, at the supreme crisis of the expedition, selected this man for a position of momentous responsibility. This is all the more surprising because of the fact that it was a matter of common notoriety that Mr Stanley disliked Barttelot as much as Barttelot disliked him. What is to be thought of Mr Stanley when under all these circumstances he turned his back upon Yambuya, assuring Barttelot that he had made a 'wise choice in selecting him to guard the interests of the expedition during his absence'. A wise choice it was in one sense, for Major Barttelot was a true British soldier, in as much as with a splendid loyalty to the best traditions of his service as to the obedience of orders he held sacred every instruction of Stanley's to the last. Nevertheless, Major Barttelot was only thirty years of age, hot tempered to a degree, and, of his own confession, frequently and most publicly made, abhorring everything in the shape of a black man. So careful was Major Barttelot to observe orders that in the face of starvation he refused to open stores of food which Mr Stanley had warned him were essential to the expedition. With disease and death hard at work all around him, he refused to open the case which meant relief and life; and yet Stanley accuses this man of disloyalty. Barttelot obeyed his orders to the very letter. He would not give us stores; he would not touch the medicines. Why? Because he had been told by his superior officer that they were essential to the advance column. There was no other reason for it but the man's stolid sense of discipline. He was told that the advance guard wanted these things, and that they were to be kept for them, and he would not touch them. People will argue that we should have taken the law into our own hands under the circumstances. This, however, would have been mutiny, and would assuredly have led to general bloodshed; for it must be remembered that the fifty odd Sudanese who were the soldiers of the expedition, and who were the only armed force in the camp, were under Barttelot's sole control. He had served in Egypt with them, and their feelings towards him were those of extreme loyalty.

If Mr Stanley, then, will come back to the original question which he started, and apportion the blame of the disasters of the rear guard as it should be apportioned, he must take at least a fair share of the blame, if blame there be. By his example on the march up he initiated his staff in indifference to human suffering and his load-bearers in the fatalistic acceptance of their lot as mere beasts of burden. By his appointment of Major Barttelot under all the existing circumstances he deliberately risked disaster, to use no stronger word. By the vague instructions which he left he placed Major Barttelot in a position of bewildering alternatives. By the alleged agreement with Tippu-Tib he put Barttelot more or less at the Arabs' mercy.

Let Mr Stanley give up publishing affidavits from his negro valet as to the demerits of dead men and answer for himself whether he should not bear some responsibility for the disasters of the rear guard. Whatever he may have said or may know as to the conduct of individual officers, the main question of responsibility is not affected. I am, Sir, your obedient servant,

HERBERT WARD

Yet only a fortnight after this letter was published, Stanley was giving a lecture in New York entitled 'The Full Story of the Rear Guard' in which he repeated all his earlier allegations and threw in a few more for good measure; and *The Times* duly published large portions of it.

But by now no one was interested any more—no one, that is, apart from those directly involved and the relatives of those who had died. Andrew Jameson wrote a couple of letters of protest at the treatment meted out to his brother by both Stanley and Bonny, and Bonny replied to the effect that he had only spoken after others had broached the distasteful subject.

And so, for want of fresh fuel, the controversy burnt itself out in mutual and petty recriminations while the public turned its attention elsewhere.

PART THREE

The Survivors

'WILL YOU be good enough to write the recommendation
you wish, and let me see if I can endorse it and if I can, without
prejudice to my soul, you may be sure I will . . . I certainly
wish you well, I do not see why I should not. What you could
do to the height of your faculties I believe you did, and did it
with good will, and good will covers a multitude of errors. At
the same time I tell you that you are one of the most incomprehensible of men, and if I lived fifty years I doubt very much if I
should know you thoroughly. I never met your equal for sweet
smiling complacency . . . I am, my dear Bonny, Your Friend,
H. M. Stanley.'

Letter dated 'Villa Victoria, Cairo,
28.2.1890.'

The controversy over the rear column gave Bonny a passing
celebrity comparable, perhaps, to his moment of glory at Banalya
when he had imagined himself, at least, as 'WILLIAM BONNY,
Commanding'. Nine months before the scandal broke, he had
written to Stanley in Cairo, soliciting his help in finding employment and expressing anxiety about the kind of write-up he would
give him in his book:

You told me that you did not intend to speak very complimentary of me. Please reconsider your decision—it will do me
harm and do the Expedition no good . . . It is my earnest hope
that the affairs of the Expedition will pass off in satisfaction to
everyone—I shall not be the first to throw the stone . . .

Stanley had replied:

What sort of employment do you wish? . . . If I had a sinecure
to give you I would certainly give it to you . . . but no big work
of trust away from me would I trust you with . . . it is better in
a man to know the right thing to do without being told. This is

all I have against you except a fierce exhibition of temper now and then. It is for you to tell me what kind of employment you would like to have. It will be for me to tell you whether you are fit for it.

Throw stones as much as you like—but always with due regard for the consequences. You cannot hurt any member of the Expedition, neither Barttelot nor Jameson nor Stanley . . .

At that time, of course, Stanley had no inkling of the furore that would follow the publication of Major Barttelot's *Diaries and Letters* later in the year, when he would need Bonny as his main witness. After that, there was no question of him ever again assuming quite the same tone of lofty superiority.

When Bonny appealed to him once more, at the beginning of 1893, for help in finding a job, 'anything in East, West or South Africa' (and thanked him for a present—of money), Stanley wrote him a very flattering reference, saying he was 'exceedingly well qualified to be placed in charge of a military station in a new country, or a frontier post, or a police detachment'. On the strength of this recommendation Bonny obtained an interview in Brussels with Captain Thys.* But nothing came of it.

By May, Bonny was 'at his wit's end'. He apologised to Stanley for not replying to a letter of his sooner. 'I was not at home,' he explained, 'but at Tunbridge Wells travelling in advertisements with very little success. I am closely pressed and am ready to take any post . . .' But even Stanley, it seems, was powerless to help him.

A year later Stanley received a letter from a Mr Henry King of 13 Clarendon Street, Pimlico, who begged to be forgiven for troubling him, but thought he ought to know that his 'old colleague' was 'in sore distress' and owed money to his landlord. 'May I beg of you,' King wrote, 'to render him some *immediate* assistance as I fear the worst may happen.'

Stanley handed over £20 and King sent him a receipt for the rent which had been overdue. He wrote, 'Mr Bonny was so bad on

* Thys was 'the great man himself', who interviewed Joseph Conrad in 1889. In *Heart of Darkness*, Conrad dismisses him contemptuously as 'pale plumpness in a frock coat'. Others found him more formidable. The Belgian socialist, Emile Vandervelde, called him 'a sort of capitalist Pizarro or Cortez'.

Monday last that I got him into Westminster Hospital on Tuesday . . . He does not know that I have seen you.'

Bonny, when he got out of hospital, far from being grateful for his friend's concern over his condition, was furious with King for what he had done. He wrote to Stanley, 'If anyone should at any time call or write [to] you on my behalf I must [ask that] you will let me know to prevent fraud. I have never sent anyone to you.'

In the autumn of 1894, Mounteney Jephson began to take an interest in Bonny's predicament. Apart from Stanley himself, Jephson was now the sole survivor of the advance column and his relationship with Stanley had developed into one of near filial intimacy.* He wanted to see Bonny 'and help him if possible'. On 9 October, he reported to Stanley:

> This morning I drove to his address and saw him for a few moments, and asked him to come and have lunch with me. In the meantime I drove off to see his landlord who is butler at the Carlton Club. He seems a very respectable person and most friendly and considerate to Bonny, who (except for not paying his rent) has always acted with perfect propriety. He told me that Bonny's friend Mr King, who has a good position at Novello's music shop, had paid Bonny's rent up till last July.

Jephson tried to see King, but found he was out of town on business; he wanted his advice on how best to use the £15 which he had put aside for Bonny. His letter to Stanley continues:

> Bonny came and had lunch and we had a long talk. He is still out of employ, I am sorry to say. He looks ill and rather red and puffy and has lost all his smartness. Poor Bonny, he was so humble and unlike his former self-assertive personality that it went to my heart and I came very near to handing him over the little sum I had for him. But fortified by a good lunch and a bottle of claret he went back to his old sententious way, so I hardened my heart and kept my hand out of my pocket.

* Nelson and Stairs had both returned to Africa and died there in 1892; Parke, though he remained in Britain, outlived them by only a few months—dying of a heart attack in 1893. Emin too, after an unhappy attempt to identify with the German interest in East Africa, was killed by Arab slavers in 1892, a myopic wanderer in the Ituri forest. Though his rescue had been an important event, his death went almost unnoticed.

The following week Jephson wrote from his family home in Ireland (Mallow Castle, Co. Cork) that he had received two letters from King, to whom he had given a cheque to cover Bonny's rent for a year—paying off two months' arrears and securing him free lodging for a further ten months.

King, said Jephson, 'wrote very hopelessly of Bonny and spoke about his not at one time having been very appreciative of his friends' efforts, but that we both know was always Bonny's failing. I wish I could feel in helping Bonny that I had a little more liking for the man, but I cannot manage to scrape together much enthusiasm.'

A month passed and Jephson's next letter to Stanley was dated, 'San Francisco, 22 November 1894'. He was in America to pursue his rather hopeless love affair with a girl named Anna Head, whom he had first met while lecturing in the States in 1891. He probably found it a relief to think of other things. He wrote to his old chief:

> I fear you think I was too hard upon poor Bonny and did not do him justice, but I think I have the same feeling about him that you have. Sometimes when he was talking I felt quite drawn towards him, and then he said something which spoilt it all, and one's heart hardened up against him again with that same feeling of contempt and anger which he caused us all to feel so often in Africa and elsewhere. Yet I feel as you do that there *is* something in him which evades one, something one wishes much to get hold of, for one feels one would have a better opinion of him if one could. His mind requires, I think, some sort of surgical operation, something in his composition to be cut away, or to be added, or perhaps both. But there certainly is a lack somewhere, and but for that he might have become something. But his reserve and extraordinary sensitiveness make it impossible to find out what it is, and so to really help him to help himself. He is a curious character, not in any way lovable, but one you feel *might* be interesting. I shall make a point of seeing him when I return, but I feel that anything one did for him would be but a patching up after all.

Bonny himself wrote to Stanley in December. He was still without employment: 'I regret to state that I have no post

although I have tried far and near for home or foreign occupation.'
Six months later he wrote again, this time to thank Stanley for his
'kind note containing enclosure'.

By the end of March 1896 he was back in the Westminster
Hospital. He was very weak and depressed and the doctors were
puzzled by his case. His liver was swollen; there were signs of a
tumour and there seemed to be something wrong with his
intestines. Dr Smith, the house physician, told Mounteney
Jephson that he was neither a very satisfactory nor grateful
patient. Jephson explained about his addiction to opium.

Much of Bonny's depression was no doubt attributable to his
concern over what would happen to him when he came out of
hospital, and Jephson was careful to explain to Dr Smith that he
could not—as he later put it in a letter to Stanley—'hold out false
hopes of support hereafter from us'. The doctor quite understood.

Jephson left the hospital, promising to return later in the week;
he had another call to make, on a friend of Bonny's—not King
this time, but a man called East.

At 7 o'clock I went down to Vauxhall Bridge Road to see East.
I found an extremely comfortable and respectable lower middle
class home near Victoria Railway Station. East, who for thirty-
three years has been in the Army Clothing Department at
Pimlico, was a man after the exact stamp of King, respectful,
straightforward and a man in whom one at once felt
confidence . . . He had known Bonny before his departure for
Africa, and on his return had with regret seen him sink lower
and lower. He had helped him from time to time but spoke of
him as being a 'most peculiar man'.

I didn't, as you may imagine, quarrel with that epithet! At
length he offered Bonny the secretaryship of a Working Class
Loan Society, a sort of club of which he was the President, a
small thing, but still employment and pay. For a short time
Bonny did fairly well, but day by day he grew more drowsy and
wanting in energy until at last when [East] came to a meeting of
the club to talk over the monthly account, he found Bonny had
disappeared, leaving his account correct but in great disorder.
He went to his lodgings in Tachbrook Street and was told that
the night before Bonny had called for clean linen and had

betaken himself no one knew whither. For nearly three weeks he heard nothing of Bonny, until a few days ago he got a note, written curtly without a word of apology for his desertion, saying he was in the Westminster Hospital, ill, and that Thursdays and Sundays were the visiting days. East went therefore to the hospital and found him very ill and almost speechless. He asked him to write to you, to Lord Kinnaird, and to Lady Burdett-Coutts merely intimating that he was ill in hospital and penniless . . . Bonny's landlord told East that nothing had been received from Bonny since a gentleman— that's me—paid his rent for him, last October year. Now that he had left in that way he did not wish to receive him back again in his house. This is what is preying on Bonny's mind, the idea of going to the workhouse when he is discharged from the hospital. East seemed to think he would not recover—the doctors will tell me the chances on Saturday—but he said Bonny's great idea was to get into a convalescent home by the sea for a few weeks when he was discharged from the hospital . . . Though he only spoke kindly of Bonny I could see that he had suffered a great deal from him. He said, 'His silly talk made him the laugh of the neighbourhood,' and ended up each sentence by adding, 'Ah! he's a very peculiar man.' Bonny it appears has quarrelled with King for some reason unknown to East . . . I left with a feeling of great respect for East, and a fresh wonder in my heart that Bonny should have found three such patient and forbearing friends as King, East and his unpaid landlord, who has been most generous to him and has never pressed for payment.

Jephson returned to the hospital that Saturday. The doctors told him they were not going to operate. They were still puzzled by the case; the discovery of his opium habit had helped but not solved the problem of diagnosis. Jephson wrote to Stanley:

[Dr Smith] wished me to see Bonny, and I thought it advisable to do so, in case it might be said that no one went near him. I went and sat by him for about ten minutes. He looked a perfect wreck and had the appearance of an old man, an ungracious, unfriendly, ungrateful old man full of complaints about everything. The chief thing he complained of was the—

what he called—'hard-heartedness' of people with whom he lodged, who he said had behaved so ill to him. 'But Bonny,' I said, 'everyone thinks they have behaved so well to you— remember they have never asked you for rent these three years and a half that you have never paid them.' 'Well yes,' he said, 'in that respect perhaps, but the woman of the house was so cold-hearted she never came and sat with me or did anything for me.' In fact I found him, as he always was and always will be, a selfish, complaining, idle creature without any sense of gratitude or decency. I told him that you had asked me to see him and that Lord Kinnaird had written to you about him, and that the doctor had promised to keep him in the hospital until he was well enough to be discharged, and after that we would be disposed to send him to a convalescent home near the sea for a few weeks to get him thoroughly well. After that he would be expected to work. 'Ah!' he replied, 'I shall never be able to work again.' There was not a thank you or a word of gratitude for anything—he was the same ungrateful, sulky, self-sufficient creature he always was, even in Africa. I fear he is hopeless, but at the same time of course something must be done for him.

I have already got the £10 I promised to raise, so if you can work Lord Kinnaird and give something yourself we can, as you say, get enough to keep him for another six months.

This was the beginning of the 'Bonny Relief Fund', which Jephson would have preferred to have given another name: 'I wish I could say the Bonny Burial Fund, for that would be more satisfactory to everyone, himself included!'

For the rest of the summer Bonny was shuttled in and out of hospital and between various convalescent homes on the south coast. At the end of July his friend East wrote to Jephson to say that he was back in hospital and that there was no improvement in his condition: 'I do not think he will ever be any better in this world.' Jephson made enquiries at the hospital and discovered that Bonny was suffering from 'an ulcer in his anus which had to be operated upon'. He told Stanley that it was a 'sign that the disease was spreading'.

After a month it was clear that Bonny was not recovering from the operation as quickly as the doctors had anticipated. Dr Smith, who knew all about the Bonny Relief Fund, had an idea. 'It occurred to me,' he wrote to Jephson, 'that Bonny might go out to the Cape. £10 would take him out and another £10 or £20 in his pocket would give him a start out there. We could advise him this as a choice between life and death—to put it mildly! Let me hear your opinion.'

However attractive the idea was, Jephson must have wondered if it was quite ethical—because in his next letter Dr Smith wrote, 'In reference to [Bonny's] going to the Cape it was merely a suggestion, as I thought 6,000 miles was about as near as you would like to have him.'

In the end Jephson put it to Bonny and reported his reaction to Stanley: 'On my first mooting the suggestion Bonny seemed delighted, but two days afterwards he apparently changed his mind about it.' Bonny was only momentarily taken in; as he wrote to Jephson; 'Mr Smith cannot mean that I, a man weighing 7 st 10 lbs and otherwise helpless, should go to the Cape, which is inundated with men, with no object in view. Why, it would be worse than madness. I should like to go to the Cape or elsewhere if I was stronger than at present but my answer must be deferred until I have a chance of looking about me for a short time.'

Jephson had also introduced Bonny to an officer who might have been able to help him get a post in the Niger Protectorate, except that competition among officers was so keen that it was most unlikely an ex-sergeant would be considered—'So I think that Bonny is convinced that a billet will not be found for him there, but such is his unswerving conceit that I believe he would imagine he was capable of acting as Prime Minister of England.'

The immediate problem, however, was whether to go on paying ten shillings a week to keep Bonny in his convalescent home. 'He might remain there for the winter,' Jephson wrote, 'or until we can get him into the Home for Incurables. Good Lord! What a nuisance he is!'

Sometime at the end of 1896 or the beginning of 1897 Stanley and Jephson must have decided that they had done all they could reasonably be expected to do for Bonny. After all, there was a limit. And Bonny, not least in refusing to die when there was nothing left for him to live for, had gone beyond the limit.

For a year there was silence. Then, on 19 January 1898, an

article appeared in the *Daily Mail* entitled, THROUGH DARKEST AFRICA—A LONG WAY ROUND TO THE WORKHOUSE. An ingenious reporter had interviewed Bonny in the St George's Union Workhouse in the Fulham Road. He described him as 'an old man with sunken cheeks, grizzled moustache, and a thin, white, almost transparent hand nervously fingering the counterpane', and contrasted his fate with that of his old chief, who was said to have made £40,000 out of his book describing his own and Bonny's adventures. African exploration was a notoriously profitable occupation, so 'what had Bonny done with his share of the plunder? The answer is simple. He never had any plunder. He was three years with Stanley, and his salary was £100 a year, making £300. In addition to this he got an honorarium of £300, making £600 in all.'

Other articles followed, and there was a flicker of righteous indignation. Stanley, who had recently returned from a short visit to South Africa, wrote to Jephson that he thought it was useless to contradict such reports. Jephson agreed:

> The two articles you enclose about Bonny and the stupid anonymous letter are not pleasant reading. I expected that some such matter would happen if Bonny was not helped. In fact I remember telling you so when there was a question of our getting up a fund together for him. I recollect perfectly saying that if he were not helped the Radicals would get hold of him and would use it against you in the election . . .* It seems to me the position is very much like the Rear Column business. However wrong poor Barttelot may have been, the public would not allow you to justify yourself because of the dead man lying there, and any attempt to justify yourself seemed to be blaming him. And now, in Bonny's case, there is a sick and dying man lying there . . . We have however my correspondence with East and with you to show that Bonny, so far from having been neglected, has practically been entirely kept by us for nearly two years.

It was only after his monstrous letter to Novello accusing King of having misappropriated the money which you and I

* At his wife's insistence, Stanley had stood for Parliament as Liberal Unionist candidate for Lambeth North and won at the second attempt in 1895.

gave him to expend upon him, that I got so disgusted I would not have anything more to do with him.

Still, it is of course impossible to make the public understand all that.

In June, a Captain Beddoes launched an appeal through the columns of *The Times*. He wrote, 'It is probably not generally known that Mr Bonny, the last survivor [*sic*] of the ill-fated rearguard of the Emin Pasha Relief Expedition, is at present dying of consumption in St George's Union Infirmary . . . Surely those who contributed so generously to the Emin Relief Expedition, which was the cause of Mr Bonny's collapse, will, on the facts being brought to their notice, help to remove him to more suitable surroundings.' (Stanley's opinion, expressed in a private letter, was: 'It is a pitiable case and altogether above the help of subscriptions I am sorry to say.')

After that Bonny *was* moved, to a private home in Clapham. In August, he wrote to Stanley, still complaining that he had never seen the money that had been paid out on his behalf, still asking for help in getting a job. He also remarked that a letter he had written to Mounteney Jephson had been 'returned without reply'.

From that moment he turned on Jephson just as he had turned on King and East. During the last year of his life he wrote Stanley a number of bitter and increasingly incomprehensible diatribes against Jephson and 'the two men he employed . . . East and King, both of whom were bound to secrecy, thus not only keeping me in the dark but treating me with a vile contempt while appearing as a friend. This won't do . . .' So he jabbered on, demanding proof of the money 'said to have been spent' on him and hinting darkly at what might happen if that proof were not forthcoming.

Stanley replied that he could not 'grasp his meaning'. But he did take the precaution of writing to Jephson to get from him an account of how the money had been spent.

Jephson gave him all the details and went on:

Now sir, you tell me that Bonny has written you insolent and threatening letters and hints—to use your own words—that 'he will expose us in the Press'. Expose what? It seems to me that there is nothing to expose but patient generous kindness to him on our part . . .

I have two letters from Bonny in abuse of his former friend King, and both of them are stories of drinking in public houses, of pawnbrokers' tickets and suchlike. In fact the whole story of Bonny's life since he came back from Africa with us is a miserably squalid one clouded with baseless suspicion and full of black ingratitude. Do not trouble any more about him, or answer his insolent letters. Conscious of having behaved far more kindly to him than ever he deserved, let us leave him to do what he pleases.

But Stanley ignored this advice. He wrote Bonny a rather extraordinary letter in which he expressed himself perfectly satisfied with the account Jephson had sent him, yet went on to say there was a difference of £7 between 'verbal and written accounts', and sent a cheque for £10 to cover this supposed difference.

Bonny was in the Guards' Hospital, Rochester Row, when he got this letter. He was 'too shaky' to do more than acknowledge receipt of the cheque. But when he rallied again, he returned to the attack: 'Only a difference of £7!!! and you are satisfied with his account, good God!!! If you are satisfied comment is useless. But I am not satisfied . . .' And he threatened legal action.

His next letter, dated 1 July 1899, began in an unusually philosophical vein:

Sir, I did not complete my last letter. I felt too seedy and my back made me restless. Two years is a long time on one's back in bed. I ought to be dead I know and I have more than once wished it, but no, I still hang on and worst luck I suffer. I don't care a fig about the demise but the continuous suffering compels me to feel not like Job but like Bonny. I am ready to curse God and die . . .

But before he died he was ready to curse a few others as well, beginning with Jephson, whom he now described as 'a man who has lived on a woman the whole of his life'—a reference to Jephson's cousin, the Countess of Noailles, who had put up the £1,000 to enable Jephson to go on the Emin Pasha expedition in the first place. Bonny proceeded to fling out accusations in all directions until his letter became so rambling and hysterical that Stanley had to admit he could make no sense of it.

'I am inclined to think,' he wrote in reply, 'that your illness causes you to imagine wrongs where none exist. Be that as it may, I have to beg now that this correspondence shall cease, for it takes too vexatious a tone to be prolonged.'

Bonny wrote to Stanley once more, on 5 August. In this letter he gave vent yet again to his hatred of Jephson. He talked of his 'lying and boasting about having paid the rent' and added: 'So much for the associate you had with [you] in Africa who was not only your "incubus" there but will also be the leech here.' The rest of the letter was taken up with complaints about his treatment in the hospital. Perhaps he was hoping that Stanley would come to his rescue once again and have him transferred to a pleasanter place, but in this he was disappointed. He died in the Guards' Hospital on 25 September. He was fifty-two years old.

Even after his death, Stanley was not rid of him. Lawyers' letters passed to and fro on the subject of Bonny's diaries and eventually Stanley bought the lot for £15. He must have had a few anxious moments first, though: there might yet have been another scandal arising out of that old business of the rear column. Certainly a note which Jephson wrote Stanley in October 1899, after a conversation with Dr Smith, has a familiar ring about it: 'He told me a lot of things about Bonny and his state of mind and said that as a medical man he had no hesitation whatever in saying that he was quite out of his mind, and that he was prepared to say it in public, or write it.'

But there was no need for that. Bonny's passing was of no significance in the great world; *he* had no influential relations to fight for *his* good name. His death brought nothing but relief to those who had known him.

When one considers what a touchy man Stanley was, his patience with Bonny is all the more remarkable. The obvious explanation is that he was motivated by self-interest: that he was scared that Bonny might indeed 'expose' him (as he had 'exposed' Barttelot and Jameson). But I don't believe it was entirely due to that. Stanley knew from his own bitter childhood experience in the workhouse what it was like to be rejected, to be an outcast;

and his whole life was a struggle for acceptance, for recognition. Bonny had fallen into precisely that pit out of which Stanley had climbed with such an effort of will. Mounteney Jephson, bred in the lap of luxury, could not understand; for him Bonny was beneath contempt. But for Stanley it was probably more a question of: 'There but for the grace of God . . .'

Bonny died just when Stanley retired to the country. Stanley had not enjoyed politics and he made little mark in the House of Commons, though he did speak out occasionally on African affairs. The only things that gave him pleasure in his declining years were his family—he and his wife had adopted a son, Denzil—and Furze Hill, the large country house near Pirbright in Surrey which he had bought and lavished money upon, calling it, significantly, 'the Bride'.

Just before his retirement, Stanley had been honoured by the British government with a GCB. His knighthood had come almost a decade later than might have been expected. But Stanley had always been a controversial figure and it would not have been possible to honour him before 1892 anyway—because it was only then that he ceased to be an American subject and reverted to British citizenship.

Stanley died in 1904. It was his wish to be buried alongside Livingstone in Westminster Abbey but the Dean, Dr Armitage Robinson, refused this request. The most he would allow was a memorial service to be held in the Abbey—a service which Herbert Ward, among others, attended. Ward later wrote, 'My feelings corresponded with those of the Congo Africans, for I knew the natives would say: "It is not true; Bula Matadi [Breaker of Rocks] is not dead." '

Mounteney Jephson eventually married his American girl-friend, Anna Head, but their life together was marred by Jephson's almost continuous ill-health. His death, when it came in 1908, was hardly unexpected.

The surviving officers of the rear column, Troup and Ward, fared better in the long run. Both were still alive in 1910—a fact that Ward recorded in his book, *A Voice from the Congo*: 'Nine British officers were engaged; at the time of writing there remain but two survivors, Mr John Rose Troup and myself.'

Both Troup and Ward (like Stanley) had married soon after the expedition—Troup in early 1889 and Ward a year later. I have not been able to discover what happened to Troup after 1890, but Ward's life is better documented. He met his wife-to-be on a voyage to America (where he was going on the inevitable lecture tour). She was an American and her name was Sanford—though she was not, it seems, any relation of the General Sanford in whose company Ward had once been employed in the Congo. They were married in America and when they returned to England Ward embarked on another 'series of lecture engagements extending over a period of two years'.

It was a curious, nomadic existence. On 13 December 1890, he wrote to his wife from Warrington in Lancashire: 'On Saturday I addressed Royalty, and to-night I am speaking to miners.' But the grimness of the industrial and mining towns and countryside depressed him more than anything in Africa had ever done: 'I think this lecture business in England is the dreariest experience of my life.'

At the same time, though, he renewed his friendship with Alfred Harmsworth (later Lord Northcliffe). The two had been close friends before Ward went to Africa; they had shared lodgings then. Now Harmsworth tried to involve his friend in his various journalistic projects. In the early nineties Ward reported on the departure of two polar expeditions—Nansen's to the North Pole from Norway, and Jackson's to Franz Josef Land from Archangel—as well as writing and illustrating African stories. But he did not find journalism satisfying.

By the autumn of 1893 the Wards had three young children; yet they uprooted themselves to go to Paris for six months. It was a crucial decision. Ward had been advised to go by two artist friends, who thought he would benefit from a proper training. He took their advice and enrolled at Julian's Academy in the Rue Fontaine. Twenty years later he still had several friends from those days at the Academy. He remembered the place and its sixty students with great affection:

Among all the varied assemblies of men it has been my fortune to have lived among, I shall always recall the kindly, rowdy French art students of the Rue Fontaine. Some of my former comrades have attained distinction as artists, some have fallen by the way, and have been obliged to earn their bread in more prosaic fashion. Spontaneously generous, though with little to give—note the little model dying of consumption, the hat passed round, pennies, francs, and a gold coin or two, and then the funeral, following the coffin through the streets to the cemetery, the respect, a strange contrast to their ribald language and their light conception of morals.

On his return to England he submitted himself to a more rigorous apprenticeship—to the painter Seymour Lucas, RA, who was deeply antagonistic to the French. Lucas insisted that Ward study under him for no less than two years; and in those two years Ward 'learned the value of precision, of painting in clean colour, of taking infinite pains'. It laid the foundation for his future work.

At the end of this apprenticeship, the Ward family moved out to Lambourn Place on the Berkshire Downs. Ward was beginning to be recognised as a painter; he had had two pictures accepted at the Royal Academy. But the next two or three years were a time of conflict and uncertainty for him. On the one hand, family life, the convivial side of his nature and his love of sport attracted him to the traditional pursuits of the country gentleman; on the other, his urge to create was so strong that he would shut himself up for days in his studio.

The conflict was not finally resolved until he stumbled upon his true métier, which was to be a sculptor. One day he picked up a lump of plasticine and idly moulded it into the shape of an African head. It was a moment of recognition. As his wife wrote, 'It was then that the artist began to dominate the sportsman, and the chapter of our life at Lambourn closed with the end of the year [1899].'

They moved into London and Ward rented a studio in St John's Wood. He was lucky to have as neighbour another sculptor, W. Goscombe John, RA, who gave him advice and encouragement. The two of them became friends and Sir William (as he later became) was impressed by Ward's sense of purpose:

There was no searching for a subject; he always knew exactly what he wished to do, and he would do it in the most direct and appealing manner. He was quite an extraordinary combination of artist and man of action. As soon as the artist decided what to do, the man of action took up the matter and carried it through, without hesitation or delay. One felt that there was nothing that could prevent him from realising what he wished to do.

It was inevitable, once he had decided to become a sculptor, that Ward would return to Paris. Negro models were more easily found there, and there were better facilities for casting in bronze. So the family went to Paris for another six months, while Ward worked on his life-size figure of the 'The Charm Doctor'—*Le Sorcier*. They returned to London, but Ward was becoming increasingly disenchanted with the place. 'There is too much of frock coat and silk hat in London,' he said, 'too much of the atmosphere of three meals a day, of roast beef and Yorkshire pudding on Sunday. In Paris one has a sense of freedom, lightness and enthusiasm that one never knows in London . . .'

So it was back to Paris again the next autumn (1903), to a studio in the Rue d'Amsterdam. Only this time it was for good. 'That first winter in the Rue d'Amsterdam proved to be another turning-point to our lives,' his wife recalled. '. . . Gradually, unconsciously, stealthily, France became our adopted country.'

The next decade was a happy and successful one. They bought a house in the country outside Paris, at Rolleboise, overlooking the Seine; the family—there were five children now—grew up in idyllic surroundings; and Ward himself was at last rewarded for the years of hard work he had put into becoming, first a painter, then a sculptor. His African figures earned him a Gold Medal at the *Salon* in 1908 and another in 1910. And to crown it all, he was awarded the *Légion d'honneur* in 1911.*

---

* For details of Ward's later life, see 'Aftermath'.

[TIPPU-TIB] was a tall, powerfully built man, with short, grizzly beard, very black skin, discoloured eyeballs, thick lips, beautifully white teeth and afflicted with a peculiar nervous twitching of the eyelids. He was benevolent in appearance and gentle in his manner. He impressed me as being courteous and dignified. He seemed to be full of restrained force. To me personally he was always kind and amiable, and it is recorded that on many occasions he rendered valuable assistance to European travellers, more especially perhaps to Livingstone, Cameron, Stanley and Wissman. He was possessed of personal virtues which contrasted strangely with his professional depravity.'

HERBERT WARD, *A Voice From The Congo* (1910)

The Emin Pasha Relief Committee, in its unpublished report of 1891—unpublished because of its contentious nature (in an angry exchange of letters with Stanley, Mackinnon wrote, 'You *know* I had not read the draft of the report ... Had I read it in draft it would never have reached the stage of being printed in draft')—took upon itself the role of adjudicator and concluded: 'History will hold Tippu-Tib responsible as the principal, and the Committee are compelled to believe deliberate, cause of the disasters of the rearguard and the deaths of Major Barttelot and Mr Jameson.'

It has to be said that this judgment was based more on assertion than on argument; for instance, 'The Committee do not believe that [Tippu-Tib] ever set out for Yambuya in June or July 1887 and, considering subsequent events, they do not believe that he ever intended to supply the men.' But the essential fact remained: 'That Tippu-Tib did not fulfil his contract to supply 600 carriers to the expedition is a fact which the history of the rearguard proves beyond question.' The Committee did not regard 'the partial fulfilment of the agreement after a year's delay' as any kind of reparation. Tippu-Tib had complied to that extent, the argument ran, only because of 'the pressure put upon him from Zanzibar and the fear of public opinion in Europe'.

Tippu-Tib was of course the ideal scapegoat. In the public mind, fed on the reports of missionaries and others, he was the very embodiment of cruelty and evil—the most notorious individual of that notorious breed, the 'Arab' slavers. What was the oppressive discipline of a Barttelot, or the excessive curiosity of a Jameson, beside the actions of this hardened malefactor? He was the real villain of the piece, not the poor deluded Englishmen who were, after all, comparative innocents.

Stanley, too—in spite of publicly blaming his own officers— held that Tippu-Tib was ultimately responsible. In 1888, he had sent Selim Mohammed back from Banalya to Stanley Falls with a warning that he would institute proceedings against Tippu-Tib for breach of contract when he reached Zanzibar. And this he did, as he described in his book:

> Among my visitors at Zanzibar was a Mohammedan East Indian, named Jaffer Tarya, who is a wealthy Bombay merchant, and acts as agent for many Arab and Zanzibari caravan owners in Africa. Among others he acts as agent for Hamed bin Mohammed *alias* Tippu-Tib. He told me that he held the sum of £10,600 in gold, which was paid to him for and on behalf of Tippu-Tib by the Government of the Congo Free State for ivory purchased by Lieutenant Becker from Tippu-Tib in its name. Jaffer Tarya had thus unwittingly put the means to enable me to bring Tippu-Tib some day before the Consular Court at Zanzibar to be judged for alleged offences committed against British subjects, the gentlemen of the Emin Pasha Relief Committee, and to refund certain expenses which had been incurred by the declaration he had made before Acting Consul-General Holmwood, that he would assist the Emin Pasha Relief Expedition with carriers.

Stanley stayed in Zanzibar only a fortnight, the last two weeks of December 1889, but it was long enough to draw up an affidavit of Tippu's supposed misdeeds and obtain an order preventing the agent, Jaffer Tarya Topan, from handing over the money he held to Tippu-Tib without the consent of the court.

Significantly, in view of the rapidly changing political panorama, the first Tippu-Tib heard about the case—and the sequestration of his money—was from Europe, from the King of the Belgians in fact. He decided to leave at once for the coast, in spite of the opposition of his fellow Arabs at Stanley Falls. They argued, 'Better to have it taken out on one's goods than on oneself.' They were worried in part, as Tippu himself was, by the hostile activities of the Germans, who were just beginning to establish their authority in that part of East Africa through which, traditionally, the slave caravans passed. But Tippu, ever the realist, called his fellows fools and retorted:

Here in Manyema have we strength enough to stop the Europeans? What kind of equipment have you with you? Are these WaManyema warriors? We had little enough strength but we mastered them in no time, because this village and that were rivals. While the Arabs were powerful and rivalled the Europeans, I accepted their suzerainty, but now it is the Europeans who have limitless resources and power. Leave off your bumbling.

By this time—March 1890—Tippu's position had become virtually untenable. When the Belgians had eventually come to Stanley Falls in July 1888, one of the first things Tippu had learned from them was that they laid claim not only to Stanley Falls itself but to all the settlements in Manyema, 'which places belong to me from a long time past,' as he wrote to his brother and son in Zanzibar, 'that is since the time of Dr Livingstone . . . All the natives as well as Europeans know that these places belong to me.' With the Belgians pressing from one side of the continent, and the English and Germans closing in from the other, the situation was both threatening and more than a little confusing. The Arabs were astonished to find that the Belgians regarded their settlements in Manyema as part of their territory and Tippu, in his bewilderment, turned to 'an Englishman, who is my friend' (the only Englishman at Stanley Falls in August 1888 was Jameson) who:

. . . said that I was a friend to the Belgians who had kept me as
their governor in this place, and that all the places mentioned
above belonged to me, and he added that he did not know
whether the boundary described by the Belgians was a true one
and whether the Germans would accept it. When this was
mentioned by the Englishman, the Belgians kept themselves
quiet and said nothing and the Englishman said that I was not
the man belonging to the Belgians but that I, an independent
man, was to look after my own affairs and added that they (the
Belgians) had made me the governor of the place actually
belonging to me, and that it was not a bad thing to be friendly
to both sides, but that it would be better to be friendly with the
Germans also before they could take these places, and that when
the Germans would try to take these places, they would see
that I was a friend to them and that the places belonged to me
and that consequently they could not take them from me by
force but would do so [only] if I was willing, and that if I was
not to act so, I would lose all the places for nothing because all
the Germans were advancing very fast and so it was better to
become their friend before they arrived here. We think that
what our friend the Englishman said is true.

The Arabs all agreed that Jameson gave good advice, so Tippu
encouraged his brother to make overtures of friendship to the
Germans. He told him, 'You need not be ashamed to join with
the Europeans in as much as our Sultan has already done so.' But
their Sultan, Said Burghash, had died recently and Tippu-Tib
could no longer be sure of his own standing in Zanzibar. He
recommended caution. 'Before you do anything,' he wrote to his
brother, 'you should go quietly to see the British Consul-General.'
He wanted him to find out 'by stratagem' whether it was true
that the Germans were becoming a power in the land and that they
and the Belgians were after his territory. It was the British, after
all, who had been responsible for negotiating his alliance with the
King of the Belgians, and he questioned whether they would be
happy to see him ousted from his domain—'I know very well that
the English are my good friends. I do not think they are willing to
see me in the hands of any other people or in trouble.'
Tippu's brother's action, when he received this letter, was

hardly strategic. He simply handed it over to the British Consul-General, Colonel Euan-Smith, who promptly sent off a copy to the Foreign Office with a covering note. The Colonel wrote: 'The letter ... seems to indicate that Tippu-Tib is not wholly free from a tendency to double-dealing and from a not unnatural desire to make the best terms for himself in the conflict for territory which he evidently considers is about to take place in Central Africa between the European Powers.'

The conflict that actually took place was not of course between the European Powers, who managed the carve-up of Africa diplomatically, but between Arabs and Europeans throughout Central Africa. Tippu-Tib was the only important Arab chief seriously committed to the policy of peaceful coexistence with the Europeans, but the Belgians did not make it particularly easy for him. They were ready enough to buy his ivory without worrying about how he had acquired it, but they were determined to limit his territorial ambition and channel it in the direction *they* chose. They still did not trust him, as they clearly demonstrated when they built a fortified post at Basoko, at the junction of the Congo and the Aruwini, which Tippu considered by rights a part of his district. They had not even consulted him, and Tippu complained with some justice to Van Kerckhoven that this 'should never have occurred between good neighbours'.

Tippu, along with the other Congo Arabs, was also suffering from the ban which the State had imposed in October 1888 on the import of arms and gunpowder. With the simultaneous blockade of the east coast there was a chronic shortage of armaments, and in March 1889 Tippu sent a rather desperate letter to the British Acting-Consul Portal at Zanzibar, begging him to write to the King of the Belgians on his behalf,

> ... informing him that there is no doubt that I am under him, and that I am the agent for him; telling him also to provide me with some arms for my own use, which may be required in case he may order me to perform some work, because on the mainland it is not possible to remain without arms. Therefore tell him to send me some arms.

Tippu went on, with mounting bitterness, to stress his own isolation:

And now all the Arabs are my enemies. They say I am the man who gave up all the places of the mainland to the Belgian King. What I earnestly wish from the Belgian King is that he should not leave me alone. Oh, my friend! now, when all the Arabs have become my enemies, how can the Belgian King leave me to my own resources? This is not good on His Majesty's part. Let this be known to you [him?] and send me the answer. And I attribute what has happened to me to the English, who put me in the friendship of the Belgian King. And you know all about this.

King Leopold, as it happened, did have a scheme for which he required Tippu-Tib's co-operation. Just as the Arabs had used Stanley as a pathfinder and followed in his wake, so the King hoped to use Tippu-Tib to open up and pacify the unexplored region of Bahr-el-Ghazal to the north-east of the Congo where state boundaries were of necessity a little uncertain. His ultimate objective was to push his north-eastern frontier right up to the Nile itself. That was his dream. Once the Arabs had pacified the area and set up stations, the Europeans would take over. The financial inducements were such that the Arabs would be amply recompensed for their labour; the King's idea was 'to get the Arabs, in return for money, to serve my policy'. Tippu agreed to the project, but as the State would give him neither arms nor soldiers to carry it through, nothing came of it.

In the meantime, the new State post at Basoko had become the focal point of discontent. The influx of Europeans and Arabs in the vicinity had created a food shortage and other related problems; just as the relationship between Barttelot and Selim Mohammed had deteriorated dramatically at Yambuya, so the Europeans and Arabs at Basoko became increasingly hostile towards one another. Once again there was a policy of 'peaceful diplomacy'; once again it proved completely unworkable. The State agents began to take a tougher line with what they called 'Arab insolence' and Tippu-Tib was once more under fire from both sides.

Providentially perhaps, it was at this moment that the news of Stanley's lawsuit reached Stanley Falls and gave Tippu an excuse to depart and hand over the governorship to his nephew Raschid.

Tippu-Tib's autobiography is, on the whole, a disappointing and rather perfunctory document, but there is, fortunately, a first-hand account of his state of mind as he crossed the African continent for the last time in the reminiscences of an Englishman called Alfred Swann. * Swann spent many years in Central Africa; a former master mariner, he was in charge of the London Missionary Society's steamers on Lake Tanganyika; later he was to become Senior Resident Magistrate in Nyasaland. Although he was totally opposed to Tippu's way of life, he had reason to be grateful to him personally.

At the beginning of 1890 he came back to the Arab settlement of Ujiji from the east coast with a party which included his wife— their child died *en route*—a doctor and two Jamaicans, none of whom, apart from Swann himself, had been in Africa before. They had a difficult journey through country aroused by the hostilities between the Germans and the coastal Arabs, and when they reached Ujiji Swann was surprised and unnerved by the absence of any sort of welcome, which was quite contrary to his previous experience. Even the doctor, though a newcomer, noticed and remarked on it.

Late that night a messenger came to the courtyard where they had taken refuge and demanded that Swann, and Swann alone, go with him to see Rumaliza, who had just arrived from across the Lake. Rumaliza was the chief Arab of Ujiji and trading partner of Tippu-Tib, a man of considerable power and influence. His real name was Mohammed bin Khalfan. Jameson had met him once when he came to visit Tippu at Kasongo just before they returned to Stanley Falls and described him then as 'a very light-coloured Arab, almost as fair as a white man, and, were it not for the scars of smallpox, [he] would be a good-looking fellow; his manners are those of an English gentleman . . . [He] is a quiet-looking man, but from all I hear is a very devil at fighting the natives, and feared accordingly.'

Swann was loath to leave his companions and his apprehension increased when, after following the messenger through dark

* A. J. Swann, *Fighting the Slave-Hunters in Central Africa* (London, 1910).

231

streets and along corridors, he found himself alone in the Arab's harem. Even when Rumaliza himself appeared and dismissed the girls with an airy gesture, he hardly knew what to expect. It was definitely not the usual thing for a white man to be invited into an Arab's harem.

After a few polite preliminaries Rumaliza held out a letter: 'This letter came to me ten days ago. I was then 200 miles from here. I have been travelling as fast as I could, so as to arrive at the same time as yourself, or before, if possible. It is from Tippu-Tib my partner, who is now on the Congo. These Ujiji Arabs have lost a great deal of property at the coast, in the war against the Germans, and many of their relatives have been killed. In order to be revenged they decided to intercept your party at the last river and to kill you all.

'The calico was to be equally divided between them. Your arms and ammunition were to come to me, whilst the vessels on the lake were to become the property of Tippu-Tib. On receipt of this news Tippu-Tib sent special messengers to me, requesting that I would at once go to Ujiji, stop all this nonsense, and inform these Arabs that if they would not listen to me, I was to place myself and people on your side, and, together with his retainers, defend you and your property. I only arrived yesterday at your station, persuaded the white man to give me a passage here, stopped as we passed Ujiji, and sent on shore my messenger, who only reached the Arabs just in time to stop their action.'

'Will you tell me,' asked Swann, 'why both yourself and Tippu-Tib took our part?'

'Because we have no quarrel with you. We have assisted every Christian traveller who has been to Ujiji. If these Arabs had killed you, there would have been much trouble.'

About a month later Tippu-Tib himself turned up at Ujiji. Swann went to see him at his request and found him 'bursting with indignation' over the summons he had just received from the Consular Court at Zanzibar.

'Look at that!' he said, pointing to the letter, 'It is a note ordering me to be at the coast in two months. Stanley accuses me of hindering him on his journey to find Emin Pasha, and alleges that this was the cause of Barttelot's death. If I had wished to stop him, I should not have played with the matter by sending 400 men instead of 600, as per contract; I should have killed him years ago. I do not simply *hinder*, I *destroy*! If I assist, it is at all costs.' He held out his hands and, counting on his fingers, said: 'Who helped Cameron, Speke, Livingstone? Who sent Gleerup from the Congo to Sweden? Who saved your life, and those of all your party; was it not me? Have I attempted to hinder any missionaries, although they are not of my religion and hate my business of catching slaves? Tell me! Is there a single European traveller who can honestly say I was not his friend?'

Swann tried to reassure him but Tippu's fury was not so easily abated. He had not finished what he wanted to say: 'I am mad with anger when I think of what we did for Stanley during his first and second journeys through this country.

'In order to make a big work out of nothing, he went up the Congo to find Emin Pasha; why not have walked up the much less expensive road from the East Coast? He came to Zanzibar and begged me to go round the Cape with him, and to bring my people, all expenses to be paid by himself. I did not desire to go, choosing rather to walk, as I have always done, and to transact business as I passed my various depots; but he would take no denial, so, out of courtesy, I accompanied him.

'He needed my assistance to obtain porters and, because only 200 out of the 600 men I sent ran away, I am accused of wanting to hinder him. Do they not desert from all Europeans, as well as from Arabs? The truth is, your countrymen are criticising his work and the loss of Barttelot, and he is wanting to blame me. Barttelot lost his life through bad temper; it was entirely his own fault. I was hundreds of miles distant, and lost money through the cannibal porters running away. I cannot understand Stanley. Without my help he could never have gone down the Congo; and no sooner did he reach Europe than he claimed all my country. Surely your people must be unjust!'

Swann replied to him, 'Stanley has been talking into one ear of Europeans, now you go and speak into the other. They will listen to you, for we are accustomed to weigh both sides of a question and love justice.'

'Do you?' said Tippu warmly. 'Then look here—how did you get India?'

'We fought for it!'

'Then what you fight for and win belongs to you by right of conquest?'

'Yes! That is European law!'

'So it is with us Arabs. Have we ever tried to rob you of India?'

'I may ask you, in reply, do these pagans try to rob you of Ujiji? The jackal cannot rob the lion.'

'Very well, then! I came here as a young man, fought these natives and subdued them, losing both friends and treasure in the struggle. Is it not therefore mine by both your law and ours?'

'It is only yours so long as you govern and use it properly.'

Tippu-Tib then got up and demanded: 'Who is to be my judge?' to which Swann replied, emphatically, 'Europe'.

They had got down to bed-rock at last.

'Aha!' Tippu replied, 'now you speak the truth. Do not let us talk of justice; people are only just when it pays. The white man is stronger than I am; they will eat my possessions as I ate those of the pagans, and——' Here he paused.

Swann asked:

'Well—and what?'

'*Someone will eat up yours!*'

Continuing, he said: 'I see clouds in the sky! The thunder is near! *I am going.*'

Swann realised with excitement that he was listening to the capitulation of Central Africa's greatest man-hunter. As he wrote, 'What were the trifling inconveniences of my past life compared with the intense satisfaction of being present—the only white man present—at this great Sedan?'

'Tell Europe Stanley lies; and tell them also, if they love justice, as you say, to compensate me for stealing my country.'

Swann did write a letter. He wrote to Zanzibar saying that Tippu-Tib and some of his fellow Arabs were on their way and that they would contest Stanley's claims,

. . . and, if they have right on their side, which is more than likely, I hope they will win. What Europeans say will decide their movements. I am not writing from hearsay or guessing. I have it from themselves. Through the whole business Mohammed bin Khalfan [Rumaliza] has stood nobly by us and to myself has been a staunch friend. Mind, I am not saying he is an angel, but let us be honest with these men and not swallow everything any popular man may wish to ram down our throats. It strikes me, if some of the African travellers said the moon was three cornered in Africa, many would believe them just now. I say give Tippu-Tib a hearing and two to one he opens the eyes of now blind Europe.

On his way to the coast, Tippu had such a severe attack of dysentery that for a while his life hung in the balance. He was laid up for several months and probably only survived through the care of the French missionaries at Kipalapala, who nursed him through the illness. When he recovered sufficiently to move—for the most part he had to be carried—he continued his journey as far as Mpwapwa, where the missionaries of the Church Missionary Society were on the look-out for him. They had been contacted by Mrs Jameson and Jameson's brother, Andrew; these two had come all the way out to Africa in an attempt to find out the truth about the cannibal incident which had caused such a scandal in England, but they had been dissuaded at Zanzibar from proceeding inland. They wanted the missionaries to ask Tippu-Tib himself what had happened on that occasion, if he had been there and seen Jameson buy a slave-girl, give her over to the cannibals and then sit down and sketch them while they stabbed her and tore off her limbs. Tippu wrote in his autobiography:

I told them, 'This is a lie. I was neither there nor did I hear such a thing before today. That [Stanley] should say Jameson would do such a thing! Or that I would allow it! Yet I've never seen a European nor, for that matter, any human being who is such a liar. And how is one to tell when he is lying?'

Tippu-Tib was still very angry with Stanley over the court case. He had liked Jameson and may have wished to protect his memory, as well as his family, from Stanley's insinuations and, at the same time, discredit Stanley himself. On the other hand, he may simply have been sensitive about his own reputation in Europe, not wanting it said of him that he encouraged such goings-on. Whatever the reason, Jameson's own diary and letters prove beyond a doubt that in this instance it was Tippu-Tib and not Stanley who was lying.

Once within sight of the coast Tippu-Tib did not hurry to cross over to the island of Zanzibar. He allowed himself to be fêted and lionised by the German authorities, staying several days with the Governor himself at Dar es Salaam. Only after that, towards the end of September 1891, did he go on to Zanzibar:

> There I found nothing amiss. No charges, no questions at all, except a few Europeans asking about Jameson—as a result of Stanley's lies. Mr Nicol came to tell me that there was no case between us, and was anxious that an agreement should be signed. This we did, and Stanley's charges and his lies were finished with.

All the charges against Tippu-Tib had been withdrawn, but why? And at whose instigation? Stanley had made the charges not on his own account but on behalf of the Emin Pasha Relief Committee; he claimed in his affidavit that, as well as 'great hardships and privations', the expedition 'had also to sustain great pecuniary losses which to the best of my knowledge, information and belief I estimate at about £10,000' as a direct result of Tippu-Tib's breach of contract. And the Committee itself, in its report of 1891, charged Tippu-Tib with responsibility for the disasters of the rear column. Its chairman, Sir William Mackinnon, was a businessman; and the expedition had proved such an enormously expensive undertaking that he might well have expected to recoup some of that expenditure from the wealthy Arab chief. Yet, in the event, the Committee decided to withdraw the charges.

In his pioneering and invaluable article on the case, 'Stanley versus Tippoo Tib' (*Tanganyika Notes and Records*, No. 18, December 1944), the historian Sir John Gray argues that Stanley's affidavit was a gross distortion of the truth, and that his own failure to provide ammunition was at least as reprehensible as Tippu-Tib's delay in providing carriers. Gray concludes that Tippu really had no case to answer and that would be reason enough 'for the gentlemen of the Emin Pasha Relief Committee to discontinue the action which Stanley had instituted against Tippu-Tib in the Committee's name and at the Committee's expense'.

But that, if it played any part at all in the Committee's decision, was by no means the whole story; there were wider issues involved. On 10 July 1890, Mackinnon had written to the Consul-General in Zanzibar, Colonel Euan-Smith:

Recently I have had several communications regarding Tippu-Tib from Brussels. The King is anxious above all things to get Tippu-Tib to come at once to Europe and visit him first of all in Brussels. He is anxious that you should assist in every possible way to induce Tippu-Tib to come sharp away from Zanzibar on his arrival there, without allowing him to have any contact with the Germans. I know you will do everything in your power to accomplish this, and I am about to telegraph you giving you a free hand in regard to the action raised by Stanley against Tippu-Tib for £10,000 damages. As I wrote you some time ago, I wish very much to impress on Tippu-Tib that if he accepts the King of the Belgians' invitation to come at once to Europe and to continue his services to the King, the. King will very likely be able to assure him that the action we have raised against him shall be abandoned. *

This was the moment when Leopold hoped to use the Arabs to extend his territory to the north-east; Tippu-Tib's co-operation was essential. Mackinnon was interested because his Imperial British East Africa Company was negotiating with the King for a strip of land alongside Lake Tanganyika in return for that access to the Nile which Leopold coveted. This strip of land to the west of Lake Tanganyika would link British territory to the north and south and thus provide for the possibility of realising Cecil Rhodes' dream of a Cape-to-Cairo railway. The moment passed, but while it lasted the political aspect of the situation demanded that Tippu-Tib be wooed by the various European powers, who were anyway inclined to overestimate his authority. Stanley, when consulted by the Emin Pasha Relief Committee about dropping the case against Tippu, took a high moral tone. He wrote to the

* To Stanley, Mackinnon wrote that Tippu-Tib's lawyer would almost certainly suggest that Tippu came to Europe to examine witnesses if they persisted with the lawsuit, and that would give the Barttelots and Jamesons an unwelcome opportunity to 'make a fresh attempt to vex and injure you'. Therefore, he urged, the action should be dropped.

Acting-Secretary, McDermott, from New York on 25 January 1891:

> My action in the matter, Tippu-Tib vs. the E.P.R.C. was solely in the interests of the Subscribers to the Fund, and on behalf of those who suffered by the breach of contract of Tippu-Tib. I have absolutely no interest in the matter beyond that. It is wholly at the option to press the claims to the fullest extent made, to demand that a share should be paid, or to drop it altogether. The Subscribers to the Fund may feel that £1,000 will be ample compensation to them for their pecuniary loss, but I am sure that Stairs, Nelson, Parke, Jephson and Bonny will not be satisfied. They ought to be consulted, as well as the widows and orphans of those who died at that pestful den of Yambuya. It is easy for the subscribers to decline prosecuting, but the officers who endured the toil, and the orphans and widows who have sorrowed ought in my opinion to be consulted. My application for justice was on behalf of all concerned. Personally I have no sentiment about the affair. Tippu-Tib deserved punishment as sternly as Pure Justice would demand. He was conveyed to Stanley Falls upon the strength of his promise. The men died at Yambuya, the Major was shot, and Jameson succumbed, and all that ruin followed, because the officers of the rear column persisted in believing that he would keep his promise. Therefore the breach of the promise caused all this calamity.
>
> That is the case, and the only view to rightly take of it, but as I said, it is for the Committee to decide. I am an outsider in it, and only moved because it was the way to get justice done for others.

So Stanley washed his hands of it and the Committee gratefully dropped the case. Tippu could pick up his £10,600 from Jaffer Tarya Topan and settle into a retirement in Zanzibar which was more comfortable than it might have been, considering events about to take place on the mainland. But Tippu-Tib was as astute a businessman as he was politician. Not all his wealth was tied up in Central Africa; he had wisely bought up a considerable amount of property in Zanzibar itself and as a result he survived the break-up of the slave and ivory trade better than other Arab adventurers. If things had worked out differently, he might have been a very rich man indeed. As it was, he still died rich. His German biographer, Heinrich Brode, estimated his fortune at £50,000 just before he died.

Although he had wanted to visit Europe, Tippu never managed it. King Leopold II's desire to see him waned as time passed. In 1890, the King had been anxious to court him; he sent an envoy to meet him on the east coast with a promise of all the guns and powder he could use, as well as a large sum of money, if he would set up State posts on the shores of the larger African lakes. But Tippu—because of the near-fatal attack of dysentery he had suffered—did not reach the east coast until the summer of 1891. By that time the envoy had gone and the situation changed. Diplomatic manoeuvres and the success of certain Belgian expeditions in the Congo encouraged Leopold to think he could achieve his goal of expansion without Arab assistance.

Yet it was not the King himself who initiated the attack on the Congo Arabs which led to their downfall, but one of his junior officers on the spot. His name was Lieutenant Dhanis. This officer took advantage of the defection of a powerful chief called Ngongo Lutete, who had been Tippu-Tib's slave but had risen with Tippu's backing to a position of considerable authority on the Lomami River, and with his aid crossed the Lomami and harried the Arabs in their own territory. The Arabs, with no Tippu-Tib to restrain or unite them, fought back furiously but without an overall strategy; and all the time they lost ground. Eventually they were driven from Stanley Falls in the north and Nyangwe and Kasongo in the south. The decisive battle in the two-year campaign was fought on the river Luama to the west of Lake Tanganyika in October 1893. Aligned against Dhanis and his force was the combined strength of Tippu's son, Sefu, and his old partner, Rumaliza; but the Belgians were too much for them. Rumaliza managed to make his escape but Sefu was killed in action and the Arabs had lost the war. Leopold was delighted and Dhanis was promptly made a Baron and a high official of the Free State.

Tippu-Tib himself had never encouraged the fighting. He bitterly regretted it and, in his autobiography, loyally tried to exonerate his son Sefu from responsibility for Arab attacks on the

Belgians. He blamed Ngongo Lutete, of course, but more than him, Rumaliza, who—he claimed—ordered the Arabs to attack and kill the few European traders living among them, thus bringing down on their heads the wrath of the government.

'Now the cause of this intrigue and the root of the trouble,' he wrote; 'basically it was Rumaliza.' But Tippu bore a grudge against his old trading partner. When Rumaliza showed up in Zanzibar, penniless, after his escape, he put forward a claim to a quarter of Tippu's fortune. He produced a document, allegedly signed by Tippu-Tib, Tippu's cousin Nzige and himself, purporting to be an agreement between them to divide all their profits. Tippu-Tib was to receive half and the other two a quarter each.

Tippu and Nzige both denied the authenticity of this document and claimed that their signatures were forgeries, but Rumaliza won the ensuing lawsuit. Tippu-Tib had to hand over all his property on the coast of the mainland and, after further legal wrangling, 6,000 dollars as well. Not that it did Rumaliza much good; he was soon driven to bankruptcy by outstanding debts and legal fees. But Tippu-Tib hardly forgave him on that account.

It was Tippu's contention that if he had still been in the Congo, things would never have got out of control in the way they did. It is possible that his political acumen might have postponed the day of reckoning but it could never have prevented it, as he himself had been the first to recognise. After all, he had left the Congo of his own volition, as Alfred Swann pointed out:

By his own decision he left the interior, never lifting his hand against the white man, and doing his utmost to persuade his partner to follow his example. It has been popularly supposed that he was a kind of political prisoner at Zanzibar; this is not correct. He had no desire to return. I always paid him a visit when passing Zanzibar. The last time we parted, and shortly before he died, he gave me an autograph copy of a brief history of his life.

Tippu-Tib died in 1905, a year after Stanley. So the 'notorious slave trader' outlived the 'great explorer'. Stanley considered him 'the most remarkable man I had met among Arabs, Wa-Swahili, and half-castes in Africa', and used him accordingly, without ever quite trusting him. Tippu returned his suspicion with interest and their friendship, such as it was, was finally soured by what happened to the rear column. Each blamed the other for the tragedy.

'For a long time,' ran the *Daily News* obituary of Tippu-Tib, 'considerable suspicion rested on him in connection with the death of Major Barttelot, who, it will be remembered, remained in command of the rearguard of the Emin Expedition. The evidence, however, showed the gallant officer's death was mainly due to his misunderstanding of native character. The fatal shot, it appeared, was fired by a soldier whose wife had been threatened with punishment for disobedience to orders.'

In the end, Tippu-Tib certainly lost more than he gained through his association with Europeans. He lost an empire, after all, and history judged him harshly. Lately, however, historians have been attempting to right the balance in his favour. Yet Herbert Ward's comment, that 'he was possessed of personal virtues which contrasted strangely with his professional depravity', will still serve as an epitaph.

AFTERMATH

'The central wrong was the reduction of millions of men to a condition of absolute slavery by a system of legalised robbery enforced by violence.'

E. D. MOREL, *History of The Congo Reform Movement*

'Those who crusade, not *for* God in themselves, but *against* the devil in others, never succeed in making the world better, but leave it either as it was, or sometimes even perceptibly worse than it was, before the crusade began.'

ALDOUS HUXLEY, *The Devils of Loudun*

'The creatures outside looked from pig to man, and from man to pig, and from pig to man again; but already it was impossible to say which was which.'

GEORGE ORWELL, *Animal Farm*

E. J. GLAVE and Roger Casement were Ward's two closest friends from his pioneering days in Africa. Both were 'Stanley's men' who stayed on in the Congo after the process of Belgianisation had got under way: they, like Ward, found refuge in the American-owned Sanford Exploring Expedition. Each was to make a significant contribution to the end of King Leopold II's personal rule in the Congo and its replacement by the more orthodox colonial regime known as the Belgian Congo (which, of course, survived until independence brought renewed hostilities in our own time).

Glave was in the Congo for six years during the 1880s and he returned to Africa in 1895, this time as a journalist—and why not? Hadn't his idol, Stanley himself, first entered Africa as the result of a newspaper commission? Glave's plan was to travel across the continent, from east to west, in the guise of a hunter and to report—for *Century* magazine—on the Arab slave trade. It was a good scheme, only by the time he arrived in Africa the Arabs were finished. The European scramble for Africa had quickly and effectively put an end to the slave trade—though not, as Glave discovered, to the practice of slavery. This continued to flourish, under various euphemistic headings, particularly in the Congo.

Glave was in a curious position. Both as an old servant of the State and as a dedicated opponent of slavery, he was anxious to praise the regime which had driven out the Arabs in the name of civilisation; but he could not ignore the evidence which confronted him at every stage of his journey. The villagers in the *Zone Arabe*, he found, were preyed upon quite as much as they had been in the bad old days of Arab rule. He put it down to the absence of white men: there were far too few of them to exercise control over the Wangwana (Zanzibaris) and Arabs they employed. If the number of 'capable whites' were increased, he thought, it 'would lead to speedy peace and the rapid development of the resources of the country.'

Only gradually did Glave come to the truth. By the time he left Stanley Falls for Basoko (the station built at the confluence of the Congo and the Aruwini to prevent Arab expansion in that direction), his indignation had been thoroughly aroused and his attempts to justify the Belgian occupation lost all conviction. His disgust was no longer confined to particular acts of cruelty he had witnessed or heard about, but extended to the whole system, as he began to understand it. He wrote in his diary:

> The State conducts its pacification of the country after the fashion of the Arabs, so the natives are not gainers at all. The Arabs in the employ of the State are compelled to bring in ivory and rubber, and are permitted to employ any measures considered necessary to obtain this result. They employ the same means as in the days gone by, when Tippu-Tib was one of the masters of the situation. They raid villages, take slaves, and give them back for ivory. The State has not suppressed slavery, but established a monopoly by driving out the Arab and Wangwana competitors.
>
> The State soldiers are constantly stealing, and sometimes the natives are so persecuted that they resent [revenge?] this by killing and eating their tormentors. Recently the State post on the Lomami lost two men killed and eaten by the natives. Arabs were sent to punish the natives; many women and children were taken, and twenty-one heads were brought to the Falls, and have been used by Captain Rom as a decoration round a flower-bed in front of his house!*
>
> Basoko is in a serious position, surrounded by a powerful enemy, so close that they can hear their speaking-drums. It is the natural outcome of the harsh, cruel policy of the State, wringing rubber from these people without paying for it. The revolution will extend.

* This detail, as various commentators have noted, was used by Joseph Conrad in *Heart of Darkness*, in his description of Kurtz's house at Stanley Falls. Conrad's novella was first serialised in *Blackwood's Magazine* in 1899, nine years after Conrad himself had been in the Congo, but less than three years after Glave's diary was published in *Century* magazine.

When Glave reached his old station at the equator he was truly shocked by what he found:

Formerly the natives were well treated, but now expeditions have been sent in every direction, forcing natives to make rubber and to bring it into the stations. Up the Ikilemba, away to Lake Matumba, the State is perpetrating its fiendish policy in order to obtain profit. We are taking down one hundred slaves, mere children, all taken in unholy wars against the natives. While at the mission station, I saw a gang of prisoners taken along by the State soldiers. War has been waged all through the district of Equator, and thousands of people have been killed and homes destroyed. It was not necessary in the olden times when we white men had no force at all. This forced commerce is depopulating the country.

The ugliness of the overall situation was reflected in such little incidents as one which Glave witnessed at the Equator station:

The *commissaire* of the district is a violent-tempered fellow. While arranging to take on the hundred small slaves, a woman who had charge of the youngsters was rather slow in understanding his order, delivered in very poor Kibanji; he sprang at her, slapped her in the face, and as she ran away kicked her. They talk of philanthropy and civilisation! Where it is I don't know.

Part of the confusion, or mystification, was semantic. This aspect of totalitarian control, which Orwell analyses in *Nineteen Eighty-Four*, was already operating in the Congo in 1894 (and for at least a dozen years after that). Glave spells it out in a letter he wrote towards the end of his journey:

The occupation of the territories of the Congo Free State by the Belgians is an enormous expense, and the administration is making most frantic efforts to obtain a revenue of a size sufficient to enable it to pay its way. In the fighting consequent upon this policy, owing to the inability or disinclination of natives to bring in rubber, slaves are taken—men, women, and children, called in State documents *libérés*! These slaves, or prisoners, are most of them sent downstream, first to Leopold-ville. There the children are handed over to a Jesuit mission to be schooled and to receive military training from a State officer established at the mission for that purpose. In two years this Catholic mission has buried 300 of these poor, unfortunate little children, victims of the inhuman policy of the Congo Free State. In one month seventy-three new graves were made. On the *Ville de Bruxelles*, the big State boat upon which I descended the Congo, we took on board at the equator 102 little homeless, motherless, fatherless children, varying from four years to seven or eight, among them a few little girls. Many of them had frightful ulcers which showed no sign of having been attended to, although there was a State doctor at the Equator station. Some few had a tiny strip of cloth, two or three inches wide, tucked in a string around the waist to hide their nakedness, but half of them were perfectly naked. As they were huddled together on the lower deck of the boat on the damp, chill mornings, shivering with cold, death was marking many more for hasty baptism and a grave at the Jesuit mission near Leopoldville. By the time we reached Kinchassa, Stanley Pool, there was a great deal of sickness among the children, principally fevers and coughs; many were hopelessly ill. If the Arabs had been the masters, it would be styled iniquitous trafficking in human flesh and blood; but being under the administration of the Congo Free State, it is merely a part of their *philanthropic* system of *liberating* the natives!

Unfortunately, Glave himself fell victim to a sudden fever and died at Matadi when his bags were already packed and loaded on board a homeward-bound steamer. But his indictment remained to inspire others.

One of the last entries in his diary referred to the missionaries and their difficulties *vis-à-vis* the State:

Mr Harvey heard from Clarke [an American Baptist], who is at Lake Matumba, that the State soldiers have been in the vicinity of his station recently, fighting and taking prisoners; and he himself has seen several men with bunches of hands signifying their individual kill. These, I presume, they must produce to prove their success! Among the hands were those of men and women, and also those of little children. The missionaries are so much at the mercy of the State that they do not report these barbaric happenings to the people at home. I have previously heard of hands, among them children's, being brought to the stations, but I was not so satisfied of the truth of the former information as of the reports received just now by Mr Harvey from Clarke.

Some of the braver missionaries no longer consented to remain silent; and the information that began to filter out of the Congo was put to good use by such campaigners as Fox Bourne of the Aborigines Protection Society and, above all, Edmund Morel, whose Congo Reform Movement was an example of how extraordinarily effective the constant reiteration of certain basic and unpalatable facts could be (in the long run) in bringing down a regime.

Ward also played a modest part in the Congo Reform Movement. He financed the publication of Morel's pamphlet, *The Congo Slave State*, and he was responsible for introducing Morel to the author of the famous consular report on the atrocities in the Congo—Roger Casement. The first meeting between these two champions of the cause of humanity took place in Ward's house in London. Ward himself was not present; he had already moved to France.

In fact he was in his studio in the Rue d'Amsterdam in Paris when he received his copy of Casement's report, with its grim catalogue of atrocities. The date was 24 February 1904, and Ward wrote in the letter-diary he kept for his wife's benefit whenever they were apart:

I could not stop reading until I got to the end of it. All the old names of people and places mean so much to me. I cannot describe how strange it is to suddenly lose oneself, as I did just now. I seemed to be out in Africa once more, to hear the sounds, to smell the strange odours, and to feel that these old friends of mine were very close to me. It is all so very sad, what he writes, dreadfully sad, and it makes one's heart go out to those poor creatures who have harmed no one, and who simply wish to be left alone. What hypocrisy it does seem this so-called civilisation of savage countries! It is always the same story, but not quite so bad as in this case of the Congo. I am writing to Casement, and sending a donation to the funds of the Association. I am sure it will do some good, although so much harm has already been done by the white man and the Arabs, in their mad quest for ivory and rubber. But money can't give back those severed hands, nor the children who were killed before the eyes of those poor distracted mothers. One's heart aches with the thought of their despairing suffering. How few there are, who have not been there, who can realise even in a small degree what it all means!

Six years later, in the 'Envoi' to his book, *A Voice from the Congo*, Herbert Ward wrote:

There are two sides to the subject of Congo affairs: the political side, which has been dealt with so ably by honest, fearless men, who have sought to ameliorate the condition of a persecuted race. The second side, it appears to me, should relate to the race in question—their nature, their habits and customs, and their personality. If a perusal of the foregoing pages serves to call forth a feeling of interest and sympathy for my African friends, I shall be more than content.

Certainly Ward's best work—his African figures, whether warrior or sorcerer, chief or slave, man, woman or child—is remarkable for the degree of sympathetic understanding it reveals. Sympathy, with or for others, was Ward's predominant characteristic; all his friends remarked on it. They spoke of his simplicity, his directness, his love of adventure, his essential modesty, but above all, of his 'genius for friendship'. Yet in one instance—and perhaps only in one—genius failed and friendship was found wanting: not in the case of Stanley, who had been a revered leader rather than an equal; but with Roger Casement, who was his close friend for thirty years. On 2 February 1915, at Rolleboise, his country home on the Seine which he had turned into a Red Cross convalescent home and staffed (at his own expense) with a doctor and nurses on the outbreak of the First World War, Ward wrote in his letter-diary:

I see by the papers that Roger Casement is in Berlin. The enormity of his action is beyond exaggeration. He is a traitor pure and simple, and he will probably be shot when he is taken, if he does not run foul of trouble beforehand. It is a great blow to me, and I have made up my mind to turn him down forever. What an ending to what promised to be a brilliant career!

His decision was irrevocable. In 1916, after Casement's capture and trial for treason, when his appeal had failed and he was condemned to be hanged, Sir Arthur Conan Doyle organised a petition to try and persuade the government to grant a reprieve. It was signed by all sorts of eminent people, mostly writers; but Ward, though he was approached, refused to have anything to do with it. Of all the refusals to sign the document, this was the one that apparently hurt Casement most. All attempts at a reconciliation, right up to within days of Casement's execution, met with failure. Ward's obduracy was unshakeable.

In his defence it must be said that the war affected him as deeply as it affected anyone. He had made his home in France; he had more or less handed over his house to the Allies as part of the war effort; his family had been evacuated when the Germans threatened to overrun that part of the country; his second son—who was only seventeen years old, but had joined the Royal Flying Corps—was reported missing, 'killed or wounded'. And then, when the news came that he was alive and had escaped to Switzerland, it was almost immediately eclipsed by the official notification of the death of his eldest son, aged twenty-two, who had been serving in the infantry on the Western Front. Ward himself, though over fifty, had joined the British Ambulance Committee and served as a lieutenant in No. 3 Convoy in the Vosges. After six months of service, 'the oldest man in the entire three sections of the British Ambulance Convoy', as he described himself, he had an accident and the resulting injury forced him go to Paris for surgical treatment. But his courage and eagerness to help the Allied cause gained him official recognition: he was both mentioned in despatches and awarded the *Croix de Guerre*.

After his injury, he turned to propaganda work. He went on an exhausting lecture tour of the United States and put together his last book—*Mr Poilu: Notes and Sketches with the Fighting French*—extolling the virtues of the ordinary French soldier. In such circumstances it is hardly surprising that he was caught up in the loyalties and animosities the war inspired.

Ward died in 1919, exhausted by his war effort—he had finished the war as British delegate to the French Red Cross. His sculptures and his large collection of African *objets* (which he insisted should be exhibited together) were presented to the Smithsonian Institution in 1920 and housed in the National Museum in Washington. And his widow, as an act of piety, wrote his biography and called it—not untruthfully—*A Valiant Gentleman*.

ACKNOWLEDGMENTS

I would like to express my gratitude to Sir Brian Barttelot, who was kind enough to let me go through his family's private collection of papers relating to the rear column controversy—including the original manuscript of Major Barttelot's diary. This contains one or two derogatory references to his fellow officers which were tactfully omitted from the published version.

My thanks also to the Librarian of the School of Oriental and African Studies for permission to examine the Mackinnon papers housed there. This interesting collection includes many letters written by and about the officers of the rear column as well as a large number of Stanley's letters.

It was my good fortune to meet Richard Hall on the publication of his biography of Stanley—*Stanley: An Adventurer Explored* (Collins, 1974)—which contained a few surprises for me in spite of my own—as I thought—extensive researches: for instance, I had no idea that Bonny was addicted to opium until I read it there. Richard Hall most generously lent me notes he had made about Bonny and the rear column while going through the Stanley papers.

This encouraged me to write direct to Richard Stanley, the explorer's grandson, to ask if I might look at those papers in his archive which related to William Bonny. I wrote without much expectation of success as I felt obliged to admit at the outset that my book was not likely to be very favourably disposed towards his grandfather. But Mr Stanley replied that I was welcome to seek the information I wanted; he was generous with his hospitality as well as extremely helpful in unearthing the documents I was after. I recall my visits to Furzehill Place with great pleasure.

A word of thanks, too, to the Reverend Herbert Ward, the sculptor's son, who entertained me one memorable lunchtime with stories of his father's— and his own—life. Sadly his father's papers seem to have disappeared when the family house at Rolleboise fell into German hands in 1940.

Christopher Fyfe read a draft of the Historical Introduction and helped save me from making a fool of myself. My debt to my wife, Jenny, is beyond summary.

Finally, I would like to acknowledge assistance from the Arts Council of Great Britain.

The Author and Publishers are grateful to the Hakluyt Society for permission to quote from *The Diary of A. J. Mounteney Jephson*; to the Mansell Collection for permission to reproduce the photograph of Stanley, and the engravings of the Emin Pasha Relief Committee and of the steamers *Stanley* and *AIA*; to the *Illustrated London News* for the engravings of Barttelot's interview with Tippu-Tib and of Tippu-Tib's canoes. The map was drawn by Patrick Leeson.

BIBLIOGRAPHY

MANUSCRIPT SOURCES:
Barttelot Papers, at Stopham, Pulborough, Sussex.
Mackinnon Papers, at the School of Oriental and African Studies, London.
Stanley Papers, at Furzehill Place, Pirbright, Surrey.

PUBLISHED MATERIAL:
Various newspapers 1888–1890, in particular a run of *The Times* from October to December 1890.

Books/Articles:
ALLEN, Jerry. *The Sea Years of Joseph Conrad* (London, 1967)
ANSTEY, Roger. *Britain and the Congo in the Nineteenth Century* (Oxford, 1962)
ANSTRUTHER, Ian. *I Presume: H. M. Stanley's Triumph and Disaster* (London, 1956)
ASCHERSON, Neil. *The King Incorporated* (London, 1963)
BARTTELOT, W. G. (ed). *The Life of Edmund Musgrave Barttelot, from his letters and diaries* (London, 1890)
BRODE, Heinrich. *Tippoo Tib: the story of his career in Central Africa narrated from his own account* (London, 1907)
CONRAD, Joseph. 'An Outpost of Progress' from *Tales of Unrest* (London, 1898)
   Heart of Darkness (London, 1902)
   'Geography and Some Explorers' and 'The Congo Diary' from *Last Essays* (London, 1926)
FARRANT, Leda. *Tippu Tip and the East African Slave Trade* (London, 1975)
FORESTER, C. S. *The Sky and the Forest* (London, 1948)
FOX BOURNE, H. R. *The Other Side of the Emin Pasha Relief Expedition* (London, (1891)
   Civilisation in Congoland (London, 1903)
GLAVE, E. J. *Six Years of Adventure in Congoland* (London, 1893)
   Diaries, *Century*, Nos. 53 and 54 (New York, 1896 and 1897)
GRAY, Sir John. 'Stanley versus Tippoo Tib', *Tanganyika Notes and Records*, xviii (Dec. 1944)
HALL, Richard. *Stanley: An Adventurer Explored* (London, 1974)
HINDE, S. L. *The Fall of the Congo Arabs* (London, 1897)
HIRD, Frank. *H. M. Stanley: the Authorised Life* (London, 1935)
INGLIS, Brian. *Roger Casement* (London, 1973)
JAMESON, J. S. *The Story of the Rear Column* (London, 1890)

JONES, Roger. *The Rescue of Emin Pasha* (London, 1972)

LOUIS, W. R. 'Roger Casement and the Congo', *Journal of African History*, Vol. V (1964)

LOUIS, W. R. and STENGERS, Jean. *E. D. Morel's History of the Congo Reform Movement* (Oxford, 1968)

MANNING, Olivia. *The Remarkable Expedition: the Story of Stanley's Rescue of Emin Pasha from Equatorial Africa* (London, 1947)

MIDDLETON, Mrs D. (ed). *The Diary of A. J. Mounteney Jephson* (Cambridge, 1969)

PARKE, T. H. *My Personal Experiences in Equatorial Africa* (London, 1891)

PORTER, Bernard. *The Lion's Share: a Short History of British Imperialism 1850–1970* (London, 1975)

PULESTON, Fred. *African Drums* (London, 1930)

ROBINSON, Ronald and GALLAGHER, John, with Alice DENNY. *Africa and the Victorians* (London, 1961)

ROWLANDS, Cadwallader. *H. M. Stanley* (London, 1872)

SINGLETON-GATES, Peter, and GIRODIAS, Maurice. *The Black Diaries of Roger Casement* (London, 1959)

SLADE, Ruth. *King Leopold's Congo* (Oxford, 1962)

SMITH, Frank Hopkinson. *The Armchair at the Inn* (New York, 1912)

SMITH, Ian R. *The Emin Pasha Relief Expedition 1886–1890* (Oxford, 1972)

STANLEY, Lady Dorothy (ed). *The Autobiography of H. M. Stanley* (London, 1909)

STANLEY, H. M. *In Darkest Africa*, 2 vols. (London, 1890)

SWANN, A. J. *Fighting the Slave-Hunters in Central Africa* (London, 1910)

TROUP, J. Rose. *With Stanley's Rear Column* (London, 1890)

WARD, Herbert. *Five Years with the Congo Cannibals* (London, 1890)
  My Life with Stanley's Rear Guard (London, 1891)
  A Voice from the Congo (London, 1910)
  Mr Poilu: Notes and Sketches of the Fighting French (London, 1916)

WARD, Sarita. *A Valiant Gentleman: the Biography of Herbert Ward, Artist and Man of Action* (London, 1927)

WERNER, J. R. 'The Camp at Yambuya', *Blackwood's Magazine* (Feb. 1889)
  A Visit to Stanley's Rear Guard (London, 1889)

WHITE, James. 'The Sanford Exploring Expedition', *Journal of African History*, Vol. VIII (1967)

WHITELY, W. H. (ed. and trans.) *Maisha ya Hamed bin Muhammed el Murjebi yaani Tippu Tib.* Supplement to *East Africa Swahili Committee Journals*, No. 28/2 (July 1958) and No. 29/1 (Jan. 1959)

INDEX

Abdullah Korona, Arab chief, 52–4, 57, 58, 62, 65, 138, 140, 141; attacks native villages, 58–9; camp at Banalya, 135

Aborigines Protection Society, 249

African Drums (Puleston), 73

AIA, Belgian steamer, 106–11, 123, 129, 130

Ali bin Mohammed, 54

American Baptist Missionary Union (ABMU), 18–19

Anglo-German Agreement (1886), xvi

Anstey, Roger, xvii

Arabi Pasha, xiv

Arabs, the, 31–2, 63, 67, 112, 180, 227–34; attack Stanley Falls and drive out Deane, 24, 31, 96; cause trouble at Yambuya, 50–2, 70, 76; attacks on native village, 58–9, 62, 83–4; relations with rear column, 100–3; Stanley's troubles with them, 160; attacked by the Belgians, 239–40; their downfall, 239–40; end of their slave trade, 245

Arthington, Robert, 10

Aruwini river, 30, 35, 47, 53, 54, 67, 83, 95, 107, 108, 112, 123, 135; junction with Congo, 31, 53, 229, 246

Assad Farran, 68, 79, 88, 103; Jameson's anger with him, 115, 117, 125; dismissal, 126–7, 129; testimony against Jameson, 136–7, 140, 147–8; retraction of his statement, 198; his affidavit, 195–202; Jameson's attempt to discredit him, 198–9

Association Internationale Africaine, xii, xiii, 11

Association Internationale du Congo, xiii

Baert, Lieutenant, 138, 142 and n., 146, 153, 165, 166; comments on Tippu-Tib, 119–20; and on Barttelot, 136

Bahr-el-Ghazal, 230

Balfour, Arthur, 193n.

Balfour, Gerald, 193n.

Banalya, 135, 138–40, 151, 153, 209; Stanley's return there, 158–60, 166, 183

Banana (town on coast), 97, 149, 164, 168

Bangala, 35, 63, 66, 107, 112, 118, 119, 122, 125, 131, 147, 149, 151, 158–9, 164, 166, 183; Jameson's illness and death there, 154–6, 158

Baptist Missionary Society (BMS), 10, 18–19

Baring, Sir Evelyn (Earl of Cromer), British Consul-General in Egypt, xvi, 172

Barker, Frederick, 4

Bartholomew, Zanzibari interpreter, 103; his theft, 56–7; escapes, 57; recaptured and flogged, 60

Barttelot, Major Edmund Musgrave, 27–8, 39–40, 50, 51, 61, 65, 67, 70, 71, 76, 79, 84, 86, 89, 96, 97, 104–5, 107, 108, 115, 125, 129–32, 135, 148, 151–3, 163–5, 168–71, 210, 220, 226, 230, 232, 233, 238, 241; early career, 3; second-in-command of expedition,

Bonny, William—*cont.*

100, 106, 108, 110, 124, 129, 135,
137, 138, 148, 149, 164, 179–81,
183, 195, 206, 238; sergeant in
Army Hospital Department, 8;
paid for services on Expedition, 8;
and Stanley, 8–9, 28; criticisms of
Barttelot, 27–8; relations with
Ward, 28–9; responsibilities in
camp, 50; and the natives, 52–3,
58; improves housing and sanitary
conditions, 67; insinuations to
Barttelot about others, 68–9, 94–7,
105; put in charge of medicine
chest, 69, 106; and Christmas celebrations, 72–4; and native women,
73, 90–1; teaches Zanzibaris to use
rifles, 88; letter to Committee,
96–7

in charge during Barttelot's
absence, 101–2, 105, 110; minis-
trations to Troup, 104, 129;
Barttelot's view of him, 105–6; on
Troup's condition, 109, 124; badly
swollen hand, 125, 127; and march
out of Yambuya, 133, 134; in
charge of camp in forest, 135; goes
to Banalya, 137–8; and Barttelot's
death, 138–44; and Assad Farran's
statement about Jameson, 140;
alone at Banalya, 151–3; letters to
Mackinnon, 151–3; alleged instructions from Barttelot, 153; news of
Jameson's death, 156–7

and Stanley's return, 158–9;
insinuations to Stanley, 165, 170–
2; an opium taker, 169, 213, 214;
responsibility taken from him, 170;
dissatisfied with treatment by Stanley, 120–1; Stanley's officers' views
on him, 171–2, 174–5; quarrel
with Nelson, 174; quarrel on board
ship, 175

Stanley uses his evidence, 184;
his statements, 186–9, 199–201;
and the cannibal story, 199–200;

and Jameson's preserved head of
native, 200–1

later career, 209–21; attempts to
find work, 209–13; obtains money
from Stanley and Jephson, 211,
212, 217–19; in Westminster Hospital, 211, 213–16; the 'Bonny
Relief Fund', 215, 216; in workhouse, 217, 218; *Daily Mail*
article, 217; appeal launched for
him, 218; at private home in Clapham, 218; letters to Stanley, 218–
20; turns on Jephson, 218–20; in
Guards' Hospital, 219, 220; death,
220, 221; Stanley buys his diaries,
220

Bosworth Smith, R., 191

Bourne, Fox, 249

Brackenbury, General, 13, 14; warns
Stanley against Barttelot, 6, 40

*Britain and the Congo in the Nineteenth
Century* (Anstey), xvii

British India Steamship Company,
xviii

Brode, Heinrich, 239

Brussels Conference (1876), xii

Buller, Sir Redvers, 6

Burgari Mohammed: theft of goat,
69; flogged twice, 69, 196; escape
and recapture, 86; shot for desertion, 86–7, 196

Cannibalism, 35, 66, 116–17, 200;
cannibalistic killing of girl, 116–17,
172, 182–3, 185–6, 199–200, 202

Casement (Sir) Roger, 17, 164, 245;
report on Congo atrocities, 249; in
Berlin, 250; tried for treason and
executed, 251

Century magazine, 245, 246n.

Charity Organisation Society, 169,
175

Chicotte, instrument of flogging, 60n.

Church Missionary Society, 235

Comité d'Etudes du Haut-Congo, xiii

Conan Doyle, Sir Arthur, 251

Congo Free State, xv, 11, 16, 24, 63, 172–3, 226; flotilla of steamers on Congo, xviii, 19; bans imports of arms and gunpowder, 229; and continuation of slavery, 246–8

Congo Reform Movement, 249

Congo river, xii, xvii, xviii, 4, 22, 31, 53, 98, 110, 122, 224, 246, 248; Stanley's stations, xiii; Expedition's journey up river, 11–12

Congo Slave State, The, Morel's pamphlet, 249

Conrad, Joseph, 210n., 246n.; impression of Stanley Falls, 55n.

Coquilhat, Captain, 107

Daenen, Belgian officer, 155, 156

Daily Mail, 217

Daily News, 241

Daily Telegraph, xii

Darwin, Charles, 193n.

Deane, Captain, driven out of Stanley Falls by Arabs, 24, 31, 55, 59, 96, 100, 106, 107, 118, 148

De Brazza, Count Savorgnan, xiii, 192

De Winton, Sir Francis, Secretary to Relief Committee, 6–8, 10, 18, 97, 124

Dhanis, Lieutenant, 239

East, Mr, befriends Bonny, 213–14, 218

Egypt, xvi, 3; Arabi Pasha's revolt, xiv; invasion by Britain, xiv

Emin Pasha (Edouard Schnitzer), xi, xv, xvi, 77, 148, 151 and n., 161–4, 166, 232, 233; withdrawal to Equatorial Province, xv; reports of his situation, xv; Relief Expedition set up, xvi; meeting with Stanley, 165, 166, 172–3; position in Equatoria, 172; Stanley's offers of future employment, 172–3; rebellion against him, 173; imprisoned by rebels, 173; escapes, 173; second meeting with Stanley,

173–4; Emin as suppliant, 173; fractures his skull, 174; killed by Arab traders, 211n.

Emin Pasha Relief Expedition, xi; set up, xvi; Stanley as leader, xvii; map of route, 2; membership of Expedition, 3–9; failure of Expedition, 179; Committee's unpublished report, 225–6

En Avant, Belgian steamer, 145, 147

Equator station, 130, 247, 248

Equatorial Province (Sudan), xv, 172, 173

Essington, R. W., 191

Euan-Smith, Colonel, British Consul-General in Zanzibar, 229, 237

Fighting the Slave-Hunters in Central Africa (Swann), 231n.

Floggings, 43, 59–60, 196

Fort Bodo, 160, 170

France: and Egypt, xiv; French press comments, 192; missionaries, 235

Furze Hill, Pirbright, Stanley's country house, 221

Germany and the Germans: sphere of influence in Africa, xvi, xvii, 227, 228; hostilities with coastal Arabs, 231

Glave, E. J., 17, 60n.; statement on Ward's complaints about Barttelot, 202–3; travels through Africa to report on slave trade, 245–9; on continuation of slavery, 246–8; death, 248

Godman, Mabel (Barttelot's fiancée), his letters to her, 4–6, 30, 47, 66, 105–6, 125, 134, 136

Gordon, General Charles, 193n.; mission to Khartoum and murder, xiv, xv, 19; relief expedition, 3, 173

Grant, Colonel, 9, 191

Guards' Hospital, Rochester Row, 219, 220

Stanley (Sir) Henry Morton—*cont.*

rumours of his return, 61–2, 66, 106, 108; deserters from his party, 65; thoughts and dreams of his return, 70–1; Barttelot's plan to look for him, 76–7

returns to Banalya, 158, 164–6, 193; his account of his arrival, 158–60; unreceived letters to Barttelot, 160–2; troubles with Arabs and Manyema, 160–2; deaths and sickness among his men, 160–1; reaches Lake Albert, 161; fails to meet his deadlines, 163; exonerates Barttelot, 163n., seeks to blame Tippu-Tib for Barttelot's murder, 163n.; letters attacking members of rear guard, 167–8; and Bonny, 169; summarises Bonny's career, 169, 175; takes responsibility from him, 170; seeks information from him, 170

meeting with Emin Pasha, 165, 166n., 172–3; offers him future employment, 172–3; their second meeting, 173–4; further dealings with Bonny, 174–5

triumph for Stanley, 179–80; writes his book, 179; marriage, 179–80; criticises rear column, 180; and Barttelot's *Diaries and Letters*, 180; statement to *The Times*, 180–4; allegations against Jameson, Ward and Troup, 182–4; uses Bonny's evidence, 189; protests against his statement, 184–6; his appointment of Barttelot questioned, 191, 204–6; announces he will not bring action, 192; puts documents at disposal of *The Times*, 195, 202; and Assad Farran's affidavit, 195; criticised by Ward, 203–6; repeats allegations from New York, 206

attempts to help Bonny, 209–21; in House of Commons, 217n., 221;

his family and country house, 221; honoured with GCB, 221; death, 221, 240; burial in Westminster Abbey not granted, 221

and Committee's unpublished report, 225, holds Tippu-Tib responsible for disasters, 225–6; institutes proceedings against him, 226–7, 230, 232, 234–5; withdrawal of charges against Tippu, 236–8

Stanley Pool, 4, 10, 11, 17, 18, 26, 166, 248

Stanley, S.S., 19, 27, 38, 107, 130, 137, 165, 166; at Yambuya, 47, 50, 51, 123, 125, 129

Sudanese soldiers on Expedition, 5, 17, 27, 31, 37; at Yambuya, 43, 49, 59, 60, 65, 66, 76, 77, 86, 92, 129, 184, 196; sickness among them, 69; detachment with Ward, 107; on the march, 133, 134, 137, 141

Sudi bin Bohati, Barttelot's boy, 141; thrashed by Barttelot, 134; steals his revolver and deserts, 134–5; recaptured, 135; his death, 181, 189

Swahili language, 83, 91, 112, 128, 158

Swann, Alfred, dealings with Tippu-Tib, 231–5, 240

Tabora, 166

Tanganyika, 149

Thomas, Miss E., Bonny's 'agent', 96–7

Thys, Captain, 210 and n.

Times, The, 10, 179, 195, 198, 201, 202, 206; publishes Stanley's statement, 180; letter from Ward, 185; letters from readers, 187, 189, 191–3, 202; on Jameson's letter of exculpation, 198; and statements by Bonny, 199; letter from Ward,

Ward, Herbert—*cont.*

in the camp, 86, 88–9; his slave woman, 91; chosen to take cable to coast, 93, 94; departure, 97, 98; Bonny's accusations against him, 98–9; insulting letter from Barttelot, 98–9

receives reply to cable, 130; travels to rejoin rear column, 130; finds Troup on board *Stanley*, 131; Barttelot orders him to stay at Bangala, 131; Jameson tells him of Barttelot's death, 147, 154

and Jameson's arrival at Bangala, 154; Jameson's illness and death, 154–6, 164; travels to coast to send another cable, 164; Committee's reply, 164; returns to Stanley Falls, 164–6; Tippu-Tib dissuades him from following Stanley, 166; and Stanley's letters attacking him, 167–8; recalled to England, 168; Stanley's allegations against him, 183–4; his letter to *The Times* and statement, 185; comments on Glave's statement, 202–3; private criticisms of Barttelot, 202–3; long letter to *The Times*, 203–6; criticisms of Stanley, 203–6; comments on Barttelot, 204–6; attends Stanley's memorial service, 221; marriage, 221–2; lecture engagements, 222; journalism, 222; studies art in Paris and London, 222–3; his family, 222, 223; takes up sculpture, 223; settles in France, 224; Negro models, 224, 250; awards, 224; on Tippu-Tib, 225, 241; finances publication of Morel's pamphlet, 249; on Casement's report, 249–50; Casement's trial and execution, 250–1; one son lost in First World War, 251; serves in British Ambulance Company, 251; awarded *Croix de Guerre*, 251; war propaganda work, 251; British delegate to

French Red Cross, 252; death, 252; biography by his wife, 252
Ward, Rowland, 201
Ward, Sarita, 222, 252
Washenzis (Arab word for natives), 53, 54, 70
Welle (Mobangi) river, 121
Werner, J. R., engineer of *AIA*, 106–11; and rescue of Deane, 106, 107; at Yambuya, 106, 108, 125, 126, 128–30; and Ward's arrival at Bangala, 107; comments on ivory, 109; and Barttelot, 110–11; helps to repack loads, 125, 126
Westminster Hospital, 211, 213–16
Wilson, Leonard, Stanley's private secretary, 195
Wolseley, Lord, 6, 13, 14

Yambuya camp, 30, 35, 36, 53, 57, 89; reached by Stanley, 34; construction of camp, 36–7; rations, 42; camp life, 43; problem of food, 44–5; attempts to trade with natives, 44–6; arrival of Troup and Ward, 47; deaths in camp, 49, 59, 64, 69, 76, 86, 87, 124; raid by Arabs, 50–2; snakes and rats, 64–5; sickness in camp, 69–70, 86, 124; Christmas celebrations, 72–5; worsening relations with Arabs, 100–3; visits of Belgian steamers, 106–11, 123

Zanzibar, xvii, 23, 24, 113, 114, 151n., 174, 226, 228, 229, 233, 234, 236, 238, 240; Expedition collects porters at, 4, 5, 43; voyage to mouth of Congo, 4–5
Zanzibaris on Expedition, 5, 13, 17, 19, 28, 31, 76, 77, 88, 100, 104, 129, 133, 136, 137, 141, 166, 169, 171, 180; Stanley's No. 1 Company, 27, 50; Barttelot's disgust at them, 40; and manioc, 42; at Yam-

Zanzibaris on Expedition—*cont.*
buya, 43, 49, 52, 59, 60; their rifles taken away, 65; sickness among them, 69; and Manyema women, 91–2; detachment with

Ward, 107, 108; incidents with Manyema, 124; troubles and desertions on march, 134
Zerilli, Stanley's courier, 195
Zingiti, *see* Stanley Falls